COLOUR AND EXPERIENCE IN NINETEENTH-CENTURY POETRY

Also by Richard Cronin

SHELLEY'S POETIC THOUGHTS

Colour and Experience in Nineteenth-Century Poetry

Richard Cronin
Lecturer in English Literature
University of Glasgow

M
MACMILLAN
PRESS

First published 1988

Published by
THE MACMILLAN PRESS LTD
Houndmills, Basingstoke, Hampshire RG21 2XS
and London
Companies and representatives
throughout the world

Printed in Hong Kong

British Library Cataloguing in Publication Data
Cronin, Richard
Colour and experience in nineteenth-century
poetry.
1. English poetry—19th century—
History and criticism   2. Colour in
literature
I. Title
821'.7'0936   PR585.C6
ISBN 0–333–44337–3

To my mother and father

'That stone is red; this stone is blue.'
'But how d'ye know it's blue?'
James Clerk Maxwell
in conversation with his nurse

'I wish you or Benson could eradicate the insane trick of reasoning about colours as identified by their names. People seem to think that blue is blue, and one blue as good as another.'
'I think a good deal may be learned from the names of colours, not about colours, of course, but about names'
James Clerk Maxwell
in conversation with C. J. Monro

Contents

Acknowledgements   ix

Introduction   1

1   Dull Red   7

Part One   The Romantics

2   Awful Newton   19

3   A Rainbow in the Sky   29

4   Blue, Glossy Green, and Velvet Black   36

5   Woven Colours   46

6   Purple Riot   64

Part Two   Robert Browning

7   Blind Hope   83

8   Rainbow Flakes   96

9   Seven Proper Colours Chorded   104

10   The Subtle Prism   116

11   The Red Thing   130

12   By White and Red Describing Human Flesh   144

13   The Crimson Quest   160

Part Three   Gerard Manley Hopkins

14   Pure Blues   171

Contents

15	Two Flocks, Two Folds – Black, White	180
16	Dappled Things	190
17	Gold-Vermilion	202
Conclusion		211
Notes		220
Index		226

Acknowledgements

I have debts to friends and to people I know only from their writings. Of the second group my primary debt is to Bernard Harrison, whose book *Form and Content* first set me thinking about colour words. Stephen Prickett's *The Poetry of Growth* first awakened me to the importance of the rainbow as a Romantic symbol. My view of Keats was decisively influenced by the two essays on Keats in John Bayley's *The Uses of Division*. Of the first group it was Philip Drew who rekindled my interest in Browning, and J. A. M. Rillie who talked about Hopkins so movingly that I went away and read him carefully for the first time. As always I have a debt to the friends who let me talk to them about my work, and who made me grateful all over again for working in an English department that has so many nice people in it. Ingrid Swanson, the department secretary, taught me how to use a word-processor, an achievement the magnitude of which those who do not know me will be unable to form an impression. I am very grateful to her.

Introduction

It is as obvious that something important happened in the arts towards the end of the eighteenth century as it has proved difficult to fix on any adequate description of what that something was. This will not be one of the many books that confront this problem, but it is a book about nineteenth-century poetry, and such books always assume some account of Romanticism.

I tend to begin with *Tristram Shandy*, because *Tristram Shandy* reveals more outrageously than any other eighteenth-century document that the age of reason was also the age of sentiment. In *Tristram Shandy* a mechanical empiricism so complete that for Mrs Shandy sexual intercourse has become a metonym for the winding of a clock is conjoined with an ethic that values a man in so far as he shows tender care for the well-being of a household fly. Between the two is an empty space inhabited only by Sterne's frenetic laughter. It was the Romantic project to establish some less volatile connection between the world of fact and the world of value, and it was this project that they, rather in the spirit of Mr Casaubon bequeathing to Dorothea his heap of jumbled manuscript, consigned to their successors.

In the nineteenth century, experience, the world as it is impressed upon our senses, becomes a problem, becomes the crucial problem that poetry addresses. Take, for example, John Clare's poem 'The Lark's Nest':

> From yon black clump of wheat that grows
> More rank and higher than the rest,
> A lark – I marked her as she rose –
> At early morning left her nest.
> Her eggs were four of dusky hue,
> Blotched brown as is the very ground,
> With tinges of a purply hue
> The larger ends encircling round.
>
> Behind a clod how snug the nest
> Is in a horse's footing fixed!
> Of twitch and stubbles roughly dressed,
> With roots and horsehair intermixed.
> The wheat surrounds it like a bower,

1

And like to thatch each bowing blade
Throws off the frequent falling shower
– And here's an egg this morning laid!

It may seem odd to suggest that Clare's naïve and charming poem is
problematic – it is certainly hard to imagine a reader being puzzled by
it – and yet it is surely also true that such a poem could not have been
written before the nineteenth century. An eighteenth-century
reader, confronted with this poem, would, one imagines, have been
at a loss, not because he would have found it difficult to understand,
but because he would not have known what it was for.

What Clare's poem lacks is generality. His effort is to distinguish
larks from other birds, and this lark from other larks – not all larks
build their nests in a hoof-print out of horse hair. The
eighteenth-century reader was, of course, accustomed by Thomson
and by Cowper to enjoying natural description scarcely less
particular than Clare's. Clare may note 'tinges of a purply hue' on the
lark's eggs, but when Cowper describes the leaves of the willow as 'of
a wannish grey' he is no less precise. The difference is that Clare,
unlike Thomson and Cowper, offers no general scheme within which
his particularities achieve point. He does not imply, for example, that
the workings of nature are worthy of minute consideration because
an appreciation of the delicacy of the mechanism will increase our
reverence for the great mechanic. A pious reader might well find in
Clare's poem support for his delight in God's handiwork, but Clare
does nothing to encourage this response. His is not a religious poem.
Why, then, do we take a pleasure in it that we could not confidently
expect an eighteenth-century reader to share?

The obvious answer is that we relish the accuracy of Clare's
description, that we have come to accept a faithful and minute
representation of nature as valuable in and for itself. This is true, I
think, to this extent – that Clare's poem could be disproved. It could
not survive a discovery that lark's eggs are a consistent light blue in
colour and that larks always nest in trees. Clare's accuracy is, then, a
condition of the reader's pleasure, but it surely cannot be its cause,
because few readers will feel the need to verify Clare's observations
before they can take pleasure in his poem. For most of us it is enough
to trust that Clare has got it right.

If I were to badger an admirer of Clare in this manner, insisting that
he tell me what he likes in the poem, he might be driven to argue that
as one reads the poem one has a dim and pleasurable awareness of the
symbolic value of the nest. Clare's delight in the nest is an

expression, perhaps, of his yearning for security, for a small, warm place in which he might snuggle and quietly attend to the business of hatching his family. The poem was written in 1835, three years after Clare had moved from his native Helpston to a village three miles distant, a journey between parishes that disoriented him quite as much as if it had been a journey between planets. 'The Lark's Nest' is only one of a series of poems about birds' nests that Clare wrote at this time, and it would be easy to guess that the precarious safety of nests expressed for Clare some of his feelings for his lost home. For the reader aware of the sad facts of Clare's life some such awareness will probably be unavoidably present as he reads the poem, but to argue that it is an awareness prompted by the poem itself is surely to disregard the complete absence of wistfulness in the delight that Clare expresses.

There are, of course, kinds of symbolic reading that cannot be refuted. The objects that Clare describes, it might be said, function as metaphors for his poem, which is woven, like the bird's nest, from humble natural materials, and yet is able, like the new-laid egg, to delight by its freshness and the perfection of its form. I cannot refute this reading – I even share it – but in itself it seems to me meagre. The poem becomes an egg, but a sterile egg, never hatching out into the real world.

Perhaps all that one can confidently say about the meaning of Clare's poem is that it shows how the man who looks at nature hard and humbly is rewarded for his efforts with a surprising and beautiful gift. Clare looks closely at the lark's nest, and because he looks closely, he finds the new egg. But interpretation collapses at this point into paraphrase. Clare's particularities – the 'black clump' of wheat, the blotches on the eggs – resist and finally defeat the interpreter's impulse to dissolve local facts into a larger meaning, just as Clare resisted his publisher's attempt to soften his knobbly dialect words into standard literary English.

Clare's things refuse to be sublimated into values: his facts refuse to be evaporated into meanings. It is through denying himself the consolation of organising the natural world into a sympathetic response to his personal worries that he achieves the emotion that characterises his poem, the emotion that Will Ladislaw regretted the lack of in Dorothea, 'a neutral delight in things as they are'. Clare does not seize on the metaphorical possibilities of the lark arising at break of day from sullen earth, and neither does he incorporate himself in the scenery that he describes, swooning away in a communion with nature that relieves him from constriction within the painful limits of his individuality: 'A lark – I marked her as she rose –'. There is the lark, and there is Clare, and the joy in which Clare's poems ends is earned by accepting, not by denying, that distinction. It is a 'neutral delight'.

In the work of the high Romantics such moments of neutral vision are represented most often as evidence of imaginative loss. This is from a fragment by Shelley, a description without a context, but expressing surely a natural world felt as alien, deaf and blind to human yearnings:

> There is no dew on the dry grass tonight,
> Nor damp within the shadow of the trees;
> The wind is intermitting, dry and light;
> And in the inconstant motion of the breeze
> The dust and straw are driven up and down,
> And whirled about the pavements of the town.

> ('Evening: Ponte Al Mare, Pisa', 7–12)

In most of Shelley's descriptive writing the world of feelings seeps into the world of things through metaphor, and these lines too are dominated by metaphorical activity, by its absence. The absence is felt, and the result is to transform Clare's neutral delight into a chill sense that the world encounters with bleak uninterest the sorrows and pains of those who live in it.

D. G. Rossetti's poem 'The Woodspurge' mediates between Shelley and Clare:

> The wind flapped loose, the wind was still,
> Shaken out dead from tree and hill:
> I had walked on at the wind's will, –
> I sat now, for the wind was still.
>
> Between my knees my forehead was, –
> My lips, drawn in, said not Alas!
> My hair was over in the grass,
> My naked ears heard the day pass.
>
> My eyes wide open had the run
> Of some ten weeds to fix upon;
> Among those few, out of the sun,
> The woodspurge flowered, three cups in one.

> From perfect grief there need not be
> Wisdom or even memory:
> One thing then learnt remains to me, –
> The woodspurge has a cup of three.

The poem is emotionally opaque, a quality that – one suspects Rossetti knew rather too well – is easy to mistake for sophistication. Rossetti is sunk in the intense self-absorption of grief. At the moment that his concentration on his own predicament relaxes enough for him to notice the tiny patch of vegetation under his eyes the woodspurge burns itself into his consciousness. He is released, as it were, from a world of feelings into a world of things, but he teasingly refuses to integrate his perception of the woodspurge with any human sense of value. The woodspurge impinges on his grief, but this serves only to confront Rossetti with the riddle of human experience, the riddle of being a feeling creature in a world of objects, a sign-seeker in a world of insignificant things.

I do not offer these two minor poems and a fragment as adequately characteristic of nineteenth-century poetry. I choose them only because they illustrate what seems to me the central problem that more important nineteenth-century poems work with; how is the self, the feeling, thinking human consciousness, related to the world in which it lives? The world impresses itself on us through our senses: we see, hear, taste, touch and smell it. That we think of the senses as both active and passive, as exploring the world when we reach out to stroke a cat, or appreciatively sniff a rose, or as passively receiving the imprint of things outside, as when some rank odour is wafted into our nostrils, is the sign that it is at this level, the level of our sensory experience, that the drama of the self's engagement with the world is most persistently acted out. That is why, I think, nineteenth-century poets almost without exception establish their literary credibility by proving their expertise in rendering sensory experience. Success in this becomes for them the primary test of literary merit, not necessarily the most important, but the first, the test on which all their other achievements depend.

This is a book about how the world of facts is related to the world of values in nineteenth-century poetry. But that is a grand theme, even grandiose, and it is in the nature of such themes that they are resistant to precise handling. I begin, then, with the premise that this engagement of fact and value takes place first, or most primitively, at the level of our sensory experience, and that when a poet seeks to record that engagement his basic tool-kit is the vocabulary of sense-impressions: hard and soft, sweet and sour, yellow and green and light and dark. But that, too, is a large theme. It seems to me possible to take just one kind of sense experience, the kind that is received through the eye, impressions of colour and of light and shade, and the vocabulary that denotes these impressions, in the confidence that one kind of sense impression may represent all the others. This will be a book about how words for colour are used by nineteenth-century poets. In particular, I shall be concerned with those instances in which fact merges with value, in which words for colours, words for primary sense impressions, tremble on the verge of becoming metaphors. The first chapter is preliminary. Thereafter the book is divided into three sections; the first concerns the Romantics, the second Browning, and the third Hopkins.

1
Dull Red

When Kipling returned from India to England he took lodgings in a down-at-heel area of London. From his window he witnessed one day a particularly brutal incident:

> Once I faced the reflection of my own face in the jet-black mirror of the window panes for five days. When the fog thinned, I looked out and saw a man standing opposite the pub where the barmaid lived: on a sudden his breast turned dull red like a robin's, and he crumpled, having cut his throat. In a few minutes – seconds it seemed – a hand-ambulance arrived and took up the body. A pot boy with a bucket of steaming water sluiced the blood off into the gutter, and what little crowd had collected went its way.[1]

The passage is oddly impressive, and its impressiveness has everything to do with the quality of attention it manifests. The suicide's breast 'turned dull red like a robin's'. The precision with which Kipling notes the colour is crucial, for it is this, and this alone, that distinguishes his response from that of the brusquely indifferent pot boy and the casually curious onlookers. They may see a man die, but Kipling attends to it. Such attentiveness is surely not just a deft touch of realism: it approaches an act of piety. As acts of piety go it is bleak enough. It is as if in London, in an area where men live alone in dingy lodgings unlinked by any sense of shared community, the observance demanded by the death of a neighbour has become brutally literal. Kipling observes the man's death, and in doing so he presents himself, so quietly that one would rather say he was recognised, as a human witness in an inhuman world.

Kipling looks at the scene through a window, a perspective that readers of nineteenth- and twentieth-century literature have been taught to suspect, for it has become a symbol of the disingenuous distance of the bourgeois from a reality that he claims to see clearly despite the fact that his sense of his own prestige requires that he remain detached from it. Thackeray could look kindly on affable loungers in the bay-windows of their clubs, but a modern reader is more likely to think of the well-heeled diners at an Alpine resort,

7

secure and superior within 'the plateglass windows of the sports hotel', and thrill with Auden at the imminence of the geological catastrophes from which they are so insecurely defended. It is the perspective, of course, of the realist novelist, who sits at his writing desk and looks at a life that he believes he may represent truly while retaining a wise narrative detachment, shielded from its reality, as it were, by an unseen pane of glass.[2] The realist novel is the art form, perhaps, of a society peopled with individuals whose participation in the life of their communities is signalled only by a twitched lace curtain. It may be very sad that all one can do is to look at one's fellows living and dying rather than to feel their lives as a part of one's own. But given that this was the case, and still is, then Kipling, in attending, in observing, can claim to be fulfilling a minimal human duty.

There are two stories in Kipling's passage: one is about a man cutting his throat, the other is about a man looking out of a window. For five days he has stared at the window, but the thick fog outside has made the panes of glass a mirror, and he has seen only the reflection of his own face. The suicide's story is a realist fiction, but the story of the man in the window is a fable. Kipling, on his arrival in London, sank into an egocentric depression. The clearing of the fog signals, as it so often does in nineteenth-century fiction, his recovery of a properly human sense of duty.[3] His business as a man and as a writer is to look through windows, not into mirrors: he must observe the world outside rather than sit in a solipsistic communion with his own face. The two stories are ironically counterpointed, for at the very moment that the fog clears and Kipling looks through the window to note with keen accuracy the dull red stain spreading on the suicide's shirt the suicide himself retreats into the final isolation of death. Both stories, as it were, record escapes from the prison of self. Kipling sees his own image fade, and is released into a proper attention to the world outside. The suicide violently does away with a self and with a world that he can no longer tolerate. The moral of the passage is clear enough. Kipling witnesses the suicide's death, and his act of attention is a type of the behaviour that will save him from a similar fate.

However Kipling's passage is read, and I grant that it can be read with a lot less fuss than I have chosen to make over it, one thing seems to me crucially true. The passage expresses an escape from a shadowy phantasmal world of private imaginings into a public world of shared reality, and the sign that the escape has been successfully effected is the single phrase 'dull red'.

This may seem odd on two counts. A colour will seem a peculiarly unlikely escape hatch to the real world for those brought up on Newton and Locke. For Newton colour has no existence outside the eye. Red, for example, is just the eye's response to the stimulus of certain wavelengths of light. For Locke colour is only a secondary quality, not 'out there' like size and solidity, but possessed only of the shadowy reality of a mental impression. Second, a colour word like red may strike us as a particularly verbal sort of word. What would we say if a blind man asked us what red was like? We might reply that it was the colour of pillar boxes, of strawberries, of blood. But such an answer would do no more than acquaint him with some specimen usages of the word. We could hardly offer any answer that did more than establish that red was a word for a particular colour, and this is somewhat unsettling. We would hardly be reduced to telling someone who asked what a fork-lift truck was that it was a word for a particular sort of vehicle. How then is it that a word like red, so very verbal a word, can provide a jolt to shake a reader out of a dream into a bracing confrontation with the world of things?

I am uneasily aware that at least two classes of readers will be supplying peremptory answers to my questions. One reader will be muttering that there is no problem here. Our sense of colour is proverbially a last line of defence for our grasp of reality. As sure as skies are blue, we say, as long as grass is green. To such a reader I can only say that it may be of some interest to explore how this came about and what its importance might be. Another group of readers will be comfortably aware that my problems stem from a naïve failure to recognise that the shock of realism I locate in the phrase 'dull red' is only a shock of 'realism', and requires for its understanding neither a knowledge of colours, nor of robins, nor of blood, but of that system of codes through the application of which realist fiction is produced. I would be recommended to an attentive reading of Barthes's *S/Z*. But what I hope to indicate is that a description of realism that takes no account of reality is necessarily as incoherent as a description of realism that takes no account of language.

Suppose Kipling had written: 'on a sudden his breast turned greenish red like a robin's'. There would be a shock certainly, but just as certainly it would not be a shock of reality. That, it might be said, is because the phrase 'greenish red' is ungrammatical. I use the term not because I understand it, but because I have read it often in similar contexts.[4] I suppose it to mean that 'realist' writers obey certain rules in their use of colour terms that prohibit the phrase 'greenish red' while admitting phrases like 'dull red' or 'brownish red'. The problem with such a position is surely that such rules could be defined only in one of two ways; either by listing all outlawed colour phrases, in which case the rules would not in any ordinary sense be rules but simply a list of random prohibitions, or by stating that in a realist text no colour can appear in a phrase conjoined with another colour with which it is discontinuous in the spectrum. That looks like a rule, but what it amounts to is this: 'greenish red' is not a possible description of a colour in a realist text because greenish red is not a possible colour.

I can best return to my original argument by asking a silly question: how many colours are there? Seven, is the reply that springs immediately to most people's lips, and that it should do so is a tribute to the authority of Newton, even when exercised in distinguishing indigo from violet in order to arrive at a magically portentous number. But in any case Newton's colours are only those observed when a beam of light is refracted through a prism. They comprehend all the colours of the rainbow, but rainbows do not display all colours. There is no purple in the rainbow, no black, no brown. I might be told, of course, that there are three primary colours, which might be identified variously as red, yellow and blue, or as red, green and violet. But this is no more useful than it would be to tell someone who asks me how many people there are in my family that I am not sure, but that I know that I have two parents. Not everyone has been so unhelpful. D. R. Hay, for example, projected a classification of 388 colours, although in his *Nomenclature of Colours* published in 1845 he succeeded in naming and illustrating only some 240. His ambition was modest in comparison with that of M.E. Chevreul, a director of dyeing at the Gobelins, who some years earlier had designed a mechanism that would, in the unlikely event that it had ever been constructed, have registered 14,420 colour variations.[5] The more colours the merrier, it might be thought, but any number, however large, will be arbitrary.

Most sensible people would deny that my question made any sense. Colour is, after all, subject to three variables; hue, saturation or purity, and tonality or brightness. In consequence the total possibility of colour may only be represented by some kind of three-dimensional solid such as Runge's colour sphere, within which all possibilities of colour are represented in a continuous range from pure white at one pole to pure black at the other. There is, one might conclude, not a number of colours, but rather an infinite series. But if this were the case then I ought to be as incapable of describing the colour of my tie as I would be of describing the number 437. In fact, I have no such difficulty. I am wearing a dull red tie, I say, or perhaps a greenish-blue tie shot with purple.

The only sensible answers that I have come across were offered by two American anthropologists and my four year old son. My son thought it a reasonable question, counted the colours he knew, and arived at the number twelve. The Americans, Brent Berlin and Paul Kay, find that there are eleven basic colours in English: white, black, red, green, yellow, blue, brown, purple, pink, orange and grey.[6] Their findings differ from my son's because he forgot pink and grey, but added gold, silver and fawn. The common ground between them is their premise, surely a correct one, that my question is about language. We can find out how many colours there are by counting the words we have to describe them.

A visit to a paint shop is enough to indicate that the range of terms that may be drafted into service as colour descriptions is infinitely extensible, but for all that there can be only a limited number of basic colour terms which, used singly or in combination, embrace all possibilities of colour, for if it were otherwise we would meet colours that were within the existing limits of the colour vocabulary indescribable, and this is never the case. Some colours certainly seem more difficult to describe than others. We may often feel that the available words are inadequate to a particular colour experience. But we are never struck dumb. We may quarrel about how to distinguish between the limited number of basic colour terms and the infinitely extensible series of derived terms. Most readers will, I suppose, disagree with the status that my son ascribes to fawn, preferring to think of it as a shade of brown. But however difficult it may be to define, the distinction must surely exist. Colour names on cans of paint – avocado and terracotta and so on – are so far from being basic colour terms that it is possible to doubt whether they are descriptions of colour at all. The band of specimen colour on the tin makes description unnecessary, and the names become a species of politeness, complimenting the purchaser on his choice by implicat-

ing him in a refined taste for posh starters and primitive earthen-
ware.

Colours, then, are hues that we have names for, more particularly
the hues named by those basic colour words that Berlin and Kay and
my son made reasonable attempts at identifying. We have a feeling
that red is a fairly stable quality, and that feeling persists despite the
fact that we know full well that we would be unable to say where the
territory of red ends and that of the neighbouring colours begins.
Our confidence has nothing to do with any facts about colour, and
everything to do with the secure status of the word red. Colours, as
opposed to colour, exist only in the process of being named.

This is not, of course, to claim that the word red and the quality
red are the same. If that were true then we would have to agree with
Dugald Stewart that colour-blindness is simply the product of an
inadequate training in the use of colour words. What it indicates is
that the way in which we use colour words can be explained only by
reference to the system of colour that they describe and to the words
themselves. We may say that greenish-red is the description of an
impossible colour because green and red are not continuous in the
spectrum, and we may also say that it is a description of an
impossible colour because the words green and red operate in
relation to the words orange and yellow, not independently of
them. Each of these statements relies for its force on the other. We
can known that a phrase like greenish-red is improper in a realist
text because it names an impossible experience, but we can
recognise the impossibility of the experience only if we understand
how the words green and red work.

When we describe colours our language and our experience are in
peculiarly close relation, mutually dependent, each achieving
significance only through the other. Colour words reach out to the
flood of colour impressions that bombard us all our waking hours,
and impose on them an organisation that derives in part from
language, but in part too from the nature of the qualities that the
words describe. The same is true, of course, of our words for smell,
touch and sound, but our colour vocabulary is more sophisticated
than our vocabulary for, say, smells, presumably because of the
relatively greater importance in conscious experience of the sense of
sight than the other senses. That colour is an immediate sensual
perception, that it seems so little the product of reflection, is one of
the reasons for Locke's relegation of colour to the status of a
secondary quality. But it is also the reason why colour words are

peculiarly well fitted to perform certain tasks. Kipling, sunk in a painful meditation on his own reflection, escapes from self-consciousness into a consciousness of the life, here ironically the death, around him, and the colour phrase 'dull red' is able perfectly to express that initial moment of attention.

Colour, then, and the words that we use to describe it, are on the frontier of the self's encounter with the world. More than that, they are at the frontier between the private world of impressions that take place sealed in the brain, and the public world of language. There are those who would deny that what goes on in our heads can ever be tied to the words that we use to describe it. They would argue that whenever we agree on a colour description, agree with Kipling perhaps in finding a robin's breast dull red, we have established only that dull red is a phrase that we have agreed to attach to a particular impression, and have no assurance that the impression, as opposed to the phrase, is common between us. John Wisdom, for example, imagines a man called Smith:

> Smith, of course, when asked the colours of the Union Jack, replies, 'Red, white and blue,' because he has been taught to call the colours he then sees 'red', 'white' and 'blue'. But does he then see the same colours red, white and blue as we do or does he see, say, black, green and yellow?[7]

Wisdom is surely mistaken, and his mistake is to imagine that colour words function independently of one another. For the normally sighted speaker, for example, red and blue merge into each other as purple, and his use of the terms red and blue is dependent on this fact. If a robin's breast is dull red, then this means among other things that it is not purple, that the possibility of it being purple has been entertained, and discounted. Now Smith who sees red as black and blue as yellow, if he were to maintain his secret through his life, would have to see yellowish black as purple, and this he could not do, because yellowish black could not exist. Nor is it the case that Wisdom has just chosen his transposed colours clumsily. Suppose, for example, he saw red as orange, orange as yellow, yellow as green, and green as blue. This might seem an undiscoverable error, but it is not so. The areas of the colour system that we describe by our simple colour terms are not identically shaped. The colour blue, for example, names a larger area of the colour system than the colour yellow: it comprehends more colour experiences. A colour so dark that it had ceased to be yellow would still be blue. The result is that no transposition of colours, no substitution of one colour for another, is possible that would not result in linguistic differences between Smith and the rest of us. It seems to be the case, then, that people with a similar ability to discriminate between colours have a similar experience of colours. When Kipling looks out of the window and sees a dull red stain like a robin's breast spreading across the suicide's shirt he emerges from an unspeakable world, a world imprisoned in the depressive's skull, and enters a world where experience, because it is common to most of us, can be expressed undisguised within our common language.

There is a problem with Kipling's passage that I have not yet mentioned. To compare a man who has just cut his throat with a robin redbreast is to stumble on the edge of – some readers will think it is to fall into – a grotesque lapse of taste. A more sensitive writer than Kipling would no doubt have avoided a comparison that risked seeming so incongruously witty. But if the passage survives the infelicity – and I think it does – then surely it owes its survival once again to the flat little phrase 'dull red'. Suppose Kipling had written, 'on a sudden his breast turned as red as a robin's'. Most readers would flinch immediately from such callous facetiousness. But the suicide's breast turned 'dull red like a robin's', and the tiny change is enough to convince the reader that Kipling's business was looking hard, and looking exactly. His very failure to notice that the simile he arrives at risks being misconstrued might even be useful as an indication that his concern is not at all with good taste but with looking, and with passing on as clearly as possible what he saw. His ability to note and to name a colour can stand as the badge of his whole endeavour.

To turn the mind outwards, to be distracted from self-absorption to the study of the world outside, seems to Kipling self-evidently a good. But not everyone would agree with him. When the hero of Shelley's *Alastor* awakes from a dream in which he has enjoyed a blissful union with a visionary maiden, an ideal version of himself in woman's form, he cries to sleep again. He opens his eyes on an alien landscape:

> Roused by the shock he started from his trance –
> The cold white light of morning, the blue moon
> Low in the west, the clear and garish hills,
> The distinct valley and the vacant woods
> Spread round him where he stood.

(192–6)

His perceptions are as sharp as Kipling's, but they wound rather than heal. Their clarity is painful because it shatters his dream. The two passages are as different as the two writers. Colours may be crucial in both, but they serve very different purposes. And yet there is still something in common between Kipling's use of the phrase 'dull red' and Shelley's use of 'cold white', 'blue', and 'garish'. In the chapters that follow I shall try to indicate a range of purposes to which the vocabulary of colour may lend itself, and also to indicate that within the nineteenth century, the period roughly framed by the passages from Shelley and from Kipling, these various purposes have something in common.

Part One
The Romantics

2
Awful Newton

In 1798 the Royal Academy for the first time allowed quotations to appear in the catalogue of the summer exhibition. The quotation Turner chose to illustrate *Buttermere Lake*, one of the paintings he exhibited that year, was less than startling. The painting shows a boat drifting, as the rowers contemplate a sombre landscape that has been blessed by a pale rainbow. Turner chose the lines from Thomson's *Spring* which were the most famous of all eighteenth-century attempts to explain the contribution made by Newton's *Opticks* to the aesthetic appreciation of natural appearances:

> Till, in the western sky, the downward sun
> Looks out, effulgent, from amid the flush
> Of broken clouds, gay-shifting to his beam
> The rapid radiance instantaneous strikes
> The illumined mountain, through the forest streams,
> Shakes on the flood, and in a yellow mist,
> Far-smoking o'er the interminable plain,
> In twinkling myriads lights the dewy gems.
> ...
> Meantime refracted from yon eastern cloud,
> Bestriding earth, the grand ethereal bow
> Shoots up immense; and every hue unfolds,
> In fair proportion running from the red
> To where the violet fades into the sky.
> Here, awful Newton, the dissolving clouds
> Form, fronting on the sun, thy showery prism;
> And to the sage-instructed eye unfold
> The various twine of light, by thee disclosed
> From the white mingling blaze. Not so the swain:
> He wondering views the bright enchantment bend,
> Delightful, o'er the radiant fields, and runs
> To catch the falling glory; but amazed

Beholds the amusive arch before him fly,
Then vanish quite away.

(189–96 and 203–17)

But if Turner's choice of quotation is predictable, the version of it
that he gives is odd:

Till in the western sky the downward sun
Looks out effulgent – the rapid radiance instantaneous strikes
Th'illumined mountain – in a yellow mist
Bestriding earth – The grand ethereal bow
Shoots up immense, and every hue unfolds.[1]

The oddity is not in Turner's wrenching of sense and metre, which
is entirely characteristic, but in the content of his lines. He omits
not only Thomson's references to Newton but all those lines in
which Thomson describes Newton's discovery that the spectrum is
an analysis of white light, its seven colours the 'various' threads
that together form the white 'twine' of light. Turner's painting may
be enough to explain why he tinkered with Thomson's lines. His
rainbow is peculiarly ill-adapted to illustrate the principle of
refraction, for it is composed simply of white paint stippled with
yellow, and seeks not at all to render the 'fair proportion running
from the red / To where the violet fades into the sky' that
Thomson notes in his bow. It is at a far remove from the bows
depicted by Thomson's illustrators, who specialised in arches
neatly divided into seven distinct bands of colour. Nevertheless, it
may be worth considering whether Turner's cool omission of any
reference to 'awful Newton' might not be more generally significant.

It is hard to determine with any certainty what exactly Turner's
response to Newtonian thought might have been.[2] The chief
evidence consists of the terse annotations scribbled by Turner in
his copy of *Goethe's Theory of Colours*, and the still more cryptic
caption that he appended to his lost painting *Fountain of Fallacy*.[3] In
addition there are the companion pictures *Shade and Darkness* and
Light and Colour (Goethe's Theory) but these are difficult in themselves, and the reference to Goethe, whether it applies to both
paintings or only to the second, is obscure.

Turner's annotations to Goethe have been read as essentially Newtonian. This is not demonstrably wrong, but strikes me as unlikely. Turner quite misses the tone of outraged patriotism mingled with scientific contempt that characterised the typical English response to Goethe's theory. He notes where Goethe's position is not distinct from Newton's, but when he does so he seems irritated rather than pleased. Most interestingly, when Goethe subscribes in a careless moment to Newton's fiction that each ray of light is a bundle of seven coloured rays, Turner comments 'what advance[?] on Newton – one ray suffices to light the World'. I cannot attach much sense to this, but it reads most easily as an expression of exasperation that Goethe, for all his anti-Newtonian trumpetings, still has not relinquished this crucial part of Newton's theory.

The lines affixed to *Fountain of Fallacy* are these:

> Its rainbow-dew diffused fell on each anxious lip,
> Working wild fantasy; imagining;
> First science in the immeasurable abyss of thought
> Measured her orbits slumbering.

The most authoritative Turner scholars agree that science is represented here as 'a stabilizing force against "wild fantasy"', and reject Jack Lindsay's suggestion that the lines express a Blakean contempt of Newton's sleep.[4] But Lindsay must surely be right. Science cannot stabilise fantasy because it is represented as itself a fantasy, a closed system occupying a mental space, devoid of reference to any world outside the brain. Science measures 'her orbits' rather than the orbits of planetary bodies, and her orbits wheel in 'the immeasurable abyss of thought', subject only to mental, mathematical control. It is impossible not to detect irony in the opposition between 'immeasurable' and 'Measured', and in the final, dismissive 'slumbering'. Science is a dream that can be entertained only when the eyes are closed against the world of appearances. Turner's lines invoke the opposition between the 'true' world available to the mathematician and the delusive world of appearances inhabited by the multitude that figures so often in eighteenth-century nature poetry, Thomson's opposition between the 'sage-instructed eye' and the eye of the 'wondering swain' tricked by the rainbow's 'amusive' light. But Turner invokes the opposition only to deny its point. We, the anxious-lipped, dream waking: they, the scientists, dream asleep. Turner allows no egress from the world of fallacy, least of all through an abstract, mathematical space.

In associating colour, 'rainbow dew', with fallacy, Turner maintains a conventional eighteenth-century notion. Newton and Locke, after all, both insist that colour is an experience that takes place in the mind: it is not a direct experience of a quality that has an existence outside the self. It was a short, if illogical, step from this position to Addison's belief that things seen 'in their proper figures and motions' would not be coloured. Colour becomes a gracious device by means of which a world that would otherwise 'make but a poor appearance to the eye' is rendered 'agreeable to the imagination':

> In short our souls are at present delightfully lost and bewildered in a pleasing delusion, and we walk about like the enchanted hero of a romance, who sees the beautiful castles, woods, and meadows; and at the same time hears the warbling of birds, and the purling of streams; but upon the finishing of the same secret spell, the fantastic scene breaks up, and the disconsolate knight finds himself on a barren heath, or in a solitary desert.

Addison does not make it clear how the magic spell could conceivably be broken, and we be plunged into a dismal world without light, colour, sound and so on. Nor is his attempt to describe what a world that cannot be experienced might be like all that convincing. But, whatever one might think of it, Addison's uneasy sense that colour is not a quality of the 'proper' nature of things, that because it is an experience that begins and ends in the mind it is somehow fictitious, is an expression of a very general prejudice. The neoclassical championing of white marble, of line over colour, owes at least as much to this as it did to any study of the antique.

When, in *Colour and Light (Goethe's Theory)*, Turner peoples his canvas with queer little heads enclosed in iridescent bubbles, he seems to be offering a visual representation of Addison's position. But there are two crucial differences. First, Addison's anxiety is play-acted. Colour is a 'pleasing delusion', a delusion that we all share, and for which we should be grateful. But Addison's tone suggests that it yields pleasure for our idle hours and to an idle faculty, the imagination. The references to romances, enchantment and spells work to associate our need for colour with our childishness. Addison may politely implicate himself in the general craving for delusion, but his is a false modesty. The mere fact that he can see such childishness for what it is indicates his superiority to it. In their adult capacities, Addison suggests, when men think rather than imagine, they are content to conceive of things 'in their proper figures and motions'. Colour is one of 'The Pleasures of the Imagination', and such pleasures are harmless, even estimable, but not to be taken too seriously.

The truth for Turner is quite different. The iridescent bubbles that surround the heads of his homunculi do not distinguish them as childish idlers, but define their representative humanity. One is reminded more of Shelley in *The Triumph of Life*:

> Figures ever new
> Rise on the bubble, paint them how you may;
> We have but thrown, as those before us threw,
> Our shadows on it as it passed away.

(248–51)

But Shelley will sometimes envision an escape from the delusive world of appearances into the permanent truth of 'white radiance', even if, as in *Adonais*, such truth is fully available only in death, 'white death'. Turner is sceptical of any such salvation.

Turner's *Regulus* shows Carthage, its wharves crowded with citizens assembled to witness the departure of Regulus for Rome. But the painting is dominated by a fierce white sun, just rising. Turner was watched as he approached the canvas with 'a large palette, nothing on it but a huge lump of flake-white' and 'two or three biggish hog tools' and began 'driving the white into all the hollows and every part of the surface', until it became a picture of 'brilliant sunshine absorbing everything', shooting out in strongly ruled rays from the central sun which was 'a lump of white, standing out like the boss of a shield'.[5] The large pat of flaky white that Turner applied so violently to the canvas grimly reminds us of the fate awaiting Regulus, when, his negotiations having failed, he nobly insists on returning to Carthage and imprisonment. His eyelids will be cut off, and he will be forced to stare at that pulsing sun until he is blinded. The painting alludes to Regulus's heroism, but it does not represent it. What it represents is white light, white radiance, and it suggests a sceptical answer to any Shelleyan faith that in the contemplation of such light we may extricate ourselves from the fallacies of colour. Regulus escapes from colour into darkness, for to stare at white radiance is to be blinded.

Colour, then, is fallacious: it offers no trustworthy knowledge of the real world. So far Turner is in agreement with a conventional line of eighteenth-century thought. A painter who subscribed to this notion might be expected to eschew colour, to adopt a linear style capable of representing solid truth, to aspire, perhaps, to a style something like Flaxman's in his illustrations to Homer. But Turner is the greatest colourist of English art, the first painter to organise whole pictures in terms of colour rather than of form, and he is a colourist not in spite of but because of his suspicion that colour, 'rainbow-dew', has its origins in the fountain of fallacy. Turner prizes colour precisely because it is fallacious, and therefore an apt symbol of the fallacies that define human experience.

It is possible to understand the mangled quotation from Thomson that Turner appends to *Buttermere Lake* as signalling, if only accidentally, a decisive break with a characteristic eighteenth-century mode of thought. Marjorie Hope Nicolson has shown that throughout the eighteenth century it was Newton's *Opticks* rather than his *Principia* that exercised the stronger hold on the poetic imagination.[6] In particular, poets were fascinated by Newton's discovery of the constitution of light. She does not explain why this should be so, and any explanation is bound to be speculative, but she provides the evidence on which any speculation must be founded. She notes, for example, that tributes to Newton's optical discoveries tend to begin with a hymn to light echoing one of Milton's several celebrations of light in *Paradise Lost*, most commonly the invocation to Book III. Such echoes work to sustain the traditional association between light and divinity, so that when poets such as Mallet and Thomson proceed from a celebration of light to a description of the various colours derived from it, the movement is felt as a transition from the infinite to the finite, from the heavenly to the earthly. Newton's *Opticks* became crucial as metaphor, for as metaphor Newton's discovery sustained the premise on which philosophical nature poems of the eighteenth century rest. The colours of the natural world are an analysis of invisible white light. The business of arriving at a knowledge of the infinite through a study of the finite, of a knowledge of God through a study of Nature, may be construed as a simple process of rational deduction, which may be both symbolised and illustrated by Newton's discovery of the relationship between light and colour.

I put the matter baldly to expose what is surely true, that no English poet of the eighteenth century aspired to a deism so shallow. Thomson, the greatest of these poets, is also their representative. He distinguishes 'the brutish gaze' that is aware only of the sensual manifold of experience from 'the sage-instructed eye', aware of the rational laws that organise the apparent chaos of sensory impressions. But Thomson knows that even the sage cannot penetrate to the ultimate order underlying human existence, that such an order is made visible not by the white light analysed by Newton but by the 'light ineffable' of God. The analogy associating the two lights must in the end be abandoned. But God's light is 'ineffable'. The epithet is precise. Thomson can acknowledge the need for such a light, but he can otherwise take no account of it. In consequence *The Seasons* is a deistic poem that registers its awareness of the limitations of deism only by substituting for a conclusion a silence. The order perceived by the 'sage-instructed eye' is incomplete in comparison with the order perceived by God, but the divine order may only be contemplated, not spoken. The *Hymn to the Seasons* ends when that higher duty is begun:

> Come then, expressive silence, muse His praise.

Attacks on Newton in the Romantic period are traditionally illustrated by mention of Blake's prayer to be protected from 'one-fold vision and Newton's sleep', and Keats's assertion that Newton had 'destroyed all the poetry of the rainbow by reducing it to its prismatic colours'. Blake was mad, and Keats drunk, so there seems little need to ascribe such sentiments to anything more than a rash contempt for the scientific mind, which may, or may not, be generalised into a characteristic Romantic attitude. But this is inadequate. Goethe and Coleridge, who could be accused of a contempt for science only if science is very precisely defined, joined in the condemnation of Newton's *Opticks*. It helps to explain, if not to excuse, their foolhardiness if we understand that their objections are as much to the mode of thinking of which Newton's optical discoveries had come to act both as an example and as an illustrative metaphor, as to the theory itself.

Goethe denied that colour could be explained simply in terms of the decomposition of light. Rather, colour was the product of a conflict between light and darkness. He adduced various experimental findings in support of his belief, but he could present this evidence as convincing only by misunderstanding Newton's methods so completely that his mistakes seem wilful rather than obtuse. His argument seems to be impelled by a need to reconcile scientific truth with an intuitive faith in a set of beliefs common in the neoplatonic and mystical traditions. Newton must be revised in order to sanction the metaphors of such men as Plotinus and Boehme. This may seem an outlandish ground for objecting to Newton, but it was oddly widespread.

One urgent problem seems to have been that to represent colour simply as the product of the decomposition of light compromises light's unity. This did not worry eighteenth-century Newtonians. Richard Savage speaks of 'promiscuous white', Thomson of a 'white mingling blaze'. But these are unfortunate epithets for those who wish to think of light as a metaphor for the divine and who take their metaphors seriously. If colours were, on the other hand, the product of a conflict between light and darkness, then the multiplicity of colour need not compromise the unity of light. Goethe seems to have felt this, and there were those among his readers prepared to sympathise. Coleridge, writing to Tieck, is excited by news that Goethe has published an attack on Newton's *Opticks*. 'I never could believe', he writes, 'that light was a mere synodical individuum.'[7] Like Goethe, Coleridge needed an optics that sanctioned the opposition between the one and the many. White light must remain a convincing metaphor for the One so that the multitude of colours might figure the multiplicities of the finite world. It may be that something like the same thought lies behind Turner's obscure counterblast to Newton: 'one ray suffices to light the World'. Shelley may seem the least likely of the Romantic poets to have denied a scientific truth on the ground that it was metaphorically inconvenient, but the best known stanza from *Adonais* scarcely bears this out:

> The One remains, the many change and pass;
> Heaven's light forever shines, Earth's shadows fly;
> Life, like a dome of many-coloured glass,
> Stains the white radiance of Eternity,
> Until Death tramples it to fragments.

(460–4)

These lines are normally glossed to bring them into line with scientific orthodoxy. The dome is understood to refer to the earth's atmospheric cocoon which refracts sunbeams to produce the blue of the sky. But blue sky is not much like 'a dome of many-coloured glass'. It seems more apt to note that in the second line 'Heaven's light' is posed against 'Earth's shadows'. Life is held by an age-old tradition to partake of the natures both of Heaven and Earth, and similarly colour, in the anti-Newtonian tradition, is explained as the product both of heavenly light and earthly shadow. The dome 'Stains' white radiance. The verb suggests that white light is modified rather than simply analysed by contact with the gross atmosphere of mortal life. Indeed, it could hardly be otherwise, for were Shelley's 'white radiance' like Savage's 'promiscuous' it could not very well act as a proper type of the One.

The attack on Newton was necessary, it seems, to preserve the authoritative contrast between the One and the many. But it was not simply this. Newton's *Opticks* both figured and illustrated a static, mechanical view of the world. Newton has light that can be analysed into colours, and colours that may, in theory though he does not know how, be compounded into white light. Light may be taken apart as colour, and colours may be put back together again as light. The theory figures the notion that a whole may be dismembered into parts, which, skilfully assembled, will reconstitute the whole. It runs counter to the dynamic, organicist thrust of Romantic thought. When Goethe insists that darkness as well as light is necessary for the production of colour, he rejects a static model in favour of a dynamic model. Light and dark become warring contraries: colour the product of a dialectical struggle. If one is looking for a third term, darkness seems the obvious choice. Colours, after all, seem darker than light and lighter than darkness. Coleridge, typically, scorned the obvious and plumped for gravitation. 'Colour', he writes obscurely '= light under the praepotence of gravitation'.[8] I have no notion of what he might mean, unless it is simply an unhelpful reference to the refractive effect of the earth's atmosphere. But the remark at least serves to illustrate how eagerly the Romantics sought an optics that fitted their favourite modes of thought. Light and colour, it seems, were metaphors too precious to be left prisoner in the camp of the deists.

Newton believed that colours were simply the eye's response to different wavelengths of light. In the rays separated by the prism 'there is nothing else but a certain Power and Disposition to stir up a sensation of this or that Colour'. When we see that grass is green, the sky blue, or strawberries red, what prompts our perception is 'nothing but a Disposition' in the grass, sky or strawberry 'to reflect this or that sort of Rays more copiously than the rest'. Various sorts of rays 'propagate this or that Motion into the Sensorium', and these motions are then experienced as sensations 'under the Form of Colours'.[9] But this, if it is idealism, is idealism of a much too empirical kind to satisfy men like Goethe and Coleridge. Newton's 'sensorium' is little more than a super-efficient translating service, interpreting each of the infinitely variable wavelengths of light as one of the infinitely variable possibilities of colour. Its role is essentially passive. Hence Coleridge's irritation. He arose from a study of Newton's *Opticks* confirmed in the opinion that 'Newton was a mere materialist – *Mind* in his system is always passive – a lazy Looker-on on an external world'.[10]

Goethe's *Farbenlehre* is best seen as a concerted attack on the passivity of the Newtonian model of perception. He begins by drawing attention to the flecks and splashes of colour that may be produced by a blow to the head, or by tightly shutting the eyelids, or that may occur casually. Such phenomena had often been noted but dismissed as trivial. For Goethe they are crucial. They allow him to make a radical distinction between subjective experiences of colour and objective experiences. He associates the two through another phenomenon long known but little considered, the phenomenon of complementarity: the fact that if one gazes attentively at a red circle on a white background, one sees, immediately on closing one's eyes, a green circle on a black background. This demonstrates to Goethe that all our experience of colour is dynamic: the eye responds to the colours of the outside world with colours of its own. It strives continually for spectral completeness; stimulated by red it will respond with green, stimulated by yellow it will respond with purple, and so on. Complementarity becomes for Goethe a type of the mode in which the opposition between the self and the world generates human experience.

In the Romantic response to Newton the history of science becomes entangled with the history of metaphor.

3

A Rainbow in the Sky

My heart leaps up when I behold
A rainbow in the sky:
So was it when my life began;
So is it now I am a man;
So be it when I shall grow old,
    Or let me die!
The Child is father of the Man;
And I could wish my days to be
Bound each to each by natural piety.

Stephen Prickett is the historian of the Romantic rainbow. In his *The Poetry of Growth*,[1] he identifies the rainbow and various related phenomena as Wordsworth's and Coleridge's central symbols for the imagination. Coleridge's definition of the symbol as the 'translucence of the infinite through the finite' suggests how the rainbow may represent the defining activity of the poet's imagination, for, in the rainbow, light, the type of the infinite, shines through a translucent water-drop to produce the bow. The rainbow becomes, in this reading, a symbol of peculiar authority, for it is the symbol of the symbol-making activity itself. It is not a figure peculiar to Coleridge.

In *The Triumph of Life* Shelley has Rousseau describe how his memories began when he awoke from sleep. It was dawn. The sun streamed through a cavern, and was reflected from the waters of a well:

there stood
Amid the sun, as he amid the blaze
Of his own glory, on the vibrating
Floor of the fountain, paved with flashing rays,
A Shape all light, which with one hand did fling
Dew on the earth, as if she were the dawn,
Whose invisible rain forever seemed to sing
A silver music on the mossy lawn,

> And still before her on the dusky grass
> Iris her many-coloured scarf had drawn ...

> (348–57)

The 'Shape all light' stands on the water where the sun's reflection burns, and flings dew. She embodies the process which creates the rainbow that Rousseau sees before him on the grass, and Rousseau responds to her with loving awe. She symbolises, as Coleridge's rainbow does, the process of symbol-making,[2] and for the same reason. She is the sun shining through dew-drops, the translucence of the infinite through the finite, and the badge of her activity is the 'many-coloured scarf' that Rousseau sees before him on the grass. He reverences the Shape because she embodies the process of symbol-making, the defining characteristic of his own, the poet's, calling.

What follows is a bitter anecdote. The Shape offers Rousseau a cup. He drinks from it, and suddenly his brain becomes 'as sand'. The Shape fades and disappears as a new vision bursts on Rousseau, a vision of the supernaturally bright chariot of life which binds all men, or almost all, to follow it in a hopeless progress towards death. The sequence of events that Rousseau records can be understood as a commentary on Wordsworth's *Immortality Ode*, and on Wordsworth's little lyric on the rainbow which summarises the ode to which it became an epigraph. Rousseau recognises the 'Shape all light' as his muse, the peculiarly Romantic muse that binds its adherent to the service of a vision that can be glimpsed only fitfully, only in intense but short-lived moments of symbolic apprehension. Rousseau drinks from the cup that the Shape offers to mark his election of her as his muse. Immediately, and as a matter of course, the chariot of life bursts on him, for to choose the 'Shape all light' as one's muse is to render the rest of life a meaningless temporal sequence: it is to be burdened with the knowledge that life is only a futile, linear progress from day to day. When the chariot approaches, the Shape fades and disappears, like the morning star at dawn. But ever afterwards its presence is 'felt by one who hopes / That his day's path may end as he began it':

> So knew I in that light's severe excess
> The presence of that Shape which on the stream
> Moved, as I moved along the wilderness,
> More dimly than a day-appearing dream,

The ghost of a forgotten form of sleep,
A light from heaven, whose half-extinguished beam
Through the sick day in which we wake to weep
Glimmers, forever sought, forever lost ...

(424–31)

The 'Shape all light' fades, as rainbows fade. To fade is the nature of both of them. Nevertheless, Wordsworth and Shelley both attach their faiths that life might amount to more than a wearying succession of days, that a man's days might be 'bound each to each', that his day of life might 'end as he began it', to the momentary vision, for only in such visions, when the finite is recognised as a translucent medium through which the infinite shines, is time redeemed, life fraught with intimations of immortality. For all that Wordsworth's calm prayer is tonally at odds with the febrile pathos of Shelley's Rousseau, 'My heart leaps up' and *The Triumph of Life* may be read as commentaries on one another.

Prickett's book has a second theme, which he illustrates by quoting an epigram by Hopkins:

It was a hard thing to undo this knot.
The rainbow shines, but only in the thought
Of him that looks. Yet not in that alone,
For who makes rainbows by invention?
And many standing round a waterfall
See one bow each, yet not the same to all.
The sun on falling waters writes the text
Which yet is in the eye or in the thought.
It was a hard thing to undo this knot.

No two men see the same rainbow because the rainbow is produced both by the sun shining through water and by the eye that witnesses it. The rainbow becomes the symbol of the knot binding together the mind of man and the world in which man lives. It becomes the appropriate emblem for Wordsworth's whole achievement, for his peculiar theme is 'the discerning intellect of Man / When wedded to the goodly universe', his poetry is 'the spousal verse / Of this great consummation'. The rainbow for Prickett is a capacious symbol, figuring both the process of symbol-making that defines the poetic imagination, and also the interfusion of man's mind with the natural world.

Prickett is not much concerned with the rainbow as a traditional Christian symbol, but Wordsworth's rainbow gains the symbolic resonance it has partly because Wordsworth secularises or naturalises a traditional Christian symbolism. That this is so becomes clear if one compares Wordsworth's lyric with some diffuse and undistinguished lines by Thomas Campbell entitled 'To the Rainbow'. Campbell's poem dilutes Wordsworth's sentiments and at the same time reasserts their Christian orthodoxy. Wordsworth's joy, his leaping heart when he sees a rainbow, presents as natural an emotion that an orthodox Christian has a pious duty to feel. 'In that heavenly circle', writes Ruskin, 'which binds the statutes of colour upon the sky, when it became the sign of the covenant of peace, the same hues of divided light were sanctified to the human heart forever'.[3] For Wordsworth as for the Christian the rainbow marks a covenant, though between man and nature rather than between man and God. In the Bible God promises that the covenant will be kept 'for perpetual generations', and Wordsworth naturalises, too, the term of the contract. He prays only that it may last throughout his life. Wordsworth grounds the religious myth in the facts of his own human nature, and in doing so he binds together not only all his days, but himself with the long tradition of Christian believers winding behind him through the centuries. It is surely this that allows a poem that begins as a slight, subjective lyric to end so naturally in a massive impersonal prayer that Wordsworth intones not for himself alone, but as a priest, on behalf of us all.

Prickett treats Hopkins's poem as an elucidation of a knotty problem in epistemology. It is that certainly, but it surely has wider implications. It is a meditation on the rainbow in the guise of a knot. The rainbow is both a hard knot to undo and a 'text'. 'Text' is from *textus*, that which is woven or knotted, but the word cannot be confined to its etymological meaning. The whole poem is concerned with the relationship between the world of the mind and the world outside the mind. The word 'knot' comes to Hopkins, I suspect, weighted by his memory of Donne's 'subtle knot', the knot that ties together the body and soul, that implicates the spiritual with the physical. Such a knotting is the condition of beauty, and the rainbow is its apt symbol, for the rainbow's beauty is the product of spiritual light shining through physical water-drops. The word 'text' reminds us, too, that the rainbow figures in a biblical text. When God sanctified the rainbow by choosing it as the sign of his covenant with man, he implicated one with another, knotted

together, the two texts to which Hopkins is devoted, the Bible and
the natural world. God indicates in that crucial passage how the
rainbow is to be read: he makes the rainbow a text, so binding
together again, as they were bound together by the divine fiat *logos*
and *geos*, God's word and his creation. Campbell makes a similar
point in his final stanza:

> For, faithful to its sacred page
> Heaven still rebuilds thy span,
> Nor lets the type grow pale with age
> That first spoke peace to man.

'Type' is, of course, a pun, but in one of its senses it describes the
world as an ancient book, the ink of its type unfaded. Like Hopkins,
Campbell marks the rainbow as the point at which God's two texts,
the Bible and the world, intersect. The covenant God made with
Noah prefigures the later covenant sealed by the life of Christ. The
rainbow is a type of Christ, which is why, in Christian iconography,
Christ may be represented seated on a rainbow. But the typology is
not simply conventional, for the refraction of divine light through a
water-drop appropriately figures God's assumption of human
form, his majesty accommodated to human powers of understanding. The knot so hard to undo on which Hopkins meditates is in part
the divinity knotted with the humanity of Christ. The fact that no
two pairs of eyes see the same rainbow delicately figures the truth,
important to Hopkins, that Christ is for all men yet also for each
man, so that although he is revealed, he must yet be by each of us
discovered: 'He is all the world's hero, the desire of nations. But
besides he is the hero of single souls.'[4]

The Christian tradition plays around almost all nineteenth-century rainbows that aspire to be anything more than picturesque, and
this is true whether or not the rainbow-maker is a Christian.[5]
Turner, for example, makes free use of the traditional Christian
symbolism, even though he uses it either secularly or ironically. Eric
Shanes suggests that the rainbow in his *Nottingham* celebrates the
new covenant between the government and the people sealed in the
1832 Reform Bill, and the rainbow in *Stonyhurst College* celebrates
the emancipation of the School's Catholic pupils and teachers in the
Bill of 1829.[6] When Turner was old, and the labour of preparing
new canvases for the Academy's summer exhibition at last became
too much, he took up once again a stormy seascape that he had

painted thirty years before, *The Wreck-Buoy*, and he painted over the
buoy, the grim memorial of a foundered ship and drowned sailors, a
wide arching rainbow Its function is ironic; to point the hollowness
of the promise made to Noah. The rainbow here becomes one more
symbol of the fallacies of hope.

Constable was at a far remove from Turner in matters of religion
as in much else. Evident throughout his correspondence, but
especially in his letters to his wife and to his friend John Fisher, is a
deep and orthodox piety. The rainbow is a recurrent motif in
Constable, the landscape of Salisbury Cathedral crowned with a
bow being only the most famous example. That bow may well alude
topically to the successful negotiation by the Church of one of those
threats to its security over which Fisher and Constable show
themselves in their letters to have been in a recurrent state of
anxiety. But it figures a more general truth. The painting marks the
friendship of Constable and Fisher as symbolic, for the landscape
painter and the clergyman are both priests, each with a duty to
interpret one of God's two texts to men, and if Fisher's task finds its
proper emblem in his church, the great cathedral, then Constable's
vocation is fittingly symbolised by the rainbow that crowns it.

The rainbow meant to Constable much more than a single natural
phenomenon: it reached out to include the whole range of natural
appearances that he had taken it as his particular task to render. He
came to recognise Rubens as his most important predecessor, and it
is in his lecture on Rubens's landscapes that the full significance he
attaches to rainbows becomes clear:

> By the Rainbow of Rubens, I do not allude to a particular picture,
> for Rubens often introduced it. I mean, indeed, more than the
> rainbow itself. I mean dewy light and freshness, the dissipating
> shower with the exhilaration of the returning sun, effects which
> Rubens, more than any other painter, has perfected on canvas.[7]

Constable is modest. 'Dewy light and freshness' were his own forte,
noted alike by his admirers and by those who spoke contemptuously of Constable's 'snow', the flecks of white paint with which
he scatters light over his canvasses. In this extended definition of
the rainbow it comes to signify the interfusion of light and matter
that it was Constable's chief ambition to realise. Leslie speaks of
Constable's refusal to accept that the sky ought to be 'a white sheet
thrown behind the objects', his insistence that 'the sky is the source

of light in nature and governs everything'.[8] In a Constable landscape the sky and the objects that the sky makes visible are interfused, and for him the rainbow symbolises this interfusion. It is an aesthetic ideal: the sky, the source of light, is recognised as the force that establishes the organic unity of the landscape. But I doubt whether it is merely aesthetic. Constable after all admired Poussin because he believed his landscapes to be 'full of religious and moral feeling'. Every successful landscape is, in Constable's extended definition of the word, a rainbow recognised, and keeps for him, I suspect, something like the significance of the archetypal rainbow. In a Constable landscape sky and land are married by light, and their wedding becomes the fitting badge of the original covenant by which God bound himself to man and to man's world.

4

Blue, Glossy Green, and Velvet Black

A French critic caterogised Constable's work as Shakespearean rather than Homeric. Constable, he argued, had an unclassical concern for naturalistic detail at the expense of the harmony of the whole. It is an early version of the distinction Arnold was to make between the Hellenic genius, characterised by its architectonic power, and the Celtic genius, defined by its power of natural magic. Constable went a long way towards accepting the criticism. But the same could be said, he added, of most modern poetry, the same could be said of *The Ancient Mariner*, 'the greatest modern poem'.[1] Though I can find no evidence to support this, Turner, too, must surely have found *The Ancient Mariner* congenial. Jack Lindsay has identified 'the sunset ship', the helpless or storm-battered hulk silhouetted against a crimson sun, as Turner's focal image,[2] and *The Ancient Mariner* contains the mightiest description in verse of such a vessel.

But the two painters would, one suspects, have admired rather different poems. Constable, who declared that he had never seen an ugly thing in his life, would have understood immediately how 'slimy things that crawled with legs / Upon a slimy sea' must be recognised as beautiful before the heart might be healed. The mariner's natural piety – 'He prayeth best who loveth best / All things both great and small' – he would surely have accepted as holy simplicity. But Turner's imagination would have been seized by the ghastly glamour of the skeleton ship outlined against a bloody sun, and a game of dice over the fates of men in which the best that may be hoped for is that death wins.

The Ancient Mariner sorts as easily with Turner's gloomy scepticism as with Constable's earnest piety, and this points to its place as, if not the greatest, then at any rate a central Romantic poem. I have no quarrel with the often repeated and commonly accepted reading of it.[3] The mariner, in shooting the albatross, commits a crime against the sacramental unity of life, 'the One Life within us and abroad'. He wantonly and irreverently breaks the bond that ought to bind us each to each as living denizens of a living world. For this crime he is punished, most tellingly by isolation from his fellow men, and by isolation from God. He is rescued from his plight when he suddenly recognises the beauty of the water snakes, and finds himself able to pray. Then he is magically returned to his home port, and to the joys of human society, delighting to 'walk together to the kirk / With a goodly company'. Various cruxes remain: what the game of dice played between Death and Life-in-Death might betoken, whether the mariner's subsequent existence, passing 'like night from land to land', ought to be understood as a continuation of the curse against him or as a mission which he is privileged to carry out, and so on. But with these I will have little to do. They seem to me in any case a good deal less intractable than they have been made to seem. My concern is simply to establish through a discussion of Coleridge's poem my general point, that the contrast between light and colour is a part of the grid within which the Romantic imagination structures itself, and to indicate in some detail how, in this one instance, the contrast operates.

From the outset of the voyage the mariner's ship is blown south. It crosses the equator and is driven all the way to the Antarctic ice-cap. It is there that the albatross appears, the sole living creature in the icy waste. It is hailed by the sailors 'in God's name', shares their food, and is then shot by the mariner with his cross-bow. The mariner's action is unmotivated, perverse. It takes place in a world of white; white snow, white fog, white moonlight:

> Whiles all the night, through fog-smoke white
> Glimmered the white Moon-shine.

> (77–8)

A white bird, bathed in white moonlight, flies through white fog over a white landscape. At least, I take it that the bird is white. Coleridge's story, as Wordsworth who suggested it to him points out, derives from an incident recorded by Captain Shelvocke in his account of his voyages. Shelvocke's mate shot an albatross thinking it to be responsible for the contrary, tempestuous winds from which the ship was suffering, and Shelvocke describes the bird as a 'disconsolate black Albitross'. But the mate took against the unfortunate bird because he 'imagined from his colour that it might be of some ill omen'.[4] The reaction of Coleridge's sailors is quite the reverse: they greet the bird 'As if it had been a Christian soul', and when, soon afterwards, 'a good south wind sprung up behind', they take the albatross to be a bird of good omen. But what clinches my case is that Coleridge could only have been more sensitive to etymology than Shelvocke. The word albatross is a variant of 'alcatras'. It has not been found before 1769, and it seems to have established itself within the language because it offered a means of distinguishing various large white sea birds, which could be called albatrosses, from the black frigate bird that English sailors called the alcatras. The pressure establishing the form 'albatross', and defining its use, was surely an association with the Latin 'albus', white, and the pressure is so strong that Coleridge, in not gainsaying it, yields to it.

I believe, then, that the albatross is white. When the mariner shoots the bird, staining its feathers with blood, we have an instance of the colour combination, white and red, which recurs several times in the poem. The bride, whose wedding the mariner's victim fails to attend, we would ordinarily think of as white, virginally white. But Coleridge says, 'Red as a rose is she'. Red is superimposed on bridal white. Life-in-Death has red lips garishly slashing a skin 'as white as leprosy'. Just before the mariner sees and blesses the water snakes the reflection of white moonlight from the sea is interrupted by the ship's red shadow:

> Her beams bemocked the sultry main,
> Like April hoar-frost spread;
> But where the ship's huge shadow lay,
> The charmed water burnt alway
> A still and awful red.

(267–71)

When the ship is returned to port, the angels who had inhabited the bodies of the dead crew leave them as crimson shadows that hover above the ship amidst white moonlight:

> And the bay was white with silent light,
> Till rising from the same
> Full many shapes that shadows were,
> In crimson colours came.

(480–3)

Most simply the contrast between red and white works just to establish as forcibly as possible the contrast between colour and whiteness. Red, the last colour to disappear in darkness, is traditionally the most colourful of all colours. It is this rather than the power of the alchemical symbolism for which he had a taste that lends what force it has to Goethe's notion that red is a privileged colour, that all other colours aspire to the condition of pure redness that he calls *Purpur*. But, more than that, white and red are easily accommodated to the ambivalent world of Coleridge's poem. White may figure purity, but it may also figure death. Shelley speaks of 'the white radiance of eternity', but also of 'the shadow of white death'. Goethe writes:

> Everything living tends to colour – to local specific colour, to effect, to opacity, pervading the minutest atoms. Everything in which life is extinct approximates to white, to the abstract, the general state, to clearness, to transparence.[5]

In *The Ancient Mariner* the white moonlight exists powerfully and recurrently as a type of purity, but Life-in-Death's skin 'as white as leprosy' is the loathsome colour of death. Similarly, red, the colour of blood, may figure energy. The redness of Coleridge's bride signifies her passionate vitality, and even the red lips of Life-in-Death offer a grim parody of liveliness. But also because it is the colour of blood, redness may figure crime: Coleridge's 'bloody sun' is red because it has been stained by the killing of the bird.

When he shoots the albatross the mariner's companions cry out against him, but the sun rises gloriously and they decide that the albatross was responsible for the fog and that it was rightly killed.

> Nor dim, nor red, like God's own head
> The glorious sun uprist.
>
> (97–8)

In the first line the negative force of the word 'nor' is scarcely felt, and an image of the bloody head of the crucified Christ prevails for a moment, until it is replaced by an image of the divine sun in his glory. But the illusion is prophetic, and by the time that the ship reaches the Equator the prophecy is realised:

> All in a hot and copper sky
> The bloody sun, at noon,
> Right up above the mast did stand,
> No bigger than the moon.

(111–14)

The sun, the fountain of white light, is, as it were, itself wounded by the mariner's bolt. The blood, which Coleridge never notices bedraggling the albatross's white feathers, is transferred to the sun, linking the sun and the bird, the life of the albatross with the source and type of all life. But whereas the bird is a helpless victim the sun wreaks a terrible revenge. The ship is fixed in a dead calm, and the sailors, their water gone, are baked dry. To kill the bird wounds the sun, and the pathos of the dead bird gives way to the vengeance of the fierce sun.

The point, I take it, is something like this. The mariner, in shooting the albatross, has brought death into the world, not because the sailors were before that crime immortal, but because the wanton killing of the bird is a denial of the unity of all life. Such a denial imprisons the mariner and, when they sanction his crime, the rest of the crew, within their sole selves. From this perspective there is no escape from the fact of death. When the albatross is hung around the mariner's neck he becomes a living emblem of the predicament of mortal man: he is fastened to a dead animal.

Death, or rather the knowledge of death, is represented as the consequence of division. In killing the albatross the mariner divides his life from the life of the rest of creation, and at the moment of separation he finds that he is born to die. Further divisions, the division of the sailors from the natural world, and of the mariner from the rest of the crew, inevitably follow. The central metaphor expressing this process is the division of whiteness, of light, into colour.

The white bird is stained red with its own blood, but in witness of the universal significance of the act, the blood stains not the bird's feathers but the sun itself: the source of white light becomes 'the bloody sun'. In place of whiteness, in place of light, there are divided colours, and colours are associated with mortality, with putrefaction:

> The very deep did rot: O Christ!
> That ever this should be.

> Yea, slimy things did crawl with legs
> Upon the slimy sea.
>
> About, about, in reel and rout
> The death-fires danced at night;
> The water, like a witch's oils
> Burnt green, and blue and white.
>
> (123–30)

'Everything living', says Goethe 'tends to colour'. The poem does not dispute this: it is just that in the mariner's guilty vision living is seen only as a process of putrefaction pointing always to death. There is Death and there is Life-in-Death, and that is all. The man and the woman that crew the skeleton ship are the Adam and Eve of an anti-paradise, for between them they exhaust the possibilities of existence.

The red sun and the green and blue waters neatly, if perhaps fortuitously, mark the division of light into its primary colours. But the waters burn 'white' as well as green and blue: they are phosphorescent. Coleridge had read in Priestley's *Optics* an explanation of this phenomenon in a chapter strikingly entitled 'Of the Putrescence of the Sea'.[6] Priestley correctly explains such light as deriving from the rotting of myriads of microscopic sea organisms. The phosphorescent whiteness of the waters acts as a ghastly parody of pure white light: the 'rotting sea', emblem here of all mortal life, mimics in its putrescence the white light from which it is divorced. It is a whiteness as unlike the pure whiteness of moonshine as is the leprous whiteness of Life-in-Death's skin.

The point is clearer if we compare the description of Death cancelled after the poem's first appearance in 1798 with the description of Life-in-Death:

> *His* bones were black with many a crack,
> All black and bare I ween,
> Jet-black and bare, save where with rust
> They're patched with purple and green.
>
> *Her* lips were red, *her* looks were free,
> Her locks were yellow as gold:
> Her skin was white as leprosy,
> The Nightmare Life-in-Death was she
> That thicks men's blood with cold.

The positive side of the spectrum, the painter's warm colours, yellow and red, are assimilated to the death-like pallor of Life-in-Death's skin: the negative side, the painter's cool colours, from green to purple, are associated with the blackness of Death. Death is figured at this point by both white and black, by the jet blackness of Death and by the leprous whiteness of Life-in-Death. The array of hues that mediates between them is only an indication of putrescence, and points inescapably either to the whiteness of death or to the blackness of death. Death is defined not as the antithesis of life but as its defining characteristic. Everything living tends to colour, and all colours are signs of putrescence. It must be so, because to recognise something as living is to know only one thing, that it is going to die.

The mariner, fastened to a dead animal, is alive in a world that yields only one significance, that everything alive is dying. It is a world without beauty, for he can recognise no beauty in the processes of corruption:

> The many men so beautiful!
> And they all dead did lie,
> And a thousand, thousand slimy things
> Lived on: and so did I!

> (236–9)

The first two lines of this stanza I have always felt to be the most moving in the poem. They bear witness to a world in which beauty is defined by its separateness from life. The bodies of the dead crew are magically preserved from corruption:

> The cold sweat melted from their limbs,
> Nor rot nor reek did they ...

> (253–4)

But they do not rot simply to preserve their distinction from the rotting mariner who looks from 'the rotting deck' upon 'the rotting sea'.

The dead crewmen are beautiful, and so is the moon:

The moving Moon went up the sky
And nowhere did abide.
Softly she was going up
And a star or two beside ...

(263–6)

The moon and the stars may be seen as beautiful for the same reason that the crew may be so seen, because they are divorced from the mariner. The commentator's splendid gloss works to fix the condition of the moon as the precise opposite of the mariner's:

In his loneliness and fixedness he yearneth towards the journeying Moon, and the stars that still sojourn, yet still move onward; and every where the blue sky belongs to them, and is their appointed rest, and their native country and their natural homes, which they enter unannounced, as lords that are certainly expected and yet there is a silent joy at their arrival.

The moon and the stars move ever onwards and wherever they move is home. The mariner is becalmed, alone, fixed as if forever in an alien landscape. He can see the beauty of the night sky and of his dead comrades, but he is isolated from both. It is a part of his despair to see beauty only in the elsewhere.

Suddenly, as he watches the water snakes, he is saved:

Beyond the shadow of the ship
I watched the water-snakes:
They moved in tracks of shining white,
And when they reared, the elfish light
Fell off in hoary flakes.

Within the shadow of the ship
I watched their rich attire:
Blue, glossy green, and velvet black,
They coiled and swam; and every track
Was a flash of golden fire.

O happy living things! no tongue
Their beauty might declare:
A spring of love gushed from my heart,

> And I blessed them unaware:
> Sure my kind saint took pity on me,
> And I blessed them unaware.

> (272–87)

Once again we are offered a complete array of colours, from 'shining white' to 'velvet black', from 'golden fire' to 'glossy green' and 'blue'. But whereas before the mariner has gagged at such chromatic displays, seeing in them only the sickly iridescence of corruption, he now finds himself, as if by the special intercession of his guardian saint, able to embrace them as beautiful.

The phosphorescence, 'tracks of shining white', assures us that the sea still rots: it is a slimy thing inhabited by slimy creatures still. But a precondition of spiritual health is the ability to recognise mortal beauty, the beauty of mortality. One may think of Turner's lyrical celebrations of Venice, the city slowly rotting and crumbling back into the stagnant lagoon. But there is always something grim in Turner's landscapes, no matter how beautiful. Constable is, in the end, more like: 'But the sound of water escaping from mill-dams, etc., willows, old rotten planks, slimy posts, and brickwork, I love such things.' Such love does not reach out to comprehend rot and slime, rather it originates with them. For they signify in Constable as in Coleridge's redeemed mariner a serene, even joyful, acceptance of the fact of death. The mariner finds beauty in the here and now, and at last he can pray rather than monotonously and hopelessly yearn. To experience beauty here, now, is to make a connection between our living, mortal experience and the absolute beauty that we can only glimpse, and such a connection is necessary before the current of prayer can flow. The mariner's blessing of the water-snakes offers an explanation of the importance that Coleridge together with the other Romantic poets attached to a just recognition of the beauty of the natural world. More than that it hints at the supreme importance of Christ, for in taking upon himself a human body and undergoing the mortal progress from birth to death Jesus established that connection between mortal and immortal beauty that makes prayer possible. As soon as the mariner prays the albatross falls from his neck. He loses that obsessive concern with his own mortality that had weighed on him, constricting his vision. The natural and supernatural forces that had been ranged against him immediately begin to co-operate towards his salvation, and the poem moves quickly towards a conclusion.

I do not propose that Coleridge self-consciously and systematically makes use of the language of colour to express his theme in *The Ancient Mariner*. All I would claim is that such a language occurs to Coleridge quite naturally as he tells his tale. The killing of the albatross, the act that ends the mariner's time of innocence is a desecration of a white bird in a white landscape. The mariner's bolt shivers that whole, unified whiteness into the array of colours that signals for him his own mortality within a mortal world. Innocence can never be recovered. Even the 'Hermit good' rests his knees on a cushion of moss that grows from a 'rotted old oak-stump'. There is no magic escape either from the fact or the knowledge of death. But for all that there is hope, for the coloured fragments of the lost white wholeness need not be spurned as evidence that to live is to be in the process of dying, but may instead be embraced, as the mariner embraces the water-snakes, whose colours are the condition of their mortal beauty.

5

Woven Colours

Attempts to implicate Keats in the transcendental concerns of his Romantic contemporaries have never seemed very persuasive. He has remained for most of his readers a master of the 'fine isolated verisimilitude', not an irritable reacher after the absolute. He remains so to me. Endymion may love 'to the very white of truth', but, as John Bayley remarks, the phrase suggests a Brazil nut rather than white radiance. Truth, for Keats, is immanent, not transcendent: it is to be found within, not beyond, human experience. I had better quote at once the passage that might seem to contradict me:

> Then saw I a wan face,
> Not pined by human sorrows, but bright-blanched
> By an immortal sickness which kills not.
> It works a constant change, which happy death
> Can put no end to; deathwards progressing
> To no death was that visage; it had passed
> The lily and the snow; and beyond these
> I must not think now, though I saw that face –
> But for her eyes I should have fled away.
> They held me back, with a benignant light,
> Soft-mitigated by divinest lids
> Half-closed, and visionless entire they seemed
> Of all external things – they saw me not,
> But in soft splendour beamed like the mild moon,
> Who comforts those she sees not, who knows not
> What eyes are upward cast.

(The Fall of Hyperion, 256–71)

There is a fairly obvious family resemblance between Moneta's face and the face of Dante's Beatrice, and, in some sense, the roles of the two women are similar. Both admonish and yet comfort the poet. But the likeness works only to underscore the crucial difference. The point is easier made if we compare Keats's passage not with Dante but with one of Shelley's symphonies in white. This is the Spirit of the Moon sitting in a chariot shaped like the crescent moon:

> Within it sits a winged infant, white
> Its countenance, like the whiteness of bright snow,
> Its plumes are as feathers of sunny frost,
> Its limbs gleam white, through the wind-flowing folds
> Of its white robe, woof of etheral pearl.
> Its hair is white, the brightness of white light
> Scattered in strings ...

> (*Prometheus Unbound*, iv. 219–25)

The whiteness of Shelley's spirit signifies its freedom from mortal contrarieties. To glimpse such a vision is to know that behind the tattered colours of earthly life a white spirit sits laughing like a child. In this life we wear motley, but we are consoled when we are allowed to see through such limiting complexity to the white radiance to which we are heir.

The whiteness of Shelley's spirit signifies its transcendence of mortal pain. Moneta's whiteness is quite otherwise. It is a whiteness that inhabits the paradoxes that Shelley's spirit transcends. Hers is a face made bright by sorrow, suffering from 'immortal sickness', exempt from 'happy death', timeless and yet time's victim, with eyes that are both benignant and blind. She is for Keats what Shelley's spirit is for him, the embodiment of an ultimate authority, but, unlike Shelley, Keats cannot imagine an authority that is defined by its exemption from mortal ills. His paradoxes establish Moneta as both within and without the mortal predicament. In the end she is more like Pater's Mona Lisa than she is like Dante's Beatrice. Or, to put it another way, the face of Beatrice is superimposed on the dying face of Keats's consumptive brother, Tom.

In my last chapter I presented the opposition between white light and colour as a means through which poets explored the relationship between the transcendent one and the finite many. It is not an opposition that much interested Keats. The description of Moneta's face is as close as he ever comes to dabbling in the metaphysics of white radiance, and it is not very close. *Lamia* is the poem in which he flirts with the metaphysics of colour.

Lamia first appears in the poem as a snake:

> She was a gordian shape of dazzling hue,
> Vermilion-spotted, golden, green and blue;
> Striped like a zebra, freckled like a pard,
> Eyed like a peacock, and all crimson barred;
> And full of silver moons, that, as she breathed,
> Dissolved, or brighter shone, or interwreathed
> Their lustres with the gloomier tapestries –
> So rainbow-sided, touched with miseries,
> She seemed, at once, some penanced lady elf,
> Some demon's mistress, or the demon's self.
>
>   (47–56)

She is 'rainbow-sided'. Like Coleridge's water snakes she embraces the whole colour spectrum: vermilion, golden, green and blue. But whereas they embody the mortal world of colour that the mariner must learn to love, Lamia seems garishly unnatural. To be marked like a zebra, or a leopard, or a peacock is to be as strikingly costumed as nature permits: to be marked like all three is to go beyond nature, to become either elvish or demonic.

Most critics have seen it as their job to decide which. When Apollonius stares Lamia out of existence he is either a meddling sophist or the exponent of a healthful stringency. Some critics have noted Keats's distrust of 'consequitive reasoning' and his hostility to Newtonian optics, and have concluded that Lamia, like poetry, is a pathetic casualty in the war of the analytic against the imaginative mind. Others quote Keats's opinion that philosophy is to be preferred to poetry for the not very philosophical reason that 'an eagle is not so fine a thing as a truth', or Moneta's view that poets and dreamers are 'sheer opposite, antipodes', and they regard the poem's story as an expression of Keats's mature conviction that the poetic imagination must found itself on a stern acceptance of reality rather than a weak nostalgia for childish illusions. But most critics hold to the restful view that the poem leaves the matter undecided, and that a poet anxious to confront the riddle of human experience can do no better than to leave his reader in a quandary.

What all these critics have in common is that they take illusion and reality to be irreconcilable, 'sheer opposite, antipodes'. Keats, they suggest, persuades his reader either to reject one of these and choose the other, or to swither between them. In *Endymion*, of course, things are otherwise. Endymion realises the futility of crying for the moon and pledges himself to the Indian princess, only to find that his human lover becomes the moon goddess that he has rejected. Keats, we are often told, outgrew such wish-fulfilling fantasies, and *Lamia* is the clearest expression of the rugged refusal to deny the harsh contrarieties of life that distinguishes Keats in his last years.

The first thing to be said about this is that it unfairly represents the argument of *Endymion*. Faced with a choice between the Indian princess and Cynthia, Endymion responds not by rejecting the ideal in favour of the real, but by rejecting both. He elects to retreat from the world and from the impossible contest between competing desires, to become a 'hermit young', and to live in 'a mossy cave'. It is true that before Endymion takes his vow of celibacy he does reject his love of Cynthia, and pledges himself to the mortal princess:

> I have clung
> To nothing, loved a nothing, nothing seen
> Or felt but a great dream!

> (IV. 636–8)

He convicts himself of presumption 'against the tie / Of mortals each to each'. He turns to the princess and kneels to her:

> Here will I kneel, for thou redeemed hast
> My life from too thin breathing.

> (IV. 649–50)

Endymion's speech is diffusely written, but seems authoritative. Keat's comment on it is shocking:

> The mountaineer
> Thus strove by fancies vain and crude to clear
> His briared path to some tranquility.

> (IV. 721–3)

Keats dismisses Endymion's decision to abandon 'cloudy phantasms' for a human love, and he dismisses it not because the decision is inconvenient or painful, but because it is vain, crude and fanciful.

'Fancies' is the crucial word. To suppose that one must choose between a real and an ideal mistress is fanciful. The sexual realist – Byron seems to have been for Keats the representative of the type – and the sexual idealist – Shelley, perhaps – are joint victims of a fanciful illusion, for human love, and in this as in much else it is like poetry, has its being only in the coincidence of the ideal and the real. This is the conclusion to which *Endymion* drives, and if it is an immature belief, a belief that Keats had to grow out of, then Keats's critics have access to mature lore hidden from me.

But it is less than convincing to rebut a reading of *Lamia* by offering a reading of *Endymion*, and in *Lamia* we find this passage:

> Let the mad poets say whate'er they please
> Of the sweets of Fairies, Peris, Goddesses,
> There is not such a treat among them all,
> Haunters of cavern, lake, and waterfall,
> As a real woman, lineal indeed
> From Pyrrha's pebbles or old Adam's seed.

> (I. 328–33)

This is, of course, a feeble pastiche of *Don Juan*. Miriam Allott suggests some lines from the second canto as its model:

> she was one
> Fit for the model of a statuary,
> (A race of mere imposters, when all's done –
> I've seen much finer women ripe and real
> Than all the nonsense of their stone ideal).

> (II. 940–4)

Byron is robustly unRuskinian, and undeniably attractive. Keats seems to try for the same effect, and most critics have been willing to accept the attempt for the achievement. They have noted the ironic placing of the passage – the real woman in question is, after all, Lamia – but have not doubted that the lines express a preference for the real over the illusory that has at any rate provisional authority. The oddity that Keats should choose to imitate a poet, Byron, and a poem, *Don Juan*, that he consistently slighted is explained, if mentioned at all, as professional opportunism. *Lamia* was, Keats confesses, his attempt to escape from mawkishness and win wider public appeal, and *Don Juan* was the least mawkish and the most popular poem of the day.

But I doubt whether this is an appropriate reading. When Lycius first sees Lamia he takes her for a goddess, and Lamia, partly to tease, partly out of policy, plays up to his mistake. She cannot stay with Lycius, she claims:

> Thou art a scholar, Lycius, and must know
> That finer spirits cannot breathe below
> In human climes, and live.

> (I. 279–81)

She sets Lycius a sexual challenge, but he does not rise to it. He faints. And Lamia, to revive him, confesses herself a flesh and blood woman:

> gentle Lamia judged, and judged aright,
> That Lycius could not love in half a fright,
> So threw the goddess off, and won his heart
> More pleasantly by playing woman's part.

> (I. 334–7)

The point is that the 'real woman' and the goddess are for Lamia alternative roles, alternative illusions. As a goddess she is a tease, as a real woman she is a 'treat'. Both are fancies vain and crude.

Hazlitt's essay 'On Poetry in General'[1] is relevant here, not only because a large part of it is taken up with a discussion of the relationship between poetry and philosophy, a theme obviously central in *Lamia*, but also because Keats echoes the essay in his poem. 'It cannot be concealed however', writes Hazlitt, 'that the progress of knowledge and refinement has a tendency to circumscribe the limits of the imagination and to clip the wings of poetry.' 'Philosophy', according to Keats, 'will clip an angel's wings.'

Hazlitt's essay is confused. He argues successively that poetry and science are both true, and that the truths they offer are independent of one another; that science, because it describes a world that is not and cannot be humanly experienced, is more properly dismissed as a fiction than poetry; and that science and poetry are antagonistic activities, so that the expanding empire of science has necessarily contracted the province of poetry. The naturalist finds a glow-worm, takes it home in a box, and when he examines it in the morning finds it to be 'a little grey worm'. The poet would do better to study the glow-worm in the evening when 'it has built to itself a little palace of light'. The naturalist's account, it seems, could scarcely threaten the poet's, nor vice versa. But Hazlitt also argues that poetry exposes philosophy and science as fictions:

> Plato banished the poets from his Commonwealth, lest their descriptions of the natural man should spoil his mathematical man, who was to be without passions and affections, who was neither to laugh nor weep, to feel sorrow nor anger, to be cast down nor elated by anything. This was a chimera, however, which never existed but in the brain of the inventor, and Homer's poetical world has outlived Plato's philosophical world.

Or Hazlitt argues that the modern, scientific world threatens poetry, in part because 'we are less exposed to the vicissitudes of good and evil', and in part because 'the province of the imagination is principally the visionary, the unknown and undefined'. This recalls Keats in his review of Kean's Richard III: 'In our unimaginative day – Habeas Corpus'd as we are out of all wonder, uncertainty and fear.'

Hazlitt betrays his uneasiness by his habit of supporting his arguments with illustrations that are obviously untrue. What sort of naturalist is it that offers no account of the luminousness of the glow-worm? Plato has so far shown no sign of being outlived by Homer. But all the same the essay is full of interest. The dismissal of Plato's philosophical man as a 'chimera' boldly accuses the philosopher of constructing those compound monsters that were the standard banal examples used by philosophers to illustrate the working of the poetic imagination. Hazlitt's point is that the poet 'represents nature as seen through the medium of passion and imagination', that nature always is so seen, and that to pretend to see nature otherwise, by the lights of 'literal truth' or 'abstract reason', is to produce chimeras, fictions that have no basis in human experience.

This is the conclusion towards which the essay presses, but Hazlitt is repeatedly diverted because he wants to make for poetry two quite different claims; that it is more beautiful than science, and that it is truer. This passage is typical:

> If poetry is a dream, the business of life is much the same. If it is a fiction, made up of what we wish things to be, and fancy that they are, because we wish them to be so, there is no other nor better reality.

The 'better' makes nonsense of the 'other'. Hazlitt wants to say that poetry offers us a golden, in place of a brazen, world, and he wants also to say that the world it offers us is the world we live in.

Hazlitt repeatedly associates the 'medium of passion and imagination' through which the poet sees with colour. The poet does not see a little grey worm, but 'a palace of emerald light'. The countryman is a poet whenever he 'stops to look at a rainbow'. 'Let who will', writes Hazlitt, 'strip nature of the colours and the shapes of fancy, the poet is not bound to do so.' Colours, for Addison, are God's gift to console us for the nakedness of facts. God is a little like Erasmus Darwin, sweetening the pill of scientific fact by dressing it up in fancy. Glow-worms are only little grubs, and cut, God knows, a poor enough figure, and so God weaves around them a gracious illusion, a palace of emerald light. Hazlitt is still half-trapped in this mode of thinking, but he wants to add that the palace of green light is what we really experience, and that there is no reality other than human experience. Hazlitt is confused, one might say, because he writes at the pivot in the history of a metaphor. Colours, that for the eighteenth century were associated with fancy, with the imagination, are groping towards a new status. They are soon to become badges of reality. Hazlitt's essay is a proper introduction to *Lamia* because *Lamia* too is set within that pivot.

Philosophy, Keats writes in *Lamia* will 'Unweave a rainbow'. The thought is always, and properly, associated with the toast Keats shared with Lamb, damning Newton for having 'destroyed all the poetry of the rainbow by reducing it to its prismatic colours'. But the objection is surely only casually to the effect that Newton has had in distracting our attention from the seamless woof of colour in the sky, in reconciling us to those distinct bands of colour with which popular illustrators slander the rainbow. Keats's complaint against philosophers must be more radical. They threaten, he suggests, the knot that weaves together the rainbow and our common humanity. When Hazlitt argues that 'the end and use of poetry' is to 'hold the mirror up to nature, seen through the medium of passion and imagination', and that therefore the countryman is a poet when he 'stops to look at a rainbow', he means, though his expression is clumsy, what Keats means when he writes that to recognise beauty is to be busy 'wreathing / A flowery band to bind us to the earth'. The rainbow is a central symbol of the wreathing of our heart with the natural world that is both the cause and the effect of our perception of beauty. If it is true that Newton threatens this, then he threatens almost everything.

Yet it cannot be true. Newton showed that what governs the rainbow's appearance is a natural law that may be given mathematical expression. The rainbow is still a rainbow for all that. Thomson and the eighteenth-century Newtonians were confident that Newton had tightened the band that tied them to the earth. Wordsworth seems not to doubt that his own interest in the rainbow is independent of anything that Newton did, or could have done. In comparison Keats and Lamb seem at best unintelligent, at worst irredeemably whimsical. How can one respect a writer who complains that he has lost his subject matter when he can no longer believe in the existence of things such as a 'gnomed mine'. I cannot claim that Keats's objections to Newton are free of such silliness, but they have a more serious aspect.

Newton established a test of reality anterior to human experience. What is real is what can be shown to result from a natural law, and natural laws are rules that can be given mathematical expression. In the eighteenth century Newtonian science became the measure against which other searchers after truth estimated their success. In particular a series of moral philosophers appeared each claiming to be the Newton of the human sciences. Some, such as Hartley, Bentham and Malthus, even lay weird claim to Newton's own mathematical methods. Theirs was not just a bizarre confusion. They seem to have felt a need to demonstrate that human experience was as real as the movement of the planets and the behaviour of light, and they did not see how this was to be done unless it could be shown that human experience was susceptible to precise, preferably mathematical, description. Unsurprisingly, they failed, but their failure left a problem.

Truth is now of two kinds; what truly seems to be so, and what truly is so, and the poet is condemned to travel only on the illusory sea. The epic voyage is across the 'strange seas of thought' through which Newton journeyed. In response the poet can offer only an ancient mariner journeying through a sea of human experience, propelled by fanciful spirits that even the poet does not believe in. It is surely anger at such a situation that prompts Coleridge's pathetic retaliation, the invention of the strangest of all branches of mathematics, the computation of how many Newtons it would take to make one great poet.[2] Hazlitt seems far saner:

> This language [of poetry] is not the less true to nature because it is false in point of fact: but so much the more true and natural, if it conveys the impression which the object under the influence of passion makes on the mind.

There is one kind of truth appropriate to poetry, and a quite different kind to science. This seems reasonable, but it is a costly reasonableness. The solid world of 'fact' is the preserve of the scientist, and the poet is confined to the shadowy world of impressions. It is the scientist who is engaged in a bracing confrontation with things as they are. The poet is concerned, and it hardly seems so important, with things as they seem to be.

This is not a happy state of affairs for poets, and nor is it for the rest of us. Hazlitt struggles against it as his argument tacks and veers. He couples the scientist with Plato. Both would confine a knowledge of reality to the privileged few, the mathematically literate or the philosophically trained. But even they encounter reality only in abstract thought. When Newton and Plato walked about the world, going about their daily business, they walked, as we do, in a dream. Both Plato and Newton work to shake our confidence in the reality of that play of sensations that guarantees for most of us our presence as living people within a living world. Both offer only abstract beauty, the beauty of ideal form or of mathematical proportion, and these seem poor gifts if, in return, we must give up our trust in the beauty that plays upon the senses and is echoed in our hearts, rainbow beauty.

Keats's central theme is, we know, the relation between dream and reality. In particular, this is the theme that dominates the 1820 volume, the volume introduced by *Lamia*. Most critics represent it as a theme through which Keats expresses his concern with the status of poetry and with the proper duty of the poet. It is that, of course, but not only nor even most importantly that. It is a theme that engages the status of the play of sensations, those truths felt upon the pulses, that is the common ground of our human experience.

'If poetry is a dream', writes Hazlitt, 'the business of life is much the same. If it is a fiction, made up of what we wish things to be, and fancy that they are, because we wish them so: there is no other nor better reality.' Hazlitt denies that scientific fact or philosophical truth may be identified with reality, 'the business of life'. I want to believe this, but Hazlitt makes it difficult, for how can reality be the same as a dream when we are usually confident of the difference between them? How can the business of life be made up of 'what we wish things to be, and fancy that they are' when our everyday experience mocks any such notion? It is time to return to *Lamia*.

Lamia lies in wait for Lycius as he walks back to Corinth from Cencheras. He is lost in thought:

> His fantasy was lost, where reason fades
> In the calmed twilight of Platonic shades.

(I. 235–6)

There is an area of the mind in which reason and fantasy part company from the solid world, and when they do so they merge, as shadows merge. The couplet foretells Lycius's fate, for he is to be the victim not of illusion nor of philosophy, but of the joint operation of the two. Colours are what fade at twilight, and their fading may be the work of Apollonius's rational stare or of Hermes's magic wand. Apollonius's philosophy will, we are told,

> Unweave a rainbow, as it erstwhile made
> The tender-person'd Lamia melt into a shade.

(II. 237–8)

Hermes's 'lithe Caducean charm' has just the same effect. He touches Lamia's serpent body, and undresses her:

> Of all her sapphires, greens, and amethyst,
> And rubious-argent ...
>
> (I. 162–3)

'His fantasy was lost where reason fades.' The line seems to oppose fantasy and reason, but the opposition is only specious: fantasy is lost where reason is lost. The two, in the act of opposing each other, reveal their essential likeness, just as Apollonius, at the moment that he stares Lamia into non-being, reveals to Lycius that he is himself a lamia; a magician, a demon, with the eyes of a snake. Keats's poem begins with another such opposition:

> Upon a time before the faery brood
> Drove Nymph and Satyr from the prosperous wood,
> Before King Oberon's bright diadem,
> Sceptre, and mantle, clasped with dewy gem,
> Frighted away the Dryads and the Fauns
> From rushes green, and brakes, and cowslipped lawns ...
>
> (I. 1–6)

Enchantment is not ousted by sober fact, but by another enchantment. One set of fairies drives out another, and this predicts the story of the poem, for when Apollonius destroys Lamia, one fantasy is defeated by another.

Hazlitt dismisses Plato's ideal philosopher as a 'chimera', a compound monster much like Lamia. He is chimerical because he is without laughter, tears, sorow and anger, and thus excluded from the web of shared experience that is, for us, reality. Apollonius is just as cut off from fellow feeling. He laughs, it is true:

> Something too he laughed,
> As though some knotty problem, that had daffed
> His patient thought, had now begun to thaw,
> And solve and melt – 'twas just as he foresaw.
>
> (II. 160–2)

But it is Hobbesian laughter, a lonely delight in his own mental superiority, sudden glory. It is the opposite of the laughter that joins men together in shared delight.

Lamia, the illusionist, no less than the philosopher threatens that fellow-feeling, that shared confidence in the continuous life of the sensations, on which our sense of reality depends. Lycius is too engrossed in Lamia to see that he walks with her to Corinth not over solid ground but through a dream:

> Lamia's eagerness
> Made, by a spell, the triple league decrease
> To a few paces ...

> (I. 344–6)

But he feels instinctively that if he is to possess Lamia he must rend the social fabric of his life. He enters Corinth, 'Muffling his face, of greeting friends in fear'.

Lamia and Lycius live together in an illusory palace, lying side by side like figures on an urn. But it cannot last. Trumpets call Lycius back to 'the noisy world'. He demands a public wedding and a marriage feast:

> What mortal hath a prize, that other men
> May be confounded and abashed withal,
> But lets it sometimes pace abroad majestical,
> And triumph, as in thee I should rejoice
> Amid the hoarse alarm of Corinth's voice.
> Let my foes choke, and my friends shout afar,
> While through the thronged streets your bridal car
> Wheels round its dazzling spokes ...

> (II. 57–64)

Lionel Trilling comments: 'the most corrupt young man of Balzac's scenes of Parisian life could scarcely have spoken to his mistress or his fiancée as Lycius speaks to Lamia when he insists that she display her beauty in public for the enhancement of his prestige'.[3] Keats maintains in this passage the astringency with which he treats all the poem's characters, but all the same, Trilling is surely mistaken. Lycius's wish that his wife should 'pace abroad majestical' is quite uncorrupt. Weddings are public: the bride and groom assemble their friends and families, and triumph each in the choice of the other. Their friends shout afar, and if their foes choke, then so much the worse for the foes, though doubtless Lycius would have been a more sympathetic character had he not relished their discomfiture. Lycius is properly human in his wish to display publicly his private love. Beauty, like colour, is a thing of the mind, and it has only a shadowy existence until it is publicly ratified. When the evening sky deepens to a particularly lovely shade of royal blue, we look around for a companion to share it with, because beauty is realised in being shared. If we are alone, we feel vaguely cheated.

Not to feel so is subhuman, or superhuman. It is not a feeling known to the gods. When Lamia makes appear the nymph that Hermes burns for by breathing on his eyes, we do not know whether he is released from, or bound in, a spell. Hermes does not care. It is enough for him that he sees his nymph:

> It was no dream; or say a dream it was,
> Real are the dreams of Gods, and smoothly pass
> Their pleasures in a long immortal dream.

> (I. 126–8)

Hermes is divinely self-sufficient. He knows only his own desires. He may be thwarted or satisfied, but he needs no witnesses to his affections. These lines are often quoted to show how the gods are free of what Keats suggests is the defining human predicament. That reading seems to me tonally rather than substantially wrong. It suggests that we should envy a god his carelessness whether what he loves is a dream or a reality, and envy, perhaps, we do, but the envy is tinged with contempt.

Christopher Ricks has celebrated those moments in Keats when the mind knows itself a part, and yet not a part, of the social world, the moment of embarrassment, when private feeling publicly emblazons itself on the face as a blush. I admire Ricks's book, and I am indebted to it, but his remarks on *Lamia* seem to be misguided. Hermes blushes:

> Ah, what a world of love was at her feet!
> So Hermes thought, and a celestial heat
> Burnt from his winged heels to either ear,
> That from a whiteness, as the lily clear,
> Blushed into roses 'mid his golden hair,
> Fallen in jealous curls about his shoulders bare.

> (I. 21–6)

Ricks compares with this Raphael's blush when Adam asks him about the sex life of angels. But Raphael's tender shyness could hardly be more distinct from Hermes's blush. The blush phallicises his face: his whole person swells into hard desire. Lamia blushes, too, when Hermes swears he will grant her her wish:

> Ravished, she lifted her Circean head,
> Blushed a live damask, and swift-lisping said,
> 'I was a woman, let me have once more
> A woman's shape, and charming as before.
> I love a youth of Corinth – Oh, the bliss!
> Give me my woman's form, and place me where he is.

> (I. 115–20)

Ricks finds in her blush the disconcerting humanity of the snake. Lamia blushes, he seems to feel, because telling her love embarrasses her.[4] I doubt this. Her blush, like Hermes's blush, is a blush of uncomplicated desire. It is the freedom of her blush from all human complexity that marks her as not one of us, as either above us, like a god, or below us, like an animal.

In Ricks's special sense Hermes and Lamia flush rather than blush, like the wedding guests when they begin to get drunk:

> Soon was God Bacchus at meridian height;
> Flushed were their cheeks, and bright eyes double bright

> (II. 213–14)

And we drink, as Ricks notes, to free us from embarrassment. We flush in order not to blush. Our flushed cheeks signal that we have lost our blushing humanity and become, depending on one's point of view, either Bacchic or bestial.

Only one character in *Lamia* blushes a proper human blush. Lycius blushes when Apollonius enters his door, an uninvited guest at his wedding feast:

> He met within the murmurous vestibule
> His young disciple. 'Tis no common rule,
> Lycius,' said he, 'for uninvited guest
> To force himself upon you, and infest
> With an unbidden presence the bright throng

Of younger friends; yet must I do this wrong,
And you forgive me.' Lycius blushed, and led
The old man through the inner doors broad-spread ...

(II. 163–70)

Apollonius feigns the embarrassment of a man morally bound to break a social rule. But his calm and measured speech is fully self-confident. Apollonius is a philosopher, and philosophy is thus far divine, that Apollonius has achieved the god's capacity for self-containment. He feels a conflict between social decorum and moral duty no more than Hermes and Lamia feel a conflict between desire and bashfulness. Lamia is Lycius's lover and Apollonius is his friend. But lover and friend are human roles – they are, as Keats well knew, the essential human roles – and Lamia and Apollonius, who are either above or below humanity, can only mimic love and friendship.

When she is transformed into a woman Lamia is a disturbing compound of new-born innocence and sexual sophistication:

Not one hour old, yet of sciential brain
To unperplex bliss from its neighbour pain.

(I. 191–2)

She entices Lycius on 'To unperplexed delight, and pleasure known'. Critics have been quick to point to Keats's mature conviction that pleasure and pain are interknitted, his sense of 'aching Pleasure nigh, / Turning to poison while the bee-mouth sips'. To demand that the one be separated from the other is to seek an illusory freedom from the realities of human experience. But this is only an incidental theme in *Lamia*. It is a truth that Lycius would have learned had he lived longer:

but too short was their bliss
To breed distrust and hate, that make the soft voice hiss.

(II. 9–10)

It is not the perplexity of bliss and pain that is central, but perplexity itself. When Lamia decorates her fairy palace in honour of her guests, she lines the hall with plantains, intertwined to signify marriage. Then she:

> Missioned her viewless servants to enrich
> The fretted splendour of each nook and niche.
> Between the tree-stems, marbled plain at first,
> Came jasper panels; then, anon, there burst
> Forth creeping imagery of slighter trees,
> And with the larger wove in small intricacies.

(II. 136–41)

She knows that such intricate weaving is what her guests will find beautiful, but she can offer only woven images. Simply by being what she is, an illusion and an illusionist, she threatens the weft that perplexes each man with his fellows, and all men with their world. When they arrive at the palace the guests marvel:

> for they knew the street,
> Remembered it from childhood all complete
> Without a gap, yet ne'er before had seen
> That royal porch, that high-built fair demesne.

(II. 152–5)

The palace is beautiful, but can any beauty compensate for the loss of what is remembered from childhood? A rent appears in a web of experience that had until then been 'all complete / Without a gap', and it leaves the guests ill at ease. They whisper low to each other, until wine accomplishes its 'rosy deed', and loosens their tongues.

The guests wonder. They find, as we say, that they cannot trust their eyes, and to lose such trust is profoundly disconcerting. Our sense of being real people living in a real world depends on a simple trust that our continuous sensations bind us at each moment to a continuous world. Reality is a web weaving one man with another, and all men with their world. It is, as Shelley says, a 'painted veil', a delicate fabric, easily torn. Lamia threatens it. Illusion, magic, call it what you will, destroys the continuity on which our sense of the real depends. Apollonius, too, threatens it. He unweaves, just as Lamia unperplexes. Both look through the web of sensations to some anterior reality, the reality of magic or of philosophical truth. Both would confine a knowledge of reality to a privileged coterie, adepts or philosophers, and consign the rest of us to the undignified position of those who, asleep or awake, live in a dream.

Lamia breathes upon our eyes, and makes us see whatever she would have us see. Apollonius stares, and her visions vanish before his withering gaze. He destroys Lamia, but he destroys us with her. Our reality is not the same as illusion, and it is not the same as scientific or philosophical truth, but it cannot be unperplexed from either. That is why colours, the colours of the woven rainbow, are its appropriate symbols. They do not exist in the dream world inside our heads, and they do not exist in the scientist's abstract world peopled by various wavelengths of light. They are not illusions, and they are not scientific facts, and yet we cannot separate them from either. We cannot extricate them from Lamia, nor from Apollonius.

Reality, then, is a painted veil, a veil so fragile that its web remains intact only by a continuous act of good faith, an act in which we all join. I use Shelley's phrase because he would tear the veil aside. He reminds us that what I have called an act of good faith has oftener been described as bad faith, a bourgeois reverence or the flimsy stuff that protects him from having to face whatever lies behind it. If that is so, the end of *Lamia* exposes Keats as a devotee of bourgeois illusions, for when Apollonius rends the veil Keats grieves. *Lamia* ends not in triumph, but bleakly, sadly, in mourning for the death of Lycius:

> his friends came round –
> Supported him – no pulse, or breath they found,
> And, in its marriage robe, the heavy body wound.

(II. 309–11)

6

Purple Riot

In *Lamia* and in *The Fall of Hyperion* colour and whiteness come close to being symbolic, qualities are all but metamorphosed into themes. But this is not so in the bulk of Keats's verse. Whiteness and colour, the absolute truth of Moneta's face and the illusive iridescence of the rainbow-sided Lamia, coexist as easily as the yellow laburnum and the white honeysuckle:

> When the dark-leaved laburnum's drooping clusters
> Reflect athwart the stream their yellow lustres,
> And intertwined the cassia's arms unite,
> With its own drooping buds, but very white.

(To George Felton Matthew, 41–4)

The whiteness that Keats registers in a gasp of naïve awe moves him not at all as an intimation of absolute truth. The phrase 'but very white' is awkward and urgent, like a fifteen year old. It awkwardly completes the couplet, and it urgently attaches itself to a sentence that seems to have arrived already at an elegant formal close. It is charged by Keats's erotic awareness of flowers. The weight of the blooms, their roundness, and their invitation to the hands to fondle them, to the face to plunge itself into them, achingly reminds Keats of a woman's body, and that awareness is concentrated into the phrase 'but very white', and the glimpse it offers of white skin, white flesh.

Oddly, when the thought is spoken the erotic charge is reduced:

> a dimpled hand
> Fair as some wonder out of fairy land,
> Hung from his shoulders like the drooping flowers
> Of white cassia ...

(Calidore, 93–6)

Keats curbs his roving adolescent imagination by safely locating the whiteness in the hand. But even here he only mimes devotion to the

Renaissance ideal of alabaster beauty, while remaining furtively preoccupied with thoughts of those secret, white expanses of skin that girls keep modestly hidden from the sun. The phrase 'but very white' aches, aches with a longing to touch that must be frustrated. It is sweaty verse, perhaps too sweaty. Keats's sweet peas are less sultry than his honeysuckle:

> Here are sweet peas, on tip-toe for a flight,
> With wings of gentle flush o'er delicate white,
> And taper fingers catching at all things
> To bind them all about with tiny rings.

('I stood tip-toe upon a little hill', 57–60)

The sweet peas are like butterflies, and the thought is happy enough to control Keats's other sense that their petals are coloured like a girl's skin, its whiteness warmed by a maidenly blush. Keats's own grasping hands are absorbed into the sweet peas' taper fingers, so that the whole description remains fresh and innocent.

Those 'taper fingers' hint what is generally true, that Keats's instinctive response to beauty is not to look, but to touch. His alertness to beauty is an affair of the whole body, a standing on tip-toe, which is why he is less consistently a colourist than one might imagine. Keats lapses into chromatic richness when his mind is focused on style rather than experience; in the very early 'Imitation of Spenser', for example:

> There the king-fisher saw his plumage bright
> Vying with fish of brilliant dye below,
> Whose silken fins and golden scales light
> Cast upward, through the waves, a ruby glow.

(10–13)

This is very beautiful in its way, but detached, quite without the shocking intimacy that is Keats's peculiar achievement. Or colour words can indicate a mere tapping of the poetic feet:

> So, with unusual gladness, on he hies
> Through caves and palaces of mottled ore,
> Gold doors, and crystal walls and turquoise floor,

> Black polished porticoes of awful shade,
> And, at the last, a diamond balustrade ...

> (*Endymion*, II. 593–7)

This is the Keats who, remarkably young, was 'an old Stager in the Picturesque': the gorgeous colours are just a mechanical richening of the texture of the verse.

Colours become vital to Keats when they are not simply given to the eye, when they become things to be touched as much as looked at. A butterfly sips at a fountain:

> with touch
> Most delicate, as though afraid to smutch
> Even with mealy gold the waters clear.

> (*Endymion*, II. 89–91)

'Mealy' is one of the many words that Keats found in Shakespeare, one more example of his unerring sense for finding himself in Shakespeare, so that time and again he can echo a greater poet, and manage it so that in those echoes he is never more truly himself. The word perplexes colour with touch. Keats feels his finger gently stroke the wing, his tongue flicks out to lick it. The butterfly's tender care for the water is his own for the insect's fragile wing. Adonis lies asleep, richly blanketed:

> And coverlids gold-tinted like the peach,
> Or ripe October's faded marigolds,
> Fell sleek about him in a thousand folds ...

> (*Endymion*, II. 396–8)

The peach-coloured blankets fall 'sleek' about him, the kind of word that Keats received from Shakespeare through Hunt. It works here with the plump peach to do away with the difference between bedcovers and skin. The goldenness of the one merges with the goldenness of the other. That is why Adonis can be represented as decorously draped and yet as 'giving' himself 'to the filled sight / Officiously'.

Keats can use colour words to charge the sensual atmosphere, but not only so. The word 'green', for example, is important in *Endymion*. It is pre-eminently the colour of the earth, 'our green earth', and gently reminds us of the green pleasures that are obscured if we devote ourselves single-mindedly to moonlight. And yet to lie sheltered within the earth's 'green nooks' is to be imprisoned in the natural. Hyacinthus dies, killed by the envious Zephyr, and his metamorphosis into a flower is for Keats an imprisonment:

> Oh, for Hermes' wand
> To touch this flower into human shape!
> That woodland Hyacinthus could escape
> From his green prison ...

> (*Endymion*, II. 66–9)

Hyacinthus loses in death the love of Apollo, and not to know the love of the gods is to be confined to 'the green earth', enclosed in a 'green prison'.

Just before Endymion is rescued from his predicament when the Indian princess reveals herself as Cynthia, he finds the solution blazoned on a tree:

> A little onward ran the very stream
> By which he took his first soft poppy-dream;
> And on the very bark 'gainst which he leant
> A crescent he had carved, and round it spent
> His skill in little stars. The teeming tree
> Had swollen and greened the pious charactery
> But not ta'en out.

> (*Endymion*, IV. 785–91)

When Endymion scored on the bark a moon and stars, he imprinted on the tree his love of silvery light, and gestured his contempt of the merely natural. But as the months have passed the green nature that he scorned has embraced its wounds, until the wound has become a part of the living tree, swelling and greening as the tree grows and flourishes. It is a happy thought, but for a triumphant reconciliation of green and silver one must turn back to the second canto:

> as when heaved anew
> Old ocean rolls a lengthened wave to shore,
> Down whose green back the short-lived foam all hoar
> Bursts gradual with a wayward indolence.

> (*Endymion*, ii. 347–50)

The green wave and the silver foam so perfectly complete each other, are each so completely a part of the wave's long, liquid movement, that the wave's nonchalant beauty becomes at once a type of all perfect experience.

Endymion takes his walk 'Through the green evening quiet in the sun', but he is no part of his landscape. He is sick with desire, his life a series of sickening plunges between ecstasy and despair. He cannot find within himself any green quietness. But nature's greenery, the tender colour that best represents the 'gentle band' that ties us to the earth, is not itself all earthly. It is the product of a chemistry that involves the dark earth with heaven's light. Plants needs light to be green, and they do not rest in green quietness. Every leaf, says Ruskin, would be a flower if it could, and every plant strives to produce in fruit or flower an incarnation of the light that gave it birth. Flowers, as Shelley has it, are 'incarnations of the stars'. A fruit, for Keats, is an incarnation of the sun. Once Endymion has known the love of Cynthia all other joy palls. What once seemed heavenly, now seems dull earth:

> Essences
> Once spiritual, are like the muddy lees,
> Meant but to fertilize my earthly root
> And make my branches lift a golden fruit
> Into the bloom of heaven.

> (*Endymion*, ii. 905–9)

Endymion spurns his previous existence, rejects it as 'muddy lees', but his rejection is wiser than he realises, for in its expression it becomes an embrace. Rhyme and botany both insist that the 'earthly root' and the 'golden fruit' are tied together. Neither can exist without the other, and the fruit must lean on the root if it is ever to be lifted into the bloom of heaven. Endymion is consistently wiser than he suspects:

> but some few days agone
> Her soft arms were entwining me, and on
> Her voice I hung like fruit among green leaves.

(*Endymion*, III. 269–71)

He is the fruit, I suppose, and her voice the leaves, but that is not how the lines work. The touch of leaf on fruit signals the tenderness of the lovers' embrace, its cool naturalness, and the refreshment it offers. Golden fruit and green leaves consort together in a harmony that Endymion seizes instinctively as a type of human happiness.

What he learns in the poem is how to be happy, which is to learn that one must not love either the natural or the divine, but both together. To be happy it is not enough to be earth-bound, rooted, nor is it enough to shine with a golden light. One must be both together. By the end of the poem Endymion has learned this, which is only to say that he has learned to understand his own metaphors: 'and – ah, ripe sheaves / Of happiness'.

The Eve of St Agnes is also a happy poem, but its ripe sheaves of happiness grow from odd soil, out of cold, danger, mortality and deceit. It is very cold, 'bitter chill', the animals live their narrowed winter lives bent only on survival, and the holy man's thoughts are on death. From the cold outside, the cold that makes the living creatures shiver, we move with the beadsman into the chapel, and the sharper cold of the dead:

> The sculptured dead, on each side, seem to freeze,
> Emprison'd in black, purgatorial rails:
> Knights, ladies, praying in dumb orat'ries,
> He passeth by; and his weak spirit fails
> To think how they may ache in icy hoods and mails.

(14–18)

The beadsman is the appropriate guide because he stands on the verge between the coldness of the living and the coldness of the dead:

> already had his deathbell rung,
> The joys of all his life were said and sung:

(22–3)

But then there is a burst of music. It flatters the old man to tears,
distracts him for a moment from his single-minded contemplation
of past sins and coming death. But he resists such blandishments,
and bends himself to a night of 'harsh penance':

> and soon among
> Rough ashes sat he for his soul's reprieve,
> And all night kept awake, for sinners' sake to grieve.

(25–7)

In the castle a feast is just beginning, but it is through the cold
night, the icy chapel, and the dying holy man that we see the
merrymaking. It is night, and the dark chapel is lined by 'black
purgatorial rails'. The gloom is lightened only by the beadsman's
lamp and the 'frosted breath' that rises white from his mouth. Into
this sombre chiaroscuro bursts 'golden music', 'silver snarling
trumpets', until:

> At length burst in the argent revelry,
> With plume, tiara, and all rich array ...

(37–8)

The metallically bright colours: 'golden', 'silver', 'argent', stridently
repel the darkness – too stridently. After the reader has shivered
with the animals, felt the iciness of death, and turned with the
beadsman away from idle revelry, the snarling trumpets are apt to
seem a heartless and a mindless denial of the encompassing
realities. Robert Gittings has argued for the influence on the poem of
Orcagna's 'The Triumph of Death'.[1] Keats shares this with Orcagna
at any rate, that his revellers seem recklessly unaware of the pain
and the mementoes of death that surround them. But Keats does
not settle into any stable medieval framework. His perspectives
begin to shift elusively.

The gorgeous chambers, dressed for the feast, are surveyed by
angels:

> The carved angels, ever eager-eyed,
> Star'd, where upon their heads the cornice rests,
> With hair blown back, and wings put cross-wise on their breasts.

(34–6)

'Eager-eyed' consorts oddly with 'stared': the one suggests excitement, the other blind eyes of stone. The streaming hair fits oddly with the demure crossed wings. It is hard to say whether we should see the angels gazing in blank disapproval at the festivities, or with keen interest. They are made of stone, and yet alert, excited.

We first see Madeline amonst the revellers. Amongst them, but not of them. Here eyes are 'Fixed on the floor', modestly bent downwards, like a nun's. She does not reject the advances of 'many a tiptoe, amorous cavalier', it is just that she does not see them: 'She danced along with vague regardless eyes'. Not 'eager-eyed', not 'staring', but the reverse; and not carved stone, frozen into stillness, but moving with a charming living looseness, dancing along. Like the beadsman, Madeline chooses not to feast, but to do penance. She will go 'supperless to bed'. The beadsman hopes to be rewarded in death for his self-abnegation: Madeline's reward will come in her dreams. Virgins who perform correctly the appropriate rituals will 'Upon the honeyed middle of the night' enjoy 'soft adorings from their loves'. The beadsman prays to the Virgin Mary. Madeline prays to Agnes, another virgin saint. Both reject common pleasures, the pleasures of the feast, sacrificing present happiness in the hope of a more refined joy in death or in sleep. And yet ought we to compare them or contrast them, for after all the beadsman prays for Heaven, whereas Madeline prays for erotic dreams? Does her isolation from the revelry signal, like his, an awareness of a truth that the revellers are blind to, or is she blinder than they, 'Hoodwinked with fairy fancy'? But such questions remain latent in the poem. They are never asked, because Madeline is too charming to be problematic.

From Madeline and the revellers we move to Porphyro, from the revellers' general carelessness of mortality to Porphyro's individual recklessness of death. Porphyro's family is at feud with the lords of the castle. If he is discovered, he will be killed, but he risks death just for the chance that he may see Madeline. Just as Madeline is first paired with the beadsman, holy age with fairy youth, Porphyro first meets Angela. His youthful idealism contrasts with the horse sense of the old woman. The thought of Madeline playing the 'conjuror' makes her laugh, him cry.

Angela leads Porphyro aside for safety into a little room:

> He found him in a little moonlight room,
> Pale, lattic'd, chill, and silent as a tomb.

> (112–13)

The room is lit by moonlight, pale, quite other than the dark chapel, but both are cold, both tomb-like. It is there that Porphryo has his idea:

> Sudden a thought came like a full-blown rose,
> Flushing his brow, and in his pained heart
> Made purple riot …

> (136–8)

Porphyro blushes, as well he might given the strategem he is about to propose. But it is not just a blush, it is summery warmth and colour bursting into a pale, cold room. We respond to Porphyro's thought before we know what it is, and we respond so simply that Angela's moral qualms, entirely reasonable though they may be, seem too sophisticated to be anything other than diversions. We wait for her to be won over, and Porphyro safely stored in Madeline's closet.

Angela is only just in time:

> Her falt'ring hand upon the balustrade,
> Old Angela was feeling for the stair,
> When Madeline, St Agnes' charmed maid,
> Rose, like a mission'd spirit, unaware:
> With silver taper's light, and pious care,
> She turn'd, and down the aged gossip led
> To a safe level matting.

> (190–6)

Madeline moves as if in a trance. She is a 'mission'd spirit', but for all that she turns and helps her nurse downstairs. She is poised poignantly between other-worldliness and being a good young girl. She helps Angela downstairs 'With silver taper's light and pious care', and the phrasing marks her action as at once ritualistic and kindly. This kind of effect is preserved throughout the following stanzas. Porphyro gazes at 'her empty dress', and the phrase makes achingly palpable the absent body. But when he speaks to Madeline it is to 'my love, my seraph fair', and all her warm, weighty physicality is dissolved in the light formality of the address.

Her room is 'silken, hushed, and chaste'. As she enters her candle goes out, and the room is lit only by pallid moonshine. She is silent – it is a necessary part of the ritual that she remain so – but her heart, like Porphyro's, riots:

> her heart was voluble,
> Paining with eloquence her balmy side,
> As though a tongueless nightingale should swell
> Her throat in vain, and die, heart-stifled, in her dell.

(204–7)

The silent birdsong has the same relation to the silver snarling trumpets that the purple riot in Porphyro's heart has to the pomp of the feast. Both suggest that somehow the deep austere inwardness of the beadsman and the extrovert glitter and blare of the festive trumpets might not between them exhaust the possibilities of human experience.

But Madeline herself is bathed in purple:

> A casement high and triple-arch'd there was,
> All garlanded with carven imag'ries
> Of fruits, and flowers, and bunches of knot-grass,
> And diamonded with panes of quaint device,
> Innumerable of stains and splendid dyes,
> As are the tiger-moth's deep-damask'd wings;
> And in the midst, 'mong thousand heraldries,
> And twilight saints, and dim emblazonings,
> A shielded scutcheon blush'd with blood of queens and kings.
>
> Full on this casement shone the wintry moon,
> And threw warm gules on Madeline's fair breast,
> As down she knelt for heaven's grace and boon;
> Rose-bloom fell on her hands, together prest,
> And on her silver cross soft amethyst,
> And on her hair a glory, like a saint:
> She seem'd a splendid angel, newly drest,

> Save wings, for Heaven: — Porphyro grew faint:
> She knelt, so pure a thing, so free from mortal taint.

(208–25)

These stanzas are the chief legacy that the Pre-Raphaelites received
from Keats, and they and Tennyson were surely the proper heirs.
The stanzas are thematically rich, but pictorially so much richer that
it would be tactless to allow a symbolic understanding of them to
intrude into a simple appreciation of the image. That 'tiger-moth',
for example, might in any other context be felt as oxymoronic,
ironically hyphenating Porphyro's predatory lust with Madeline's
fragile helplessness, but the opulence of the wings, their colour and
texture, is realised so finely that we are aware of the symbolic
possibility only in so far as it makes us blink to remove from the
image an irritating speck of meaning. Throughout the description
meanings are suggested only to be refused, and the refusal is
important only as it peels the reader's sensual eyes. It is Keats's
version of Shelley's image, not a dome, but three arches of
'many-coloured glass', and it stains the white moonlight. But in
Keats's version the image is sublimely free from metaphysical
implications, and if we remember our unease at the revellers
repelling with the strident colours of the feast the stark reality of an
icy moonlit night, it is only to assure ourselves that here such a
response is utterly inappropriate.

When Porphyro comes from his closet and lays out his stock of
exotic dainties, the noise of the communal feast intrudes for the only
time into Madeline's silent chamber:

> The boisterous, midnight, festive clarion,
> The kettle-drum and far-heard clarinet,
> Affray his ears, though but in dying tone: —
> The hall door shuts again, and all the noise is gone.

(258–61)

The music threatens to disturb Madeline's sleep, but it sounds only
that the hall door may shut, and the lovers be confirmed in their sole
possession of the closed world of Madeline's chamber. The
boisterous public feast is quite unconnected with the feast that
Porphyro silently prepares for Madeline. The pleasure it offers

seems gross in comparison with a feast so delicately rich that it need not even be tasted:

> candied apple, quince, and plum, and gourd,
> With jellies soother than the creamy curd,
> And lucent syrops, tinct with cinnamon.

(265–7)

It melts in the mouth as its ingredients are named, a feast so fairy that it is eaten just by being pronounced.

As John Bayley remarks, Keats moves throughout this poem with cat-footed sureness, and the test in these stanzas is the completeness with which he confines the reader in the world of appearances. If we think about it we know, of course, that the rose-bloom that falls on Madeline bathes her only in warm colour, and that the air is still cold. But we do not think, and 'the warm gules on Madeline's fair breast' repels the icy moonlight. When seeming is so rich, it is a perverse reader who looks through it to an indigent reality.

Bathed in red light Madeline mimics Porphyro's blush. His brow was flushed like a 'full-blown rose'. 'Rose-bloom' falls on her hands and on her breast. We might point the contrast. Porphyro's redness is the colour of his lust. It spreads from his seething heart in 'purple riot', until it flushes his whole body. Madeline, on the other hand, kneels down to pray, and redness falls on her. She is to be the passive victim, he the active aggressor. He shines, but she only reflects. Or we might understand Madeline's rosy blush as exposing her self-deception. As she kneels to pray she is both virginally pure, and alive with erotic desire, and this is signalled when there falls 'on her silver cross soft amethyst'. But our minds are not so busy. Madeline is not Imogen, and neither is she Belinda: she is neither the object of our moral concern nor the victim of our irony. She is just beautiful.

Porphyro watches her undress:

> Of all its wreathed pearls her hair she frees;
> Unclasps her warmed jewels one by one;
> Loosens her fragrant boddice; by degrees
> Her rich attire creeps rustling to her knees.

(227–30)

The lines flicker between formality and unnerving intimacy, between the distant charm of 'wreathed pearls', and 'warmed jewels' that thrill with the subtle contact of hard gems on soft flesh. It is not at all like Donne:

> Off with that girdle, like heavens Zone glittering,
> But a far fairer world incompassing.
> Unpin that spangled breastplate which you wear,
> That th'eyes of busie fooles may be stopt there.
> Unlace your self, for that harmonious chyme,
> Tells me from you, that now it is bed time.

> (*Elegie: Going to Bed*, 5–10)

Donne's sexuality is fine and open, and also curiously unmoving. His mistress takes off her clothes and resumes her proper state of nakedness. Donne frankly joys in her; admires her clothes much, her body more. We watch her, as Donne watches her, openly. We watch Madeline with Porphyro, in a hot stillness of repressed desire. She teases, but she does so in all innocence. Our admiration is not exactly furtive, but neither is it exactly open. When her dress slips she stands 'Half-hidden like a mermaid in sea-weed'. Keats may have in mind a particular painting here, but in any case the line works to place Madeline within the pictorial tradition of the marine nude. The peculiar quality of such nudes is that they are quite unembarrassing because quite unembarrassed. Nudity is their proper state, so that they are quite fresh and innocent even though they have no clothes on. To use Kenneth Clarke's terms they are quite nude but not at all naked. But Madeline is not securely within that tradition. She is a mermaid, but she is also a young girl caught in a moment of poignant awkwardness, her dress slipped to her knees. She is a nude, but she is also charged with the special intimacy of nakedness glimpsed rather than displayed, the intimacy vulgarly parodied in old-fashioned pin-ups, where the half-clothed model mimics startled dismay, as if the photographer had suddenly opened the door.

Madeline is soon in bed, 'trembling in her soft and chilly nest'. There she lies 'In sort of wakeful swoon perplexed', until she enters 'the poppied warmth of sleep'. Then she is:

> Blinded alike from sunshine, and from rain,
> As though a rose should shut, and be a bud again.

> (242–3)

Porphyro's thought came 'like a full-blown rose'. It bursts from his heart out into his face. Madeline knelt at the window, 'rose-bloom fell on her hands', and she absorbs it, encloses it within herself, as a rose-bud sheathes its redness in cool green leaves. The rose-bloom disappears, and Madeline asleep is robed in virginal blue and white:

> And still she slept an azure-lidded sleep,
> In blanched linen, smooth, and lavender'd ...

> (262–3)

The moon shines softly on her: 'the faded moon / Made a dim, silver twilight'. Its light is no longer stained with colour. It is a cool, virginal moon and appropriately shines on Madeline as she sleeps cool and virginal in her bed. 'The splendid dyes' that had played on Madeline when she knelt before the window are taken up into the food, the dishes and the furnishings, the 'cloth of crimson, gold, and jet', the fruit, the jellies, and the syrups, the 'golden dishes' and the 'baskets bright / Of wreathed silver', the lustrous salvers, and the 'golden fringe' of the carpet.

When the food is laid out, Porphyro wakes Madeline with a song:

> He ceased – she panted quick – and suddenly
> Her blue affrayed eyes wide open shone;
> Upon his knees he sank, pale as smooth-sculptured stone.

> (295–7)

Her blue eyes open and, fixed by her gaze, Porphyro is blanched into white marble. For a moment the lovers are frozen by fear into a white and blue tableau of virginity. Their richly coloured sensuality is spread out on the table as a feast and enclosed in their hearts as a rose, but the inward and the outward do not coalesce. They are fenced from one another by cool blue eyes and flesh like cold white stone.

Madeline has been dreaming of Porphyro. When she opens her eyes she sees him:

> Her eyes were open, but she still beheld,
> Now wide awake, the vision of her sleep ...

(298–9)

Her dream lover becomes a real lover. She dreams like Adam, and wakes to find her dream come true. But at first it feels to her like 'a painful change', and her dream a dream like the hero's in Shelley's *Alastor*, or like the knight's in *La Belle Dame Sans Merci*, a dream from which one wakes to an indigent reality. The real lover is a shrunken version of the lover in her dream. He is 'pallid, chill, and drear' and like the cold moonlit night, not like the 'poppied warmth' of the lover who came to her while she slept. Madeline is half asleep and half awake, 'In sort of wakeful swoon, perplexed'. The Porphyro of her dreams and the Porphyro by her bed coexist for her. The risk is that she will awake, her vision flee, and she will confront with open eyes an impoverished reality. Then hers will be the common human lot of making the best of it one can.

The poem has been built out of conflicts that fade before they are resolved: between the holy austerity of the beadsman and the boisterous merriment of the feast; between the cold night air without and the glowing chambers within; between a chapel and a bedroom; between Porphyro and the enemies in the castle who threaten his life; between Madeline's virginal innocence and her heart, hot with erotic desire; between Porphyro's reverential love and his furtive lust; between Madeline as a 'seraph fair' and as the vital principle that inhabits her own thrillingly palpable body; between Madeline's private fantasy and the aggressive sexuality of Porphyro that threatens it. Such conflicts appear and fade, are dissolved into the poem's quite extraordinary pictorial richness, until this crisis, when they are all pressed into the single conflict between Madeline asleep and Madeline awake, between the rose in her heart and her 'blue affrayed eyes'. And at last a conflict is resolved:

> Beyond a mortal man impassion'd far
> At these voluptuous accents, he arose,
> Ethereal, flush'd, and like a throbbing star

Seen mid the sapphire heaven's deep repose;
Into her dream he melted, as the rose
Blendeth its odour with the violet, —
Solution sweet: meantime the frost-wind blows
Like Love's alarum pattering the sharp sleet
Against the window-panes; St. Agnes' moon hath set.

(316–24)

Keats himself, through his clumsy revision of this stanza and comments in his letters, bears the main responsibility for focusing critical attention on the problem of what exactly the lovers are getting up to here.[2] But it is surely a perverse question to ask. Porphyro melts into Madeline's dream: the crisis is resolved in a 'Solution sweet'. He rises like Mars, a red star in a blue heaven, his flushed sexuality glowing against a virginal sky, and then the two melt together, 'as the rose / Blendeth its odour with the violet'. The 'purple riot' in his heart is at last enacted, but with extraordinary delicacy, as a purple scent.

Porphyro and Madeline dissolve into one another, like scents, like colours – woven scents, woven colours. This is fitting because scents, colours, the full play of sensations that marks the interface between us and the world, mock the distinction between outer and inner, reality and dream. Colours are the weaving together of our dreams and our world, not exactly in our heads and not exactly in the world, but a glowing covenant between them, the guarantee of the rich perplexity, the wakeful swoon in which we all of us live, or can live.

The lovers awake, and there is a secondary crisis as Madeline feels herself betrayed. But Porphyro stills her fears, and the two make their dream-like escape from the castle, gliding 'like phantoms'. The hostility of Porphyro's enemies is suspended: they lie in a drunken sleep. Nothing hinders the lovers. The guard dog does not bark.

The chains lie silent on the footworn stones; —
The key turns, and the door open its hinges groans.

And they are gone – aye, ages long ago
These lovers fled away into the storm.
That night the Baron dreamt of many a woe,
And all his warrior-guests, with shade and form

Of witch, and demon, and large coffin-worm,
Were long be-nightmar'd. Angela the old
Died palsy-twitch'd, with meagre face deform;
The Beadsman, after thousand aves told,
For aye unsought for slept among his ashes cold.

(368–78)

The poem ends with foul nightmare side by side with harsh death.
But the lovers are spared that gruesome choice. They 'fled away into
the storm', spared, it seems, if only by the poet's silence, the
common human lot, safe within the magic circle of Keats's poem.
And yet it is not so. We have nightmares, it is true, and we die, but
we need not conclude that life is a Gothic nightmare followed by the
pain and the loneliness of death, a grim sequence that can be
escaped only within the fictional world of a poem. We are not, at any
rate, compelled to think so. Nightmares, after all, are not true, and
death may end life but need not negate it. It is open to us to believe
that the solution sweet of the lovers is the proper type of our living
experience. We can trust the poem and judge the Baron and the
warrior-guests tossing in their troubled sleep, and Angela and the
beadsman cold in their graves, not only less happy but less real than
Porphyro and Madeline safe within their joy.

Part Two
Robert Browning

7

Blind Hope

Millais's 'The Blind Girl' is in the municipal gallery in Birmingham. It shows a blind girl, a beggar, sitting on a bank, her face raised gratefully to the bright sun. With her left hand she clasps the hand of a child who leans against her, gazing over the blind girl's shoulder at a brilliant double rainbow outlined against storm clouds in the distance. Ruskin admired the picture greatly. He describes it as an anti-pastoral; a beggar girl, just as she is, every rent in her ragged dress displayed, set amidst a neat but suburban stretch of English countryside. Madox Brown thought it lacking in finish, but all the same for him it was 'a religious picture and a glorious one'.[1] These are interesting responses, not least because they are so disparate. Ruskin, oddly for him, makes no mention of the blind girl's beauty, nor of her serene stillness, though he notes that the butterfly resting on her cloak shows that she has been motionless for some time. Madox Brown does not notice the picture's ordinariness; the uncluttered landscape, the straggle of neat buildings in the distance, the battered harmonium on the blind girl's lap, her little friend's clumsy, heavy boots. Both their responses seem to be true, for it is a picture about two kinds of seeing.

The child turns, her posture taut and restless, and looks, as we look, back towards the rainbow. But not quite as we look, for her gaze seems focused on the apex of the rainbow, and Millais has not painted that, but left it to be imagined just above the top right-hand corner of the picture. The blind girl faces us, her eyelids relaxed but not quite closed. She is, of course, untroubled by a bright sun that would pucker our eyes into a squint, and she looks with her unseeing eyes not directly at us, but rather to our right. The blind girl does not look straight at us, and her companion does not look quite with us. We are placed at an angle between their different kinds of vision. The young girl looks outwards at a natural beauty that finds its perfect embodiment in the rainbow, but the blind girl's gaze is inward. She raises her face to the warmth of the sun, but her attention is fixed on some mental landscape that we can know only by her calm, rapt expression. The butterfly that has settled on her shawl is the emblem of what both girls see. It is brightly coloured and ephemeral, like the rainbow and the natural world over which the rainbow is arched, but the escape of the butterfly from its chrysalis is the traditional emblem of the escape of the body from its mortal vesture, of release from imprisonment within the merely natural.

The painting represents two kinds of seeing, but it also suggests how they are related one to the other. The blind girl evidently relies on her companion. She needs the young girl to lead her from place to place, to collect the coppers she earns by playing her harmonium. But what we see in the picture is the dependence of the child on the blind girl. The child clutches the blind girl's hand, leans against her, shelters within the blind girl's shawl, and peeps over it to look at the rainbow. She finds the security she needs in the blind girl, who is herself serenely self-possessed. If the child were to jump up, the blind girl's posture would be unchanged. If the blind girl were removed the child would topple over. What this implies, I think, is that the child's natural vision is dependent, in some sense, on the inward gaze of the blind girl, just as the rainbow is dependent on the sun. We are not shown the sun any more than we can see what is passing in the blind girl's head, but we see her face, and it glows in the sun's light and also in the light of her own inner peace. Madox Brown was right to describe 'The Blind Girl' as a religious picture, for it adumbrates the dependence of the material on the spiritual, of the mortal on the divine.

'I am', wrote Elizabeth Barrett to Robert Browning, 'in a manner as a blind poet.'[2] She does not mean that her eyes are bad, but that she lives a sequestered life, deprived of all the busy social activity that Browning enjoyed and that he could use as materal for his plays. Elizabeth's tone is one of restrained self-pity, but it is hard not to feel that her self-pity masks a boast, for by tradition blind poets are richly compensated. Their thwarted gaze turns inwards, and its light is intensified into a blaze of prophetic fire. It is as just such a poet that Browning first hailed Elizabeth:

> You speak out, *you*, – I only make men and women speak – give you truth broken into prismatic hues, and fear the pure white light even if it is in me.[3]

He is turned, like the child, and can look only at the prismatic hues of the rainbow, but Elizabeth, like the blind poet of tradition, like

Millais's blind girl, can look direct at the pure white light of the sun. To press a comparison between Browning, solid, hairy, and so fastidious in his dress as to be something of a dandy, and the pale waif in the ragged frock who nestles close to Millais's blind girl risks being comic rather than illuminating, but it is a risk I am just prepared to take.

Of Browning's married life with Elizabeth we know little: such a life, both agreed, should remain private. Our best evidence comes before and after the marriage, in the courtship letters and in those dreadful letters in which Browning sobs out his misery after his wife has died. Two things seem clear. Browning took a wife little less dependent on him in the ordinary business of life than the blind girl is on the seeing child. He married a permanent invalid. Second, there are indications that emotionally their positions of dependence were reversed. In her letters to Robert, Elizabeth is from the first urbane, clever, easy, with a self-possession that sometimes borders on self-absorption. In comparison, Browning's letters are gauche, uneasy in tone, even somewhat frenetic. Long before he ever met Elizabeth he confessed a depth of attachment to her that would surely have frightened off a less assured woman. He may have been a man of the world and she a recluse, but his is the insecurity.

In his early letters Browning clings to Elizabeth, leans against her. He seeks her hand in marriage, and the phrase is oddly appropriate. One remember's Millais's child, looking away from the blind girl towards the outside world, yet still clutching her hand. It is a version of a relationship that Browning sketches in several poems; notoriously in *Pauline*, but also in *Sordello*, *The Ring and the Book*, *Fifine at the Fair* and *Red Cotton Night Cap Country*. One thinks of the relationships between Sordello and Palma, Caponsacchi and Pompilia, Don Giovanni and Elvire, and between Léonce Miranda and Clara. These poems are not Browning's best exactly, and they are never likely to be his most popular, but they could plausibly be represented as his greatest achievements. I am not claiming any of these poems, even *Pauline*, as autobiographical. The connection between Browning's poems and his life is so subterranean that all attempts to elucidate it strike one as merely footling. Even when one feels some connection its significance is opaque, for it might just as easily be argued that Browning occasionally imitated his poems in his life as vice versa. My claim is more modest; that the relationship between a calm strong woman and a hectic, troubled man is important to Browning, and that he associates it with the relationship between a mind focused on the stirring, restless surface of the world, and the mind that has access to some still truth that lies behind the welter of appearances. Elizabeth, like the blind girl, looks at the 'pure white light' of the sun: Browning, like the child, turns back to the dancing 'prismatic colours' of the natural world.

I doubt whether any phrases from Browning's letters are more often quoted than these, and they are not only quoted directly: they reappear in the metaphors that Browning's critics use to describe his achievement. But I have located only three attempts to unravel the significance of the metaphor, and of these much the most substantial is W. O. Raymond's essay 'The Jewelled Bow'.[4] Raymond suggests that Browning's metaphor derives from Shelley's representation of life in *Adonais* as 'a dome of many-coloured glass' staining 'the white radiance of eternity'. For Browning as for Shelley, he argues, colours figure the limitations of mere mortality, white radiance freedom from mortal constraints. But whereas Shelley feels only that colours disfigure the pure white light, for the mature Browning they enrich it 'by mellowing and humanising it into prismatic hues':

> Only the prism's obstruction shows aright
> The secret of a sunbeam, breaks its light
> Into the jewelled bow from blankest white;
> So may a glory from defect arise ...

> (*Deaf and Dumb*, 1–4)

Colour, he suggests, is for Browning the badge of the humanist ethic that Browning turned to after he had rejected the Shelleyanism of his youth. He embraces colour not because he fears white light, but because he has rejected it. It is the symbol of the platonic transcendentalism that he has outgrown. Raymond's ragged child, we might say, grows up, leaves the blind girl, and walks steadily and independently towards the jewelled rainbow, turning back to the blind girl and the pure white light of the sun only to wave goodbye.

This is, I suppose, the traditional version of Browning's career. He begins as a Shelleyan, a disciple of the sun-treader, a subjective poet. He finds himself only when he rejects Shelley, and becomes a dramatic, objective poet. He begins as a reacher after white radiance, but he learns to rest content with the prismatic hues of the world. It is the whole point, it might be said, of the late poem, the parleying *With Gerald de Lairesse*, to describe and to defend the trajectory of such a career.

Gerald de Lairesse was a Dutch painter who lost his sight, and wrote in his blindness a treatise on painting, *The Art of Painting in All its Branches*. Browning had come upon this book as a boy, and it had been a favourite of his. De Lairesse sets out to show that a painter who lives in a dull landscape, 'hemmed round by Dutch canals', need not despair. He shows how it is possible for the artist to 'descry abundant worth / In trivial commonplace'. He seems at first to be a Dutch realist, but we quickly learn that in his book he describes in words the kind of landscape that he painted, 'Holland turned Dreamland', its actuality idealised, its scenery populated with classical gods and goddesses. He escorts his reader through landscapes that the seeing, 'ignobly common-sensed', are blind to, and only the blind can see:

> Say am I right? Your sealed sense moved your mind
> Free from obstruction, to compassionate
> Art's power left powerless, and supply the blind
> With fancies worth all facts denied by fate
> Mind could invent things, and to – take away
> At pleasure, leave out trifles mean and base
> Which vex the sight that cannot say them nay,
> But, where mind plays the master, have no place.

> (88–95)

Browning looks at the book now, and wonders what he saw in it when he was a child. It is his *Swiss Family Robinson*:

> 'twas a boy that budged
> No foot's breadth from your visioned steps away
> The while that memorable "Walk" he trudged
> In your companionship.

> (44–7)

Only as a boy could Browning agree to be led by the blind, to prefer to the evidence of his own eyes the fanciful vision found in a book. When he walks now, he no longer sees a landscape littered with nymphs and satyrs, and he no longer averts his eyes from 'trifles mean and base'. But the adult's plain view of things, 'ignobly common-sensed', is not self-evidently to be preferred to the child's vision. It may be that the humdrum world that Browning now looks at is all that is left to the man who has lost the child's ability to imagine. Common sense may be the bleak refuge of a poet who lives in an impoverished world, a world where there is no place for fancy, where fact:

> Has got to – say, not so much push aside
> Fancy, as to declare its place supplied
> By fact unseen, but no less fact the same,
> Which mind bids sense accept.

(150–3)

In the world in which Browning lives the place of the charming supernatural creatures of ancient myth has been taken by the abstract laws of science. But he will have no truck with the Romantic primitivism that mourns their loss. The change from his early taste for de Lairesse to his present affectionate contempt, from de Lairesse's kind of landscape to Millais's, is progress not decline.

Browning sets out to prove it by showing that he could, if he chose, describe landscapes in the style of de Lairesse, that he can 'Boast, with the sights I see, your vision too'. If he is successful then the verdict must be that Browning has outgrown his boyhood master:

> Bear witness while you walk with me,
> I see as you: if we loose arms, stop pace,
> 'Tis you that stand still, I conclude the race
> Without you.

(174–7)

Four landscapes follow, eighteenth-century heroic landscapes recreated in verse a little like Thomson's. Prometheus undergoes his torture as dawn breaks; in the morning Diana hunts in the forest; at noon a satyr pursues a nymph; in the evening the armies

of Darius and Alexander mass for battle. The fifth landscape is only
begun. Night falls, and a ghost appears:

> There he stands,
> Voiceless, scarce strives, with deprecating hands.

> (361–2)

He breaks off. He has, he feels, done enough. He has found an
epithet that Pope might envy, and there is no need to go on:
'Enough! Stop further fooling, De Lairesse.' To make poetry from
stories that we have to pretend to take seriously is only childish
play:

> The dead Greek lore lies buried in the urn
> Where who seeks fire finds ashes.

> (392–3)

Browning moves into one of those celebrations of the onward march
of the human intellect, interspersed with hearty advice to his
readers to roll up their sleeves, that members of the Browning
Society found so edifying:

> Let things be – not seem,
> I counsel rather, – do, and nowise dream:
> Earth's young significance is all to learn ...

> (389–91)

But the poems ends more interestingly than we could expect.
Browning recalls two things. First, he remembers that, however
unsatisfactory the result, the impulse that led de Lairesse to
champion the ideal or mythological landscape was a true one. It was
an attempt to compose 'the strife / 'Twixt sense and soul', and,
though de Lairesse brought about this resolution only with the help
of trivial 'fancy', it is a necessary project, ours as much as his:

> for sense, my de Lairesse,
> Cannot content itself with outward things,
> Mere beauty ...

> (139–41)

Second, he remembers the ghost, and the pity of its weak and futile gesture. De Lairesse presents himself as the champion of 'Imagination's limitless domain' against vulgar actuality. His chief mistake is that his imagination is not at all 'limitless', but bound within the confines of a Greek mythology that, in the face of death, recoiled helplessly, waved deprecating hands. The Greeks could imagine Achilles, greatest of their heroes, content to give up all his glory if only he might 'slink / To life back'.

There are two grounds on which Browning asserts his superiority over de Lairesse. The art of the realist is higher than that of the idealist. Browning has proved it. He can make landscapes in de Lairesse's style, whereas de Lairesse, both when he could see and when he was blind, inhabited a dream world from which he could not grope his way to the real world that preoccupies Browning. Second, de Lairesse's dependence on Greek mythology left him tied to an imaginative system that crumpled against the fact of death.

The two grounds seem so incongruous that Browning's poem threatens to disintegrate. But it ends triumphantly in a lyric that unites its themes. The Greek poet contemplating the spring was reminded only that though nature may be reborn man dies. Browning offers in place of Greek melancholy modern joy:

> Dance, yellows and whites and reds –
> Lead your gay orgy, leaves, stalks, heads
> Astir with the wind in the tulip-beds!
>
> There's sunshine; scarcely a wind at all
> Disturbs starved grass and daisies small
> On a certain mound by a churchyard wall.
>
> Daisies and grass be my heart's bedfellows
> On the mound wind spares and sunshine mellows;
> Dance you, reds and whites and yellows!

> (426–34)

The song praises spring, but it praises, too, the brave innocence of Browning's eye that so boldly preserves the unadorned experience, flowers as flashes of colour on the visual plane. That is the boldness that the Greeks lacked, that de Lairesse lacked. But Browning's lyric does more than celebrate its own achievement: it also explains it.

The reds and whites and yellows dance in the breeze around a sheltered spot where there is 'scarcely a wind at all'. They dance around a grave, and Browning looks at the grave with its 'starved grass and daisies small' both unsentimentally and undismayed. He does not feel the need that the Greeks felt to hide a corpse, to deck it with a gorgeous catalogue of flowers. He can look at it with its natural covering of daisies and grass, and take what he sees to his heart: 'Daisies and grass be my heart's bedfellows.' He is at ease with death, confident – for the lyric implies no less – of his own immortality and of the immortality of those he loves. It is the sign of this confidence, and it is the effect too, that he can find happiness in the actual, in his own unadorned sensory experience: 'Dance you, reds and whites and yellows!'

Realism, Browning would have us see, is not only truer but more imaginative than the art practised by such as de Lairesse. The realist accepts his experience, he is truer. But he is able to accept it only because he has made the last leap of the imagination, because he has grasped in a blind act of faith the fact of immortality. To have failed that leap, to have failed to find in death a benediction, is to live in a world that one can never see truly, for one can look only out of the corner of one's eye at a world haunted by the appalling fact that with death life ends.

Browning does not need to be led by the hand of the blind de Lairesse. His was only a boyhood allegiance. He is now a man, even an old man, and he no longer needs what he needed as a boy. He needs more. He does not need to join de Lairesse in his feebly imaginative walk, but to walk hand in hand with a woman who died a quarter of a century before. And he needs this not simply as a grieving husband but as the condition of his art, for Browning is a realist, and it is his crucial belief that realism can exist only in the faith that love conquers death.

Fifine at the Fair is, I would be prepared to argue, one of the best long poems of the Victorian age and Browning's greatest achievement. Its merit has all to do with the reckless moral courage evident in its composition. The business of the poem's critics, from Nettleship, who distinguished those passages that must be understood ironically by printing them in italics, to Browning's modern commentators, has been to protect Browning from the consequences of his own daring by distinguishing clearly between the speaker's truth and his sophistries. This critical effort is not at all wrong-headed, for it is exactly that exercise that the poem forces on the reader. One wants to add only that the difficulty of the exercise is a fact at least as important as its result. *Fifine at the Fair* is not a dramatic monologue at all like Browning's early successes, poems such as *My Last Duchess* and *The Bishop Orders His Tomb*. They are external portraits: one listens to the duke and the bishop from a stance detached enough for moral disapproval to consort quite comfortably with relish of their monstrous vitality. *Fifine at the Fair* is an internal monologue. The speaker needs to fool himself more pressingly than he needs to fool his wife, and so we can only listen to him inwardly, testing what he says by our own experience of things. He speaks at once as an everyman and as a sleazy sexual adventurer. His is the frailty that all male flesh is heir to, but it is also a frailty that presents itself as universal only in a weak act of self-deception. In his characterisation Browning's love of human imperfection and his contempt for moral cowardice are intricately mixed, too intricately for the poem ever to become very popular.

Fifine at the Fair ends as Don Juan leaves Elvire, hurrying off in response to a note that Fifine has slipped into his hand. He promises to be back home in five minutes. As is his habit he protests his loyalty at the moment that he betrays it. But it is not clear whether he is betraying a dead or a living wife, a ghost or a flesh and blood woman:

> How pallidly you pause o' the threshold! Hardly night
> Which drapes you ought to make real flesh and blood so white!
> Touch me, and so appear alive to all intents!
> Will the saint vanish from the sinner that repents?
> Suppose you are a ghost? A memory, a hope,
> A fear, a conscience! Ouch! Give back the hand I grope
> I' the dark for!

(2306–12)

Juan can neither reject nor rest satisfied with the love of his wife, but how literally we are to construe her spirituality is open to doubt. Juan exits protesting:

> five minutes past, expect me! If in vain –
> Why, stir from flesh and blood, and play the ghost again!

(2354–5)

The poem has ended, but there remains an epilogue, a lyric that has been construed almost always as a dialogue between Browning and the dead Elizabeth:

> "Ah, but if you knew how time has dragged, days, nights!
> All the neighbour talk with man and maid – such men!
> All the fuss and trouble of street-sounds, window-sights:
> All the worry of flapping door and echoing roof; and then,
> All the fancies … Who were they had leave, dared try
> Darker arts that almost struck despair in me?
> If you knew but how I dwelt down here!" quoth I:
> "And was I so better off up there?" quoth She.
>
> "Help and get it over! *Re-united to his wife*
> (How draw up the paper lets the parish-people know?)
> *Lies M., or N., departed from this life.*
> *Day the this or that, month and year the so and so.*
> What i' the way of final flourish? Prose, verse? Try!
> *Affliction sore long time he bore*, or, what is it to be?
> *Till God did please to grant him ease.* Do end!" quoth I:
> "I end with – Love is all and Death is nought!" quoth She.

(17–32)

Elvire waits at home for Juan to return: the speaker waits in his house for his dead wife to visit him. So far the positions are reversed. But the husband's house is his body, and his spirit lives in it, alternately dumb and rancorous, 'Tongue-tied now, now blaspheming like a Turk'. His wish to leave the house with its 'crumbling brick embrowned with sin and shame', and the dreary agitation of flapping door and echoing roof is, he knows, a wish for death, and in the final stanza he writes his own epitaph, sardonically, with grim humour. But the wife, unlike Elvire, is allowed the final word:

> "I end with – Love is all and Death is nought!" quoth She.

This is a platitude, and it is a creed, movingly suspended between the two. And it stills the querulous husband, gently turns him back to the house of his body, back to the neighbour talk and the fuss and trouble of the streets, strong in the faith that death cannot restore what death cannot take away.

The lyric can be read – it is hard not to read it so – as spoken by Browning to Elizabeth, but it is also possible to understand it as spoken by Juan to Elvire. Browning writes it for himself, if you like, and then, generously, confers it on his character, rising contemptuously above the kind of critical response that will seize on just such a stimulus to read the poem as a veiled confession of shameful hanky-panky with Lady Ashburton. *Fifine at the Fair* is an example of high Victorian realism. Its condition is an unflinching openness to experience, both external and inward, both the 'street-sounds' and 'all the fancies'. Browning makes the poem by attending to what he has seen and to what he has felt, and by allowing free commerce between these different kinds of knowledge. It is a kind of realism that demands even before technical competence moral courage, and in the last line of the poem Browning names the belief that sustains his courage. 'Love is all', *amor omnia vincit*: it is a faith startling in its simplicity, and it is a blind faith.

Early in their correspondence Elizabeth told Robert that she was translating Aeschylus's *Prometheus* as an act of penance for having translated it before, and translated it very ill. Browning protests that he has not read her earlier version, only looked at it 'to see what rendering a passage had received that was often in my thoughts'. This is the passage in Elizabeth's improved (!) translation:

PROMETHEUS: I did restrain beside
          My mortals from premeditating death.
  CHORUS: How didst thou medicine the plague fear of death?
PROMETHEUS: I set blind Hope to inhabit in their house.
  CHORUS: By that gift thou didst help thy mortals well.

τυθλὰς ἐν αὐτοῖς ἐλπίδας κατῴκισα; in Elizabeth's version, 'I set blind Hope to inhabit in their house'; as Shelley has it, 'He caused blind hopes to dwell in them'. The line haunted Browning. It is 'what you hear men dissertate upon by the hour, as proving the immortality of the soul apart from revelation, undying yearnings, restless longings, instinctive desires which, unless to be eventually indulged, it were cruel to plant in us, etc. etc.'.[5] But, he notes, the chorus in Aeschylus replies only, 'By that gift thou didst help thy mortals well.' Blind hope, hope in immortality, was important to

Browning before Elizabeth died, before even he had met her. His hostility to Mr Sludge and the 'darker arts' that fascinated Elizabeth is not that of the sober rationalist, but of a man who will not have his gut feelings played with. The complicated courtship dance with orthodox Christianity that Browning performed for most of his adult life is impelled by a need stronger than most men's to believe in personal immortality, together with a need, also stronger than most men's, for belief to be grounded in experience. When one impulse predominates he shuffles forward, when the other has sway he shuffles back, swithering always between blind hope and blind faith.

The conflict between the idealist and the humanist, the transcendentalist and the realist, the poet-prophet and the poet-recorder has long been the staple of Browning criticism. The poet who wrote *Pauline*, *Paracelsus* and *Sordello* gave way, we are told, to the poet who took upon himself the task of transcribing the humdrum, the ordinary, whose subject was men and women. As Raymond has it, he turns his back on the 'pure, white light' and settles himself to a patient study of light as it is refracted through the prism of mortal circumstances. But even though one must turn one's back on the sun to see a rainbow, it remains true that the rainbow is dependent on the sun. One may choose to look at colours rather than pure, white light, but white light remains the condition that enables one to see colours clearly. In the same way, Browning's seeing eyes, his gift for human observation, depend on his clinging to a blind hope, a blind faith. I wish not at all to subvert the human reality of Browning's love for his wife, and I do not believe that it does so to suggest that his love took a form that allowed him to act out a central article of his private creed. In choosing freely to depend upon a woman who was 'in a manner as a blind poet' and who speaks out of the pure, white light of truth, Browning signalled the dependence of colours on light, of common sense on intuition, of the seeing on the blind. That is why Millais's 'The Blind Girl' is an appropriate frontispiece to his poems.

8

Rainbow Flakes

Had Browning contrived to set the seal on his allegiance to Shelley by dying at the same age, it is hard to know what we would have made of him. He would have been the author of *Pauline, Paracelsus* and *Sordello*, of that thick sheaf of pages that even now unnerves the student setting out on a serious study of Browning. He would have been one of those poets who attract a small coterie of admirers, and every now and then their missionary zeal would have forced him for a time on the attention of a wider audience. He would have ranked, I suppose, just above Beddoes and just below Clough. *Pauline, Paracelsus* and *Sordello* are all of them, in some sense, failures, but they are failures more substantial than many successes, for they are that peculiar kind of poetic failure that will not go away.

The three poems have much in common, but their most striking affinity is that all of them are concerned to express an ambition so fierce, so all but insane, that failure is its inevitable outcome. All three poems are studies of genius, of men conscious of an inner power so extraordinary that the world seems too puny an arena to permit any adequate display of their talents. They are both the victims of Romantic irony and its connoisseurs. Their power is infinite: it cannot reveal itself within a finite world. That is the condition of their failure, but it is also the condition of their sense of their own magnificence. It is an irony that they alternately suffer and fondle. They fail, and their failure at once mocks and supports their sense of their own greatness. The poems are inseparable from their heroes. Their failure is the failure of the poems in which they appear, and the failure of the poems is as paradoxical as the failure of the heroes, for Browning crumples under the weight of his own material in a manner that is both a confession of weakness and a boast. He cannot sustain his enterprise, which betrays his inadequacy, and shows too that it was an exercise so stupendous that it could not be sustained. Within the three poems success, the human success of Festus, or the success of Eglamor, for whom the craft of poetry is all in all, is envied with an envy that seldom fails to plunge into contempt. Success is the lot of the man who does not have the greatness of soul to fail.

It is hard not to feel that the man who wrote these poems was half
mad. It is also hard to connect one's impression of their author with
one's impression of the author, say, of *Ferishtah's Fancies*. And yet all
three poems, and *Paracelsus* and *Sordello* especially, are quarries
from which Browning continued to hack out poems for the rest of
his career. They are thoroughly Romantic poems – their most
important predecessors are *Alastor* and *Endymion* – and yet they are
also the poems in which Browning struggles to formulate a
distinctively anti-Romantic aesthetic.

Browning's attack on Romanticism takes the form of a thorough-
going assault on Romantic holism or organicism. Dualism, Shelley
confidently asserts, is a philosophical error of a pernicious kind, for
it is 'fatal to morals'.[1] Dualism for Browning, whether it be the
infinite soul trapped in a finite body, the contest between fact and
fancy, or the opposition between the idea and the word, is the
defining condition of human experience.

In *Pauline*, *Paracelsus* and *Sordello* Browning stubbornly insists on
a distinction between the idea and its expression. The distinction is
presented as one more aspect of the triumphant failure to which the
poems aspire, for only thought not worth expressing could yield
itself satisfactorily to language. Paracelsus can deliver to his
students the knowledge that he has gained incidentally, while 'bent
on nobler prize'. But the prize itself, the knowledge 'one, – vast,
shadowy' must remain unspoken. Paracelsus finds to his surprise
that he is ill-equipped to share even the lesser knowledge:

>   I found
> Such teaching was an art requiring cares
> And qualities peculiar to itself:
> That to possess was one thing – to display
> Another.

>   (III. 651–5)

His lectures are remarkable for their fervid obscurity. Paracelsus is
decently apologetic about it, but Browning moved on from
Paracelsus to *Sordello*, and *Sordello* might aptly be described as a
lecture delivered by Paracelsus. The frantic urgency of the speaker,
his concern to indicate the high moment of what he has to say, are
given shocking precedence over any concern that he might be
understood. And it would be quite wrong to assume that Browning

is innocent of intending any such effect, that he is suffering only from the young poet's failing of over-estimating the telepathic powers of his reader. Sordello boasts of a similar obscurity as the badge of his superiority over Eglamor. The new style that Sordello had so vigorously hammered out, 'welding words into the crude / Mass from the new speech round him', shatters at the impact of his first attempt to express within it one of his perceptions:

> Because perceptions whole, like that he sought
> To clothe, reject so pure a work of thought
> As language: thought may take perception's place
> But hardly co-exist in any case,
> Being its mere presentment – of the whole
> By parts, the simultaneous and the sole
> By the successive and the many.

(II. 589–95)

The audience is left in some difficulty: 'painfully it tacks / Thought to thought'. Readers of *Sordello* will sympathise with them.

Sordello's songs are unlike Eglamor's. In such songs as Eglamor's, 'you find alone / Completeness, judge the song and singer one'. Such completeness is for Browning deathly. In comparison, Sordello's songs are 'true works', not so much the songs he sang, but his 'dream performances that will / Never be more than dreamed'. From them:

>   escapes there still
> Some proof, the singer's proper life was 'neath
> The life his song exhibits.

(III. 624–6)

This is Romantic, I suppose, in its preference for the unwritten poem, the song unheard, but Keats and Shelley laud an art that, in refusing abrasive contact with any materials of expression, can express perfectly the artist's mind. Sordello, amazingly, approves of poems that can only be dreamt for only so can the poems preserve with sufficient clarity the distinction between the singer and the song. Sordello dreams poems that fail more superbly than any poems he can accomplish, for in poetic failure, in incompleteness, in the sense that the 'lay was but an episode / In the bard's life', is preserved that asymmetry that for Browning is the condition of all living art.

The central conflict explored in *Pauline, Paracelsus* and *Sordello* is between character and action, or rather between personality and action, for character, the individual as he is defined by what he does and what he says, is dreaded by the poem's heroes like death. The problem is most fully explored in *Sordello*. Even as a child Sordello is conscious of his genius, and he knows that his purpose in life must be to express it. He frankly admits that his one end is 'self-display'. In his boyhood it is enough to dream, confident that when the time comes the means to accomplish his project will appear:

> though I must abide
> With dreams now, I may find a thorough vent
> For all myself, acquire an instrument
> For acting what those people act; my soul
> Hunting a body out may gain its whole
> Desire some day!
>
> (I. 832–7)

His childhood is happy. All possibilities open to him, no choice taken, his sense of his own greatness is spared contact with the limiting contours of mortal life.

His first choice of profession, poetry, appeals to him precisely because it is a choice and no choice. Poetry gives him a public role in which he can win the prestige that he demands while still refusing to limit himself as he would have to do were he to become, say, a soldier. To become a poet need not be to become a particular kind of person. The poet may prove his power by his ability to enter imaginatively into the minds of an infinite number of characters and still remain himself a neutral creature. In this way he may wield power and yet refuse the self-limitation which, for other men, is the sacrifice that must be made before power can be won. To show oneself able to become another person is to prove oneself the greater man. One remembers the aged Browning proving his superiority over de Lairesse in exactly this way. When one becomes another person the other person yields:

> The world shall bow to me conceiving all
> Man's life, who sees its blisses, great and small,
> Afar – not tasting any.

(II. 425–7)

What is more, it is the poet who ascribes value to all other pursuits by consecrating them in song. Even the greatest ruler 'stoops' to the poet, because the poet is the source of all value:

> Himself inactive, yet is greater far
> Than such as act, each stooping to his star,
> Acquiring thence its function.

(II. 381–3)

It is tempting to explain Browning's subsequent career as Sordello's. He chooses to live by inhabiting a long succession of men and women, resolving thus the conflict between the infinite soul and the finite activities through which alone the soul can reveal itself, and satisfying at the same time his need for a power subtler and vaster than that of any emperor. But however tempting it would be wrong. Even Sordello gives up the attempt to live an infinite life by living life vicariously. He recognises that to choose to live wholly in the imagination is itself a limiting choice. He still feels frustrated, divided, still searches for 'the complete Sordello, man and bard'. At last he gives up his poetic career, and retreates to Goito, his boyhood home, to a life of obscurity. 'Better sure', he decides, 'be unrevealed, than / Part revealed'.

Sordello's re-emergence from retirement is the most obscure part of the poem. The agent seems to be love. Palma has been a shadowy figure in Sordello's life. She is seen and at once adored. She prompts the sudden bursts of sensual urgency to which the reader clings amidst the poem's abstract windings, as when she rewards Sordello for his first poem by giving him her scarf, 'her neck's warmth and all', and it is his love for her that seems to prompt Sordello's return from the shadowy life of Goito to the city. Mankind has been for him only a means, though a necessary means, through which he can accomplish the 'self-display' that is his only ambition. He now sees that he may achieve his end not by subjecting mankind to his will, but by submitting himself to mankind's service. If he does this, then humanity will 'supply a body to his soul'. It is no longer enough to dream his poems: his poems must become projects acted out in the world for mankind's benefit.

Ambitious as ever, Sordello conceives a stupendous poem. The Pope and the Emperor must be encouraged to destroy each other. Their mutual destruction will give Sordello the chance to found once more Rome in all its glory, a free republic of free men. But this project, too, 'Last of my dreams and loveliest', he must abandon. It is work not for one man and one lifetime, but for centuries. Palma explains:

> God has conceded two sights to a man –
> One, of man's whole work, time's completed plan,
> The other of the minute's work, man's first
> Step to the plan's completeness.
>
> (v. 85–8)

Sordello's task is to write his fragment, do his minute's work, and to abandon the futile attempt to accomplish all by himself 'time's completed plan'. Nevertheless, his ability to glimpse the complete plan is crucial, for only then will he be able to write the fragment of time's epic poem that he has it in him to write.

Sordello knows that the work of time will be to effect the mutual destruction of Guelf and Ghibbelin. His 'minute's work' is to side with the Guelfs, and to use his powers of rhetoric to persuade the warlord Taurello to throw in his lot with the Guelf cause. Taurello is Sordello's antitype. For Taurello 'Thoughts were caprices in the course of deeds'. For Sordello, as for the poem of which he is the hero, the reverse is true. Sordello's meeting with the warlord is the climax of the poem, for were the two men to be reconciled, thought and deed would be united. The sense of frustration that meets Sordello at every turn would be healed. Sordello speaks to Taurello, urgently, from the heart. Taurello, uncannily anticipating in this the response of the reading public to the whole poem, cannot make head nor tail of it. Speech-making, he knows, is a fine thing in its way, but he is confident that it has nothing much to do with the harsh actualities of political decision-making, so he is not much perturbed by his inability to make out what Sordello is going on about. Sordello offers him the opportunity to wed his sword to an idea. He responds by offering Sordello the opportunity to become himself a warlord. Both offers are declined. Sordello has failed. There is nothing left for him to do but die, and die he does.

Sordello dies a failure, like Paracelsus. He accomplishes next to nothing. Browning rescued him, an obscure forerunner of Dante, from a footnote in the history of Italian literature, just as he rescued Paracelsus from a footnote in the history of chemistry. He galvanizes both men into frenetic life, and at the last he releases them once more into the obscurity from which they had been snatched. Both lives are futile, and so, in a sense, are the poems of which they are the heroes.

Sordello is, of course, a Shelleyan hero. In the poem's first three books he is like the hero of *Alastor*, a driven man, alienated from a finite world that can offer no embodiment of his infinite dreams. In the final three books he is a Promethean hero, struggling to create a world in which he and all men may feel at home. But he is also like a hero of George Eliot's – like, say, Will Ladislaw – who begins life trying to change the world, and grows up to learn that the proper object of a man's ambition is to secure a slightly better sewage system in at least one town. Sordello's task is to 'Fit to the finite his infinity', and to do so in such a way that he will not 'Brutalize / The soul the sad world's way', and that is the task of George Eliot's heroes just as much as it is of Shelley's. In *Sordello* Browning fuses a transcendental Romantic rhetoric, a rhetoric of absolute demands, with the subtle Victorian rhetoric of compromise. The whole theme is pressed into a single metaphor:

> light, thwarted, breaks
> A limpid purity to rainbow flakes.
>
> (v. 605–6)

A ray of light encounters the obstruction of a prism and fragments into shivers of coloured light. The infinite human soul encounters the resistance of a finite world and is thwarted. But the moment of defeat is also the moment of richest consolation, for the 'limpid purity', as it is broken, gives birth to 'rainbow flakes', to the colours of mortal beauty. The metaphor is remarkably even-handed. Limpid purity is lost, broken: there is no repairing that loss. And yet for the rainbow flakes ever to come into being there must be limpid purity, and it must be broken. Browning sides neither with pure light nor with colour. He celebrates both, and he celebrates the asymmetrical relationship that joins them, for asymmetry, for him, is the condition of life.

The metaphor focuses the poem's themes; Sordello's difficulties as a poet, his whole perceptions thwarted when they meet the obstruction of language, and his difficulties as a man, his infinite self thwarted as it meets the obstruction of a finite world. It preserves the truth that Palma delivers to Sordello. God has conceded 'two sights to a man'. He can see the 'whole work, time's completed plan', and he can see also 'the minute's work', the work that must be accomplished under the conditions of our mortal life, amidst the play of coloured light that figures the fragmentariness of our living experience. There is no choosing between the two sights: the problem is to give to each its due. The blind girl looks towards the sun, her young friend gazes at the rainbow. We do not see the picture properly unless we look with both of them.

9

Seven Proper Colours Chorded

'Browning at his weakest' is Isobel Armstrong's comment on *Christmas-Eve* and *Easter-Day*, and this much seems certain, that never again will these poems occupy the privileged place in the Browning canon that they once owned. *Christmas-Eve* is a poem of confirmation. At a time of year appropriate to the beginning of a Christian life Browning chooses a church in which to worship. *Easter-Day* is apocalyptic. A red flash in the night sky scares the poet with a premonition of the end of the world. The poem is a dialogue between a soul and a recalcitrant body that accepts the soul's case, and yet pleads that it be allowed to cling to mortal things; to the beauty of the natural world, to the craft of poetry, to human love. The soul is obdurate, and at last the body yields, gives itself up. But the soul's victory lasts only as long as Browning's terror. He ends, as we would expect, celebrating the struggle rather than its outcome, thanking God that he 'finds it hard to be a Christian'. Neither poem offers much scope for the reader prepared to be interested in everything about Browning except what he thought. The value of both is heavily dependent on an interest in their arguments, and such an interest can no longer be reckoned general.

In both poem's Browning's fancy is set working by a rare atmospheric fact. In *Christmas-Eve* he sees a lunar rainbow, its 'seven proper colours chorded'. In *Easter-Day* he sees the clouds lit by a 'fierce vindictive scribble of red'. It ignites the whole sky, and fades only to flash out again. The blood-red flashes are punctuated by:

> violet intervals
> Leaving exposed the utmost walls
> Of time, about to tumble in
> And end the world.

(543–6)

Christmas-Eve is concerned with the Christian life in this world, and finds its proper symbol in the rainbow. The theme of *Easter-Day* is the chasm that separates this world from the world to come. The red and the violet, the extreme edges of the spectrum, expose the 'utmost walls' of the world. They pulse alternately to signal that the mortal world of colour is about to collapse in on itself, leaving only eternity.

Browning kept track of the developments in optics through the nineteenth century which makes it a little surprising that he should choose to repeat Newton's time-honoured but arbitrary division of the rainbow into 'seven proper colours'. But the reason is plain enough, and it is the same as Newton's. Seven in these poems is a magic number, the number of mortality, of life under the moon. In *Easter-Day* Browning defines the poet's business as 'Making the finite comprehend / Infinity'. He should properly spend:

> Such praise alone, upon his craft,
> As, when wind-lyres obey the waft,
> Goes to the craftsman who arranged
> The seven strings, changed them and re-changed –
> Knowing it was the South that harped.
> He felt his song, in singing, warped;
> Distinguished his and God's part.

> (909–15)

Browning repeats, and as he repeats travesties, a central Romantic symbol. It is a favourite technique. For Coleridge and his followers the Aeolian lyre figured an achieved wholeness; the poet fused with nature, the finite with the infinite, the human with the divine. But for Browning there is no fusion, only warping. The harp's song registers the divine only in the distinction between the singer and the song, between the craft of the man who arranged the strings and the divine artlessness of the south wind. The gap is fixed in the contrast between the wind, one, indivisible, and the seven strings. But it is in *Christmas-Eve* that Browning is most preoccupied with the number seven. The poem is built around the association between the seven colours of the rainbow and the seven-branched candlestick of *Revelation*, 'Saint John's candlestick'. The seven branches signify, we are told, the seven churches of Asia, by a natural extension the various Christian churches between which Browning must choose.[1] So much is obvious, but the business of the whole poem is to work out the relationship between the candlestick and the rainbow, between the Son of Man as John sees him 'in the midst of the seven candlesticks', and as Ezekiel sees him, as bright fire in the midst of a rainbow: 'As the appearance of the bow that is in the cloud in the day of rain, so was the appearance of brightness round about'.

Browning shelters from rain in the porch of a Congregational chapel. A service is about to begin and a parcel of unattractive lower-class worshippers edge past the poet and enter the church. He is put out by their manner of glaring at him, as at one of the damned. Sanctimoniousness is irritating, especially in one's social inferiors, and the poet, out of pique as much as anything, decides to go in:

> I very soon had had enough of it,
> The hot smell and the human noises,
> And my neighbour's coat, the greasy cuff of it.

> (139–41)

But more difficult to bear than all this is 'the preaching man's immense stupidity', and hardest of all is the evident satisfaction with which his sermon is received:

> 'Twas too provoking!
> My gorge rose at the nonsense and stuff of it;
> So, saying like Eve when she plucked the apple
> 'I wanted a taste, and now there's enough of it.'
> I flung out of the little chapel.

> (182–6)

He escapes from the hot, stuffy chapel into the cool night air. The rain has stopped and above him the night sky is a turmoil of clouds and moonlight. It is a version of the typical Romantic journey out of the tawdry social world into the purer world of nature, a walk like Wordsworth's in the opening lines of *The Prelude*. But it is fiercer than that. It is a Shelleyan and a Byronic rejection of the shabby conventionalism of established religion in favour of a communion with God achieved not through the nasal text-picking of a stupid preacher, but in natural immensity. To look at the skies is to enter God's 'church-door', not the 'lath-and-plaster' porch of the chapel with its absurdly inappropriate superscription, 'Mount Zion':

> In youth I looked to the very skies,
> And probing their immensities
> I found God there, his visible power ...
>
> (279–81)

To commune with the unbounded sky is to share its immensity, to achieve a status from which one can look with pitying condescension on those who must seek God in church or chapel:

> O, let men keep their ways
> Of seeking thee in a narrow shrine –
> Be this my way!
>
> (372–4)

It is at this point that he sees the rainbow, and his vision confirms all that he has said. It is a vision vouchsafed to him as he worships in a skyey cathedral, a vision withheld from those sitting pressed together in the chapel. He feels privileged, chosen: 'Me, one out of a world of men / Singled forth', and in gratitude for his election he offers to build mental tabernacles to the glory of God:

> Where, forever in thy presence,
> In ecstatic acquiescence,
> Far alike from thriftless learning,
> And ignorance's undiscerning,
> I may worship and remain.
>
> (415–19)

Browning projects himself as a Romantic poet, aloof in an isolated communion with the divine. But visionary isolation is no longer the badge of the prophet: it is the mark of the snob. As the rainbow's glory falls on him, it signals his mistake. It seems to be passing out of him into the ground:

> Then palely serpentining round
> Into the dark with mazy error.

(428–9)

He turns, and there is Christ, his face hidden, but his robe visible, 'vast and white'. He is struck first with joy and then with fear. He recognises his mistake: 'Me, that have despised thy friends'. But he tries to excuse himself rather than just own his fault, and when he is allowed to touch the hem of Christ's garment he feels the condescension not as a signal that he is a lost sheep, but as a mark of special distinction:

> He suffers me to follow him
> For ever, my own way – dispensed
> From seeking to be influenced
> By all the less immediate ways
> That earth, in worships manifold,
> Adopts to reach, by prayer and praise,
> The garment's hem, which, lo, I hold!

(516–22)

Holding the hem he is taken on a tour of Europe, first to St Peter's, where he follows Christ into the church and witnesses the mass, and then to Göttingen, where a professor of the higher biblical criticism lectures. Christ attends: the poet cautiously accompanies him. Both at Rome and at Göttingen he is very much the English tourist, muttering about 'Rome's gross yoke', and the dangerous German predilection for ideas. In St Peter's he witnesses a religion deprived of its head, at Göttingen a religion deprived of its heart. The second is the graver loss. He never modifies his disapproval of either Rome or Germany, but Christ's divine tolerance persuades him that, if he cannot share Catholic theology, he is at least at one with the Roman worshippers in the love they feel for their saviour. Even at Göttingen, where he cuts through German subtleties with a line of argument that would seem surprisingly blunt in anyone not so very English as Browning, he can still honour in the professor's lecture a vestige of true religious faith: 'If love's dead there, it has left a ghost'.

Christ teaches him to be tolerant, and the lesson puts him in high good humour with himself: 'This tolerance is a genial mood!'. He repudiates bigotry:

> Better a mild indifferentism
> Teaching that both our faiths (though duller
> His shine through a dull spirit's prism)
> Originally had one colour!
> Better pursue a pilgrimage
> Through ancient and through modern times
> To many people, various climes,
> Where I may see saint, savage, sage
> Fuse their respective creeds in one
> Before the general Father's throne.

(1148–57)

But no sooner has Browning won through to the kind of liberal orthodoxy with which we can feel thoroughly at ease than he rejects it. He is set down in London, and the hem escapes from his clutch:

> While I watched my foolish heart expand
> In the lazy glow of benevolence.

(1166–7)

He finds himself once again in the chapel and assumes that he had fallen asleep during the sermon. His business is clear. He cannot loftily and lazily remain neutral between the various forms of religion practised in the world. He must choose, and his choice must be a delicate compromise between accepting what is given and choosing what is best. He is, as we all are,

> Fixed to the first poor inch of ground
> To fight from, where his foot was found.

(1221–2)

We must do battle in God's cause not from the best ground, but from whatever ground we can occupy. But that does not free us from a responsibility to make our stand in the strongest position available to us. And Browning chooses the Congregational chapel, the stupid preacher and his ramshackle flock.

Sordello is disconcertingly obscure, *Christmas-Eve* disconcertingly direct. All the same, the two poems have much in common. The poet of *Christmas-Eve* just as much as Sordello demands that his soul experience the divine directly. He rejects any compromise with mortal circumstances. He gibs at the notion that he might be separated from God by some refractive atmosphere. He must learn, like Sordello, that the business of a man lies in the act of choice by which the infinite soul compromises itself with the finite world. Sordello chooses, and dies, so that his rejection of Romantic transcendentalism achieves a paradoxical Romantic glamour. His pliability is made to seem as absolute as Manfred's intransigence. But in this poem the poet must make his choice and live with it. Sordello is the creature of Romantic irony. This poet is looked at ironically too, but the irony is not at all Romantic. Sordello's reconciliation with the human race is noted with unintentionally comic earnestness: 'mankind and he were really fused'. This poet treats himself at the same moment with the rough, self-mocking humour with which he has presented himself from the first:

> I put up pencil and join chorus
> To Hepzibah tune without further apology,
> The last five verses of the third section
> Of the seventeenth Hymn of Whitfield's collection,
> To conclude with the doxology.

> (1355–9)

The breaking of limpid purity does not now produce Sordello's tragic glamour: it gives rise instead to gruff comedy. But the image remains the same:

> 'Twas a moon-rainbow, vast and perfect,
> From heaven to heaven extending, perfect
> As the mother-moon's self, full in face.
> It rose, distinctly at the base
> With its seven proper colours chorded,
> Which still, in the rising, were compressed,
> Until at last they coalesced,
> And supreme the spectral creature lorded

In a triumph of whitest white, –
Above which intervened the night.
But above night too, like only the next,
The second of a wondrous sequence,
Reaching in rare and rarer frequence,
Till the heaven of heavens were circumflexed,
Another rainbow rose, a mightier,
Fainter, flushier and flightier, –
Rapture dying along its verge.

(385–401)

The rainbow, Browning assures us, is accurately described – 'I saw that!' – but it is also emblematic. High above it is a 'triumph of whitest white', but it plays upon the ground as colour. It is, the poet knows immediately, a sign, but the story of the poem is the story of his misreading it. It seems to him, at first, to ratify his impulse to reject all established religions, and seek God instead in a vaguely enthusiastic worship of nature. Then it seems to him as a mark of special election, a vision that he is 'singled forth' to witness. But after visiting Rome and Göttingen he is inclined to understand it as recommending 'mild indifferentism'. Different religious customs are like the rainbow's different colours. If he accepts them all then he may 'Fuse their respective creeds in one', as the rainbow's colours are fused in the 'triumph of whitest white' he sees above him.

When Christ first appears to the poet, he yearns to be made pure:

The whole face turned upon me full,
And I spread myself beneath it,
As when the bleacher spreads, to seethe it
In the cleansing sun, his wool, –
Steeps in the flood of noontide whiteness
Some defiled, discoloured web –
So lay I, saturate with brightness.

(487–93)

He wants to be bleached, so that his whiteness may reflect directly the whiteness of God. The wish shows how far he is from reading the rainbow sign correctly. For a web to be 'discoloured' he can imagine only as a defilement. It is quite as if he has not just found the type of earthly beauty in the glorious discoloration of the rainbow. He has seen the rainbow, but he has not understood it. It has not made him suspect the metaphors with which he dismissed the Congregational minister's sermon. It was, he writes, 'a mingled weft / Of good and ill'. He had an absurd way of mangling texts:

> Till how could you know them, grown double their size
> In the natural fog of the good man's mind,
> Like yonder spots of our roadside lamps,
> Haloed about with the common damps.

> (225–8)

Such phenomena seem to him 'common' in both senses. He cannot connect that fog and that damp with the cloud and the rain that gave him the rainbow. When he arrives in St Peter's he is still outraged by the notion that some gross atmosphere might mediate between him and the divine. He will say of Rome only this much:

> Her teaching is not so obscured
> By errors and perversities
> That no truth shines athwart the lies.

> (616–18)

When he enters the church he does so with the intention of:

> Baring truth's face, and letting drift
> Her veils of lies as they choose to shift.

> (643–4)

Anything that comes between him and the truth is an obscuring veil that he must tear aside.

Göttingen is crucial, for the higher criticism is consistent in its repudiation of natural fog, obscuring errors, veils of lies. He witnesses a religion there that lives the hatred of refractive atmosphere to which he pretends. It is the religion of the vacuum pump:

> the Critic leaves no air to poison;
> Pumps out with ruthless ingenuity
> Atom by atom, and leaves you vacuity.

> (911–13)

If there is still something in it to honour, it is because, like all vacuum pumps, it is imperfect – a trace of atmosphere remains in the 'exhausted air-bell'.

> Truth's atmosphere may grow mephitic
> When Papist struggles with Dissenter ...

> (900–1)

But all the same Browning is forced to admit that 'atmosphere' is the necessary medium through which truth passes to men.

All churches transmit the divine light, and all refract the light they transmit, but it does not follow that we ought to be careless which church we choose. Browning can consider 'mild indifferentism' a proper cast of mind only for a moment, and even in that moment the attitude betrays itself. It may be that all Christian faiths 'Originally had one colour', but if 'duller / His shine through a dull spirit's prism', then we cannot be indifferent between them. Browning saw a double rainbow, the second the 'Fainter, flushier and flightier' reflection of the first. The sign properly read teaches tolerance, but also the limits of tolerance. If one spectrum is clearer than the others, we have a duty to choose it, to choose that religion in which:

> His All in All appears serene
> With the thinnest human veil between
> Letting the mystic lamps, the seven,
> The many motions of his spirit,
> Pass, as they list, to earth from heaven.

> (1306–10)

The mystic lamps are the seven candlesticks of St John, and they are also the seven colours of the rainbow. The candlesticks are the churches, the public religion of Christ. The rainbow is the private perception of God. It is shown to Browning alone, 'one out of a world of men', and this is not so just by chance. No two men could see the same rainbow. God reveals himself to all men through his church, and to each man, by playing on him as he played on Browning in a shaft of coloured light. But the religious life is incomplete unless private adoration and public worship can be reconciled, unless the seven candlesticks and the seven proper colours can come together as 'the mystic lamps, the seven'.

That is why Browning must choose. As he stood in the chapel door he was lit by the blue flame of a candle in a 'cracked square lantern', a 'single tallow candle' that ridiculously seemed to give itself 'the airs of a Saint John's Candlestick'. He learns by the end of the poem that that is exactly what it is. The chapel, the absurd preacher and his sleazy congregation are the 'poor inch of ground' from which Browning chooses to fight. It is from these that he must reconstitute the 'triumph of whitest white'; from the blue flame of the tallow candle, from the hectic flush of a tuberculoid young mother – 'a streak / Lay far too red on each hollow cheek' – and from the:

> tall yellow man, like the Penitent Thief,
> With his jaw bound up in a handkerchief.

> (61–2)

The rough humour of these lines reminds us that *Christmas-Eve* is, in important ways, a thoroughly unRomantic poem. But Romanticism is too amorphous to be rejected. The poet's journey clinging to the hem of Christ's robe is described very oddly:

>   as a path were hollowed
> And a man went weltering through the ocean,
> Sucked along in the flying wake
> Of a luminous water-snake ...

> (501–4 and 777–80)

He is sucked forward by a vacuum opening in front of him, and this is how the ancient mariner's boat is propelled by its spirit guardian.[2] The reference to the luminous water-snakes clinches the reference. The two poems have little enough in common, but both poets must learn to love all creatures great and small, and, although Browning has a sharp sense that it is harder to love greasy people than it is to love slimy snakes, in both poems that love is signalled by a proper love of divided light. Browning even ends like the mariner, attending 'the kirk / With a goodly company' – well, if not 'goodly', then, at any rate, good enough.

10

The Subtle Prism

In 1859, four years before Browning began writing *The Ring and the Book*, Kirchoff and Bunsen invented a new branch of chemistry. They discovered that a chemical element could be identified by the spectrum it produced. Very quickly the spectroscope became the research chemist's most important tool. In *The Ring and the Book* Browning inaugurates the art of moral spectroscopy. The Pope, an old man near death, looks around him, and, as old men do, sees everywhere evidence of moral degeneration. The glare of the world is hopelessly confused with the blaze of the divine sun:

> who distinguishes the sun
> From a mere Druid fire on a far mount?
> More praise to him who with his subtle prism
> Shall decompose both beams and name the true.

> (x. 1817–20)

Pompilia runs away from Guido, her husband, in the company of a priest, Caponsacchi. Guido chases after the pair, catches them and surrenders them to the justice of the church authorities. When the ecclesiastical court releases his wife into the custody of her parents, Guido, with the help of three hired assassins, kills both his wife and her parents. He is tried and sentenced to death, and it is the Pope's responsibility either to confirm or to commute his sentence. The Pope is less concerned with law than with justice. He needs, before he can reach a decision, to assess the moral characters of Guido and his wife, and the task is difficult. Guido's every action could be explained in terms of greed, Pompolia's every action in terms of lust. But the Pope brings a moral spectroscope to bear on the case. Pompilia, he finds, was guided by the true sun. Guido is a Druid. His is a natural religion, a religion that establishes success in the world as its one value, and a religion that demands human sacrifice.

The Ring and the Book is then a spectroscope: it analyses moral lights. But it is also a colour top. The colour top was invented by James Clerk Maxwell. It is a device to mix spectral colours by spinning a disc on which coloured plates may be arranged in any proportions. It was with his colour top that Maxwell was able to demonstrate the truth of Helmholtz's distinction between spectral colours and pigments. Spectral blue and spectral yellow, for example, combine to produce white, not green. He was also able to show experimentally that Young, and Helmholtz after him, had been right to identify red, green and blue as the primary colours of the spectrum. Red, yellow and blue were simply the primary pigments. In the Yellow Book, says Browning, he found 'a novel country', but it is not for him to choose to represent that country only in the season that suits his mood:

> Rather learn and love
> Each facet-flash of the revolving year! –
> Red, green, and blue that whirl into a white,
> The variance now, the eventual unity,
> Which makes the miracle.

(I. 1352–6)

The spectroscope decomposes light into colour: the colour top fuses colours into light. The action of *The Ring and the Book* is at once analytic and synthetic, or, to use different terms, at once dramatic and didactic. The simple story that Browning tells, indeed twice tells, in the poem's opening book, disintegrates as it is analysed into ten dramatic monologues, in each of which the characters and action of the story are differently displayed. But equally powerful is the strength and consistency with which Browning holds to his own reading of the story; announced by him in the first book, witnessed by Caponsacchi and Pompilia, confirmed by the Pope, and at the last, in the poem's final, terrible monologue, admitted even by Guido.

One more piece of equipment completes Browning's optical laboratory: the colour filter. Bottini, Guido's prosecutor, begins his address to the judges with a grandiose analogy. The judges are invited to compare Bottini with a religious painter commissioned to produce a Holy Family on their flight into Egypt. The painter begins his task in the mortuary. There he 'cuts and carves', assuring himself of the set of bone and play of muscle that alone ensure 'due correctness in the nude'. He moves on from his anatomical studies to make studies from nature; of some 'flax-polled, soft-bearded sire' who may 'simulate a Joseph', of some 'young and comely peasant-nurse' who serves to 'help his notion of the Mother-Maid', even of such incidentals as the ass, 'clouted shoon, staff, scrip, and water-gourd'. But these studies will form no part of the finished painting. Only a sorry artist would try to piece together his picture from fragmentary sketches, fastening 'here a head and there a tail':

> Rather your artist turns abrupt from these,
> And preferably buries him and broods
> (Quite away from aught vulgar and extern)
> On the inner spectrum, filtered through the eye,
> His brain deposit, bred of many a drop,
> *E pluribus unum*: and the wiser he!
> For in that brain, – the fancy sees at work,
> Could my lords peep indulged, – results alone,
> Not processes which nourish the result ...

(IX. 86–94)

The picture in the brain shows life digested, not served up raw and crude. It is:

> Less distinct, part by part, but in the whole
> Truer to the subject, – the main central truth
> And soul o' the picture, would my Judges spy, –
> Not these mere fragmentary studied facts
> Which answer to the outward frame and flesh –
> Not this nose, not that eyebrow, the other fact
> Of man's staff, woman's stole or infant's clout,
> But lo, a spirit-birth conceived of flesh,
> Truth rare and real, not transcripts, fact and false.

(IX. 99–107)

Bottini puts this account of the painter's craft to suspicious use. His own speech, he says, will be like this. He will present the facts of the case to the judges digested, not raw, filtered through his eye. He studies an 'inner spectrum' on which Pompilia is recorded as a gamesome wench, Caponsacchi as a gay dog and Guido as a sourpuss. But for all that one may distrust the analogy, it is hard not to see Bottini's as a serious and attractive account of the process of artistic creation, giving full weight to the claims of the real, but insisting that, in the end, the real must subserve the artist's imagination, observed fact must be subordinated to imagined truth.

It would even be possible to agrue that Bottini's asethetic corresponds more closely with Browning's practice in *The Ring and the Book* than does the elaborate analogy between the poet and a goldsmith that Browning sets out in Book One. Browning, after all, no more pasted together extracts from the Yellow Book than Bottini's painter pieces together 'fragmentary studied facts'. Browning understood the story as he did because of who he was. Caponsacchi became St George and Pompilia as pure as a virgin because St George and the Dragon (or Perseus and Andromeda) was one of the myths that defined Browning's imagination.[1] A print of Caravaggio's *Andromeda* hung over his desk as a young man. References to the myth recur in his poety from *Pauline* right through his career. When he eloped with Elizabeth Barrett from Wimpole Street, he seized the opportunity to become himself a St George: he acted out his ancient myth in modern dress. Browning diverts himself, surely, from the mere facts of the Yellow Book, which offer themselves so easily, as Henry James pointed out, to a humdrum, even gross, explanation, and concentrates instead on 'the inner spectrum, filtered through the eye'. Guido, Pompilia and Caponsacchi are freed from their mere historical circumstances to re-enact a timeless myth. The facts of their lives and deaths are smudged perhaps, but in place of mere factual accuracy Browning offers something grander: fidelity to his own imagined truth.

We ought, I think, to be aware of this, and to be aware too that however impressively Browning may allow Bottini to present an idealist account of art, it is not an account to which Browning subscribes. Browning is consistently suspicious of artists who scorn 'aught vulgar and extern'. He tends to allow that fact is not the same as truth, but he insists repeatedly that fact is at least truth's most important condition. Whenever Browning chooses between 'results alone' and 'processes which nourish the result', he chooses processes. The whole of *The Ring and the Book* is an immense process. Its variously coloured characters flash before us, offering the 'variance now', whereas the unity to which the poem tends is 'eventual'. The Pope's judgement is a provisional attempt to resolve the poem's process into product, but it is only provisional. After the Pope falls silent, Guido speaks again. Browning's poem ends at the moment that the ring is completed. The poem becomes product, its colours 'whirl into white', only in the reader's retrospective imagination.

It seems safe to say that Browning disapproves of Bottini's notion of art, but it does not follow that he does not share it. It may be that Bottini does not announce a creed to which an artist may give or withhold his assent, but rather describes the conditions under which any and every artist must operate. Browning may insist that to elevate imagined truth over observed fact is to deceive oneself, that imagination is just the mystifying word that artists use to describe the process by which they consecrate their own prejudices. But his knowledge, if knowledge it is, serves only to identify the predicament, not to save him from it. To know that all men are prejudiced does not free one from a common human limitation, it convicts one of it.

I had better pause to repair a deficiency. The painter, according to Bottini, broods on 'the inner spectrum filtered through the eye'. I have assumed, it may seem rashly, that the word 'filtered' refers to a colour filter. But the whole poem is the warrant for my reading. Looking through coloured glass is almost the commonest metaphor in the poem. It indicates how each individual's view of the external world is defined, or coloured, by his character. Our characters filter our experience of the outside world, and they filter it through coloured glass. The monologues, Browning tells us in the first book, will be presented to us 'each with appropriate tinge'. The various speakers show 'one tint at a time to take the eye'. Colour becomes the poem's mark of subjectivity. Each speaker describes things not as they were, but as they seemed to him, as they are imprinted on his mind's eye. Browning seems to have advanced beyond Bottini only in identifying what Bottini thinks of as a painter's knack as the inescapable condition of all human perception. Bottini recommends that the painter give up the business of grappling with the world of things, and absorb himself instead in contemplation of an 'inner spectrum'. He would have the artist turn his gaze inwards, away from the fragmentary world of appearances, towards the unified world of his own imaginings. What Browning shows in a sequence of monologues, 'each with appropriate tinge', is that we are all, whether we will or no, renaissance artists.

So it might be thought, and it is true to this extent, that this is the model of experience, each of us trapped within himself, condemned to see life only as it is filtered through tinted lenses, that the poem fights against. Browning's first tactic is to complicate the metaphor. The colour in which one sees events may not define character, it may define mood. Pietro and Violante do not live comfortably in their son-in-law's home. The inevitable domestic grievances are 'coloured by quarrel into calumny'. Caponsacchi insists that the story he tells the judges confirms in every detail his previous account. Only now that Pompilia is dying he views the same facts differently:

> I' the colour the tale takes, there's change perhaps;
> 'Tis natural, since the sky is different,
> Eclipse in the air now.

> (VI. 1620–2)

Pompilia on her death-bed is serene, 'Being right now, I am happy and colour things'. Guido, in the last minutes of his life, in an agony of fear and resentment, falls to wondering, 'From out myself how the strange colours come!' We are bound to our characters, and victims of our moods, but the same metaphor may express our moral freedom. Guido claims disingenuously that he is prepared to allow Caponsacchi that he may have been innocent of adultery:

> Concede him then the colour charity
> Casts on a doubtful cause.

> (V. 1188–9)

He points out that Pompilia and Caponsacchi will not dispute his version of the facts. They will insist only that the facts bear another interpretation:

> Only contending that the deed avowed
> Would take another colour and bear excuse.

> (V. 1879–80)

He points out that the ecclesiastical court before which the runaway pair were brought found them guilty. The effect of the verdict was to 'breathe away / The colour of innocence and leave guilt black'. Most impressive of all is the Pope's final admonition to Pietro and Violante, 'Go! / Never again elude the choice of tints.'

Colours, then, are what we project upon events. They may define our character, or our mood or our moral understanding, but in any case they are what we lend to the world. We colour our experience, but the poem insists just as forcibly that our experience colours us. Caponsacchi is introduced as a 'courtly spiritual Cupid', a man who wears 'colour of each vanity in vogue'. When he is brought to court charged with abducting Pompilia, the verdict is that he be exiled to Civita:

> There let his life skim off its last of lees,
> Nor keep this dubious colour.

(III. 1408–9)

The Pope sees Guido and his two brothers 'All alike coloured'. We colour, and we are coloured, and sometimes the two actions are united, as when Pietro and Violante rejoice in the 'tints' of Pompilia, happy that they will not lose:

> in our grey time of life, the tints
> Of you, that colour eve to match with morn.

(VII. 556–7)

Pompilia plays on them like coloured light, and she also offers them in their old age the chance to see through the eyes of a child.

Browning transforms Bottini's metaphor by complicating it. Bottini would have the artist study an 'inner spectrum' safely withdrawn from the actualities of experience. He recommends that the artist turn inwards, away from the fragmentary world of appearances towards the unified world of his imaginings. Browning, in response, offers a range of metaphors that work together to define experience as that point at which the colours we project upon the world, and the colours that the world projects upon us meet, the point where the action of the self upon events and the action of events upon the self coincide.

And yet colour is deceptive. The self distorts the world, tinges it, and in its turn the world distorts the self, dyes it a 'dubious colour'. It would seem to be the role of the judicious enquirer to see through these distorting colours; to see the world untinged, the self undyed by chance circumstances. This is what those critics imply who seek to disqualify the evidence of various speakers on the ground of their bias; of Half-Rome, say, on the ground that his judgement of Pompilia's story is coloured by his jealousy of his own wife. They assume a standard of impartial, disinterested judgement against which the opinions of the various speakers must be tested. Theirs is a point of view powerfully argued within the poem:

> To hear the rabble and brabble, you'd call the case
> Fused and confused past human finding out.
> One calls the square round, t'other the round square –
> And pardonably in that first surprise
> O' the blood that fell and splashed the diagram:
> But now we've used our eyes to the violent hue
> Can't we look through the crimson and trace lines?
>
> (IV. 34–40)

This is *Tertium Quid*, the clever, arrogant socialite, contemptuous of the mob beneath him, and contemptuous too of the aristocrats he flatters. He seeks, in his analysis of Pompilia's case, to entertain his betters, but he is too in love with his own intelligence even to do that successfully. His is the ability, he claims, to look through colour to the geometrical design that the colour obscures, to see the diagram through the blood.

He does not succeed. Indeed, the chief point of his monologue is to chart his failure. Browning would have us see that his enterprise is utterly misguided. He is emotionally untouched by Pompilia's story. He believes that this guarantees his objectivity, whereas in truth it nullifies the value of his commentary, for, to use *Tertium Quid's* own metaphor, the blood is not extraneous matter splashed on an otherwise clear design, it is of the essence of the story. Browning is not an idealist. There are the facts. They are as they are whatever people may think and feel, and the characters in *The Ring and the Book* scarcely bother disputing them. Fact is precious. In the first book Browning compares it with gold, 'the lingot truth'. But for all that it is precious, the gold is lifeless, inert. It must be adulterated with an alloy before it can be worked, and the alloy that Browning uses is his own soul:

> I fused my living soul and that inert stuff,
> Before attempting smithcraft...
>
> (I. 463–4)

Facts exist independently of our responses to them, but they exist inertly. They achieve value, meaning, only when they are felt, when they are fused with our live souls. But there is a certain rhetorical afflatus in that expression that Browning is inclined to distrust. He is ready to replace the word soul with the word 'fancy'. There are facts and there are fancies. Fancies may be capricious, but to disregard them is wrong on two counts. First, fancy, like it or not, is itself a fact of experience: 'Fancy with fact is just one fact the more'. Second, without fancy fact cannot be put to human service: the inert ore cannot be forged into a ring.

When *Tertium Quid* is true to his own enterprise he is eloquent in denial, but in assertion dumb. The values that others find in the facts he derides. He prides himself on bringing to the facts no fanciful alloy, and so they remain to him lifeless, unmeaning. He is in intention, and from time to time in fact, a moral deconstructionist. He plays with the story, finding meaning only to mock the naïvety of those who find it persuasive. The announcement of some meaning that he can assent to is always deferred. He can end only with questions, two of them. 'You see the reduction *ad absurdum*, Sirs?': the reader does, even if *Tertium Quid* does not. The second question is almost plaintive, as if *Tertium Quid* is trying to protect himself from the deflating thought that all his eloquence, his sophistication, his intelligence, may have served no purpose at all: ' 'twas not for nothing that we talked, I hope?'

But it is not a human possibility to contemplate human fact neutrally, to respond to human sexuality, human greed, human violence as though they were inert, lifeless facts. *Tertium Quid* is less successful in evading colours than he is in mixing them. His most frequent tactic is to take the bright, specific colours of human experience and mix them into muddy brown. No action is so bad or so good, so generous or so selfish, so cowardly or so courageous as people would have us believe. Did Pietro and Violante cheat Guido, or did Guido cheat them?

> Which of the two here sinned most? A nice point!
> Which brownness is least black, – decide who can …

> (IV. 626–7)

Brown is *Tertium Quid's* proper tinge: his forensic skill results at last only in the merging of the colours of life into an indeterminate, moral mud.

There is no escape from colour. The pursuit of the fact in itself as opposed to the fact as it is felt is the emptiest of all quests, for it is a quest for that which, could it be found, would have no value, would indeed negate all value. The conclusion follows, it might seem, that all perception enshrines the prejudices of the perceiver, and that any decision to embrace one perception as true and to reject another as false is arbitrary. Browning's claim to be a crucial poet and the claim of *The Ring and the Book* to be his crucial poem rest on the energy with which Browning, in this poem more than any other, struggles to deny that conclusion.

There is no escape from colour. That being so, our proper duty is not, like *Tertium Quid*, to smear human experience with a colour as muddy, as indeterminate, as possible, but to see the world in clear, bright colours. *The Ring and the Book* is a Pre-Raphaelite poem in its dislike of cloudiness, of turbidity, in its delight in pure colour and in bright light.[2] Caponsacchi begins his speech cursing smoke:

> In this sudden smoke from hell–
> So things disguise themselves, – I cannot see
> My own hand held thus broad before my face
> And know it again.

> (VI. 2–5)

Had Pompilia been his mistress, he argues, it would have been absurd of him to have eloped with her, giving up 'the safe shade / For the sunshine which men see to pelt me by'. In despising the shade where all colours merge into one, and choosing instead the sunshine, Caponsacchi is the true hero. Pompilia devotes her dying moments to clearing the cloud that has obscured Caponsacchi's bright soul:

> Yes, my last breath shall wholly spend itself
> In one attempt more to disperse the stain,
> The mist from other breath fond mouths have made,
> About a lustrous and pellucid soul ...

> (VII. 926–9)

The saddest words the Pope ever speaks come when he imagines Caponsacchi grown old, the heroic gloss of his youth dulled. Then 'the flash o' the first adventure' will have faded:

> clouded o'er belike
> By doubt, misgivings how the day may die,
> Though born with such auroral brilliance ...

> (IX. 658–60)

Celestine's sermon in defence of Pompilia's saintliness is a 'Convulsive effort to disperse the films' that have clouded her fame. His anger is as much at the way her story has been obscured as it is at Guido's evil:

> As ye become spectators of the scene –
> Watch obscuration of a fame pearl-pure
> In vapory films, enwoven circumstance.

> (XII. 552–4)

To see the world coloured is, in *The Ring and the Book*, to see it imbued with value. It is to exchange a world in which human behaviour may appropriately be described by a physicist for a world in which actions are moral decisions. It is little wonder, then, that there is a conspiracy to dull colours, for to see pure colour is to shoulder a heavy burden. Caponsacchi sees Pompilia's purity, sees her shining whiteness. He is condemned by that perception to act, and in acting to give up all the ease of his familiar life, so comfortably accommodated to the world. He is forced out of the shade into the sunshine, forced to stand up and be pelted.

Caponsacchi recognises Pompilia, sees her for what she is. Browning is in no doubt of that. But in the act of recognising her he defines, redefines himself. When women were creatures to be flirted with, he was one man. When he sees Pompilia as a woman to be reverenced, he becomes another. To see clearly is to recognise a truth in the outside world, and, simultaneously, it is to recognise a truth about oneself. There is no separating the two recognitions. Caponsacchi sees Pompilia as a saint, and in doing so defines himself and must embrace the hard lot of the hero. Half-Rome sees her as a whore, and, in doing so, he too defines himself. What Caponsacchi sees robed in heavenly white, Half-Rome sees got up in whore's red. Both their visions, for Browning, have the merit of clarity, both are preferable to *Tertium Quid's* hankering after muddy brown. But to demand only that colours are clear, easily recognisable, is no help at all in the task of choosing between them. How are we to know that Caponsacchi sees Pompilia truly, Half-Rome falsely? How can we distinguish between a divinely true intuition and a sleazy prejudice? It is a problem to which Browning found no easy answer. It baffles him in *La Saisiaz*:

> Why, here's my neighbour colour-blind,
> Eyes like mine to all appearance: "green as grass", do I affirm?
> "Red as grass", he contradicts me: which employs the proper terms?
> Were we two the earth's sole tenants, with no third for referee,
> How should I distinguish?

> (274–8)

As with colour blindness, so with moral blindness, but with this added difficulty: that whereas we may be prepared to accept the majority view in decisions about colour, in moral matters, as *The Ring and the Book* makes clear, one man may be right and the whole world wrong.

There are two men in *The Ring and the Book* whose judgements we are asked to trust, two men whose colour perceptions are presented as decisive: Browning and the Pope. Browning is the author of the poem, the Pope the authority within the poem. Both are, in some sense, infallible: the Pope because he is the highest spiritual authority on earth – within the poem he is the court from which there is no appeal; Browning because he is the poet, he constructed at once the story and its values, leaving no avenue of appeal from his understanding of the facts to the facts themselves. Both Browning and the Pope confidently insist that they have grappled with the story, brought to bear on it all their capacity for human seriousness, and have been rewarded with a knowledge of the truth. Browning has become, he tells us in the first book, the prophet Elisha. He can breathe into the mouths of his dead characters, and within his poem they live again, just as they lived three hundred years before. The Pope is more modest, but just as firm:

> All's a clear rede and no more riddle now.
> Truth nowhere lies yet everywhere in these –
> Not absolutely in a portion, yet
> Evolvable from the whole; evolved at last
> Painfully, held tenaciously by me.

> (x. 227–31)

Like Browning in the first book he presents himself as the James Clerk Maxwell of ethics. He has looked at the story as it is presented in the various depositions, looked at it through one colour filter after another, and is confident that he can, at the last, evolve from these fragmented colours the white light of truth.

Browning and the Pope, then, both assert their infallibility, and yet both too deny it. Just after Browning compares himself with Elisha he riffles once again through the old Yellow Book, and feels a spirit once again posses him:

> Letting me have my will again with these
> – How title I the dead alive once more?

> (I. 770–1)

The kiss of Elisha is unnervingly recreated as the kiss of Dracula. The poet-prohet's divine gift of resuscitating the dead becomes a grim vision of people arising from death only that they may serve the will of their master. The Pope is less melodramatic, but he too admits that his claim to know the truth may be mistaken: 'Mankind is ignorant, a man am I'. He may be mistaken, but if he has brought to his judgement all his human powers, then he cannot be held, or hold himself, guilty of any fault: 'Call ignorance my sorrow not my sin!'

In the first book Browning tells the reader about the source of the poem, the Yellow Book, and in doing so he allows, in a sense, the facts of the story to exist independent of, prior to, his version of them. The Pope reminds us that his judgement is not final. God's judgement, which is truly infallible, will follow his. Browning reminds us of a seam of crude fact that exists before the poem. The Pope reminds us of a final assessment of value that takes place after the poem. *The Ring and the Book* occupies a middle place, in which facts and values come together in an arrangement that we can at best believe, not know, to be true.

To this extent, then, the poem denies that in matters of human judgement absolute knowledge is possible. Any judgement may be mistaken. It follows that *The Ring and the Book* is a relativist poem. But to say this is to say nothing, for if relativism is defined so broadly, it is a creed from which only the insane are exempt. Relativism proper – the belief that because knowledge is not absolute it is useless to struggle towards the truth, and that if a man does so struggle and arrives at a conclusion that he earnestly believes to be true, it would be unjust for him to act stoutly on the basis of that belief – Browning resists as clearly and as vigorously as one could wish.

We must act as if we had a moral colour top, as if from the whole of our experience the truth is somehow evolvable. It may be that the white light of truth escapes us, and that poetry, in pretending to arrive at an absolute truth, amounts only to 'white lies'. Browning is prepared to admit the possibility that it is the mortal lot to see only through a colour filter. But even if this were the case, it would not free us from moral responsibility, for even to choose between different colours must not be an indifferent choice. As the Pope says when dismissing Pietro and Violante from his mind: 'Go, never again evade the choice of tints.'

11

The Red Thing

Three colours dominate *The Ring and the Book*: black, white and red. White and black are the colours of good and evil: red is the colour of human experience.

White is pre-eminently Pompilia's colour. Pietro and Violante protected her through her childhood as if it were enough to save all three that they 'keep clean / Their child's soul, one soul white for three'. The Other Half-Rome celebrates, courtier-like, her virginal whiteness, 'Lily of a maiden, white with intact leaf'. She was born into the word a 'white miraculous birth of buds'. Even *Tertium Quid* though with mocking incredulity, refers to her dying confession from which it appears 'She was of wifehood one white innocence'. To Caponsacchi she is the 'snow-white soul', 'a wonderful white soul'. He describes her approach on the night of their escape as a divine vision of whiteness. Bottini promises to prove that her flight with Caponsacchi was innocent. He will show the judges 'how white she walks / I' the mire she wanders through ere Rome she reach'. The Pope recognises her as a saint, equipped with a miraculous stain-resistant dress:

> That will not take pollution, ermine-like,
> Armed from dishonour by its own soft snow.

> (x. 677–8)

She is 'Perfect in whiteness', a lesson to all Christians how to keep 'Their robes of white unspotted by the world'. It is only fitting that she dies in 'the long white lazar-house' under 'the white hospital array'.

Black, though less insistently, is associated with Guido. It is the Pope's summary of his character:

> Such I find Guido, midmost blotch of black
> Discernible in this group of clustered crimes ...

> (x. 865–6)

Bottini's technique in prosecuting Guido will be, he says, to prove his evil in contradistinction to Pompilia's goodness:

> Beside my pearl, I prove how black thy jet,
> And through Pompilia's virtue Guido's crime.
>
> (IX. 1402–3)

When Guido bursts in on Pompilia in the room where she sleeps after her long flight, he is silhouetted against the window:

> He, the black figure, the opprobrious blur
> Against all peace and joy and light and life.
>
> (VI. 1500–1)

Guido, just before he dies, grimly asks God to erase him as a black smutch on the surface of creation:

> Do thou wipe out the being of me, and smear
> This soul from off Thy white of things, I blot!
>
> (XI. 934–5)

The opposition of white and blackness is not always so simple. Pompilia's stubborn misery during her marriage seems to Guido the 'stone strength of white despair', and the colour expresses her purity less than her petrified passiveness. There is a similar deathliness rather than purity in Pompilia's pallor after her desperate, futile assault on her husband has been thwarted: 'Dead white and disarmed she lay'. Her whiteness can be rendered gauchely erotic as in the love letters sent to her in Caponsacchi's name: 'thou art white / And warm and wonderful 'twixt pap and pap'. Similarly, blackness need not be evil. It may signify the darkness that is the necessary context of divine vision, like the black hair that frames the divine purity of Pompilia's white face. The night of Pompilia's escape from Guido is utterly dark, 'solid black'. It is out of that darkness that Pompilia appears so shining white to Caponsacchi. What proves to him that the whiteness he sees is the whiteness of her soul is that 'her body was one black'. When Caponsacchi enters the carriage and takes his seat next to Pompilia, he swoons: 'Blackness engulfed me'.

But such complications do little more than relieve the utter simplicity of Browning's moral colour scheme. What confuses it, what puts the issue of the trial in doubt, is that half the world sees in negative. Guido, to Caponsacchi, is a 'man and murderer calling the white black', and half of Rome agrees with him. Whiteness is the colour not only of unstained purity but of unbesmirched honour, and it is Guido's concern for his honour, as he represents it, that drives him to murder. His defence counsel speaks nobly of Guido's:

> natural sense
> Of human rectitude and purity, –
> Which white, man's soul is born with, brooks no touch:
> Therefore, the sensitivest spot of all,
> Woundable by a wafture breathed from black.

> (VIII. 452–6)

Pietro and Violante delivered their daughter into Guido's hands, and they did so because they wanted for their daughter a nobleman, a man of honour, or as *Tertium Quid* puts it, 'some exceptional white / Amid the general brown o' the species'. When Pompilia and Caponsacchi run away together they threaten Guido's honour, his whiteness. He kills his wife, Guido claims, only when he is sure she is an adulteress, when the stain on his honour:

> Solidifies into a blot which breaks
> Hell's black off in pale flakes for fear of mine.

> (v. 1078–9)

If to be in good repute is to be white, then Caponsacchi is irremediably blackened when he runs away with Pompilia. A man of the world like *Tertium Quid* knows as much:

> She might swim i'the whirl must bury him
> Under abysmal black.

> (IV. 943–4)

A man of honour may be violent, but, according to this way of looking at things, he is white. Guido has 'white fangs'. Pompilia flees from him as the house-martin flees from the 'white teeth' of winter. When Guido's face, as he gives evidence before the court, 'changes to all kinds of white', his pallor is not simply a ghastly parody of innocence. We should grasp at once the effrontery and the logic of Guido's characterisation of himself as 'One white integrity from heel to head'. Two rival ethical systems operate in *The Ring and the Book*: each from the point of view of the other calls white black.

The Ring and the Book is a poem in black and white, in black ink stamped on a white page. Hyacinthus imagines the Pope waiting for the man who can set down the truth of the matter in 'plain black and white', and this he sets out to do. As we write we are all like Bottini: 'with fresh-cut quill we ink the white'. Our implements may be more modern, but they figure the same truth. Naked experience cannot be written, for writing inevitably assigns values, places events within a moral scale. This is the truth that Hyacinthus and Bottini stumble on as they write their depositions, turning the paper into a pattern of black and white. But Hyacinthus is Guido's defender, and Bottini his prosecutor. Each of their patterns is a negative version of the other. Writing is no protection against the common human tendency to call white black. Writing can only judge experience, not transcribe it, and nothing guarantees that the judgement it offers is true. Browning suggests only that we should be readier to trust a judgement that arises immediately from the pressure of experience rather than a judgement that seeks to distance itself from the experience that it orders. Guido defends his killings on the ground that they reaffirmed the truth that adultery is a crime. He made the moral type more legible:

> Blackened again, made legible once more
> Your own decree, not permanently writ
> Rightly conceived, but all too faintly traced ...

> (v. 1986–8)

What makes us distrust this is the distance between his bookish metaphor and the fact of murder; between the black and white of print and the red of blood.

In *The Ring and the Book* the colour of human experience is red. Blushing and bleeding are the characteristic human activities. When we are wounded our blood splashes on to the ground, or it rushes into the face to signify that the wound is not to the body but the mind. The two kinds of wound are the proper marks of our life in this world, for they signal that living is abrasion. We blush when our privacy is exposed to others, and it is this, for Browning, that makes blushing like bleeding. He is aware throughout the poem of the shaming publicity of violence. Blood is glamorous. Pompilia on her death-bed is harassed by those drawn to her by the glamour of her wounds. Crowds fight to see her and her parents laid out in the church, and they gather again to watch Guido's bloody end. Pompilia's beauty, says the Other Half-Rome, was as unnoticed as the beauty of a red briar-rose until it was glamorized by violence, and there formed a 'pretty pool at the root, of rival red'. To be the object of such attention is shaming, embarrassing.

Blushing is important to Browning because it is an ambiguous signal. It betrays either innocence or guilt. The Other Half-Rome inclines to credit, without quite believing, that Caponsacchi's relationship with Pompilia was innocent. He only wonders at Caponsacchi's recklessness:

> oh, called innocent love, I know!
> Only such scarlet fiery innocence
> As most men would try muffle up in shade.

> (III. 890–2)

Caponsacchi flourishes 'flag-like i' the face of the world', a scarlet that most men would seek to hide, as we hide a blush. All of the Other Half-Rome's belief in Caponsacchi's innocence and suspicion of his guilt is compressed into the phrase 'scarlet innocence'. The reader does not find the phrase hard to decipher. It is exactly appropriate to Caponsacchi's indignation, his passion and his purity. It is just that when Caponsacchi blushingly and defiantly declares before the court his love of Pompilia, his innocence is at once transparent and horribly open to misunderstanding. It is the Other Half-Rome, too, who points out that Guido was disappointed when he caught up with his wife not to find her in bed with Caponsacchi. He had hoped to burst in upon 'The convicts in their rosy impudence'. Like 'scarlet fiery innocence' the phrase hints at paradox, for the wholly impudent would not blush. It is not, of course, a puzzling phrase. To be caught in adultery is to be caught acting shamelessly, and shamelessness, when it is published to the world, is deeply shaming. We understand the blush of lovers taken in adultery just as easily as we understand the blush that ignites Caponsacchi's face when he proclaims and defends his love of Pompilia. And yet to understand both is to recognise a world in which there exist both 'scarlet fiery innocence' and 'rosy impudence', a world in which moral judgement demands a Ruskinian eye for moral colour. At the moment that Caponsacchi commits himself to Pompilia's service, he feels himself reborn. It is:

> As when the virgin-band, the victors chaste
> Feel at the end their earthly garments drop,
> And rise with something of a rosy shame
> Into immortal nakedness ...

> (VI. 953–6)

The 'rosy shame' that so touchingly confirms their innocence is utterly different from, and yet so easily mistaken for, the guilty blush with which Adam and Eve signalled their fall.

Bottini's is a coarse mind. He demands that Guido be found guilty because he does not believe that old men with young and beautiful wives should be allowed to murder them just because the wives find young, handsome lovers. He feels bound to pay lip-service to Pompilia's and Caponsacchi's assertions of their innocence, but he is too sophisticated, too coarse, to believe them himself, or expect the judges to believe them. Caponsacchi, he admits, may have crept into the room where Pompilia lay asleep to gaze, enraptured, on her sleeping body, may even have stolen a kiss. Pompilia was fast asleep, her innocence uncompromised. But he adds a simile to show that he is not thinking of kissing. Pompilia sleeping was like Archimedes, so 'busy o'er a book', that he:

> Was ignorant of the imminence o'the point
> O' the sword till it surprised him.

> (IX. 757–8)

And, teasingly, it is in this state that Bottini leaves Pompilia, blushing:

> Fit place me thinks
> While in this task she rosily is lost
> To treat of and repel ...

> (IX. 763–5)

But Pompilia's rosiness is less a blush than a reflection of his own overheated imagination. He infects her with the sweaty flush on his own cheek, and the hue marks his coarseness as precisely as Caponsacchi's blush marks his delicacy and his innocence.

People blush in *The Ring and the Book*, and they also bleed. The prick of self-awareness that brings the blood rushing to the face is matched by the stab that makes the blood flow from the body. Browning splashes red violently over his poem, spatters it with blood. It is appropriate that his favourite word for stabbing is 'pinking'. The murderers are captured as they sleep, 'red from heel to head'. Guido's noble blood will run into Rome's drains, 'leaking through their scaffold plank / Into Rome's sink where her red refuse runs'. In his last hours Guido's imagination is obsessed by redness: the redness of the guillotine, 'All of it painted red', 'This kneeling place was red, red, never fear!'; the redness of the bed on which he murdered Pompilia, 'the red bed'; the red brand of the murderer that marks his brow, 'so plainly, so intolerably red'. At last the redness of the guillotine fuses with the redness of hell-fire, and sums up for him his fate. His way of life has brought him to 'the red thing we all see now', and yet it has done so as if by some monstrous accident that might have befallen anyone:

> Ay, my friend,
> Easy to say, easy to do, – step right
> Now you've stepped left and stumbled on the thing,
> – The red thing!

> (XI. 1450–3)

Blushing and bleeding are the two most obvious marks of that clash between the self and the world that defines mortal existence, but redness in *The Ring and the Book* reaches out to span the whole of life. It is the colour of callowness: Caponsacchi is exiled to Arezzo 'To rub off redness and rusticity'. But it is also cardinal red, the colour that marks the summit of the worldly churchman's ambitions, 'the red cloth that keeps warm'. The 'rosy shame' of the risen virgins marks their innocence, but red, too, is the colour of the whore: Pompilia, a prostitute's daughter, is like a doorway 'marked and crossed / In rubric'. It is the red brand on the murderer's forehead, or, as on Caponsacchi's family arms, it is the red cross that marks the soldier saint. It is dominantly the colour of blood, but blood can be like hell-fire, damning, or it may bless, like the blood of Christ. Guido bursts into Pietro's and Violante's house, and:

> wiped its filthy four walls free at last
> With a wash of hell-fire – father, mother, wife
> Killed all, and bathed his name clean in their blood.

> (II. 1426–8)

Pompilia repeats and transforms the same metaphor. Her blood erases her marriage certificate:

> this blood of mine
> Flies forth exultingly at my door,
> Washes the parchment white, and thanks the blow.

> (VII. 1699–1701)

Redness is a sign, but a bewildering sign, for it can signal anything.[1] It has no stable moral character. It can fade either into white or black. Bottini refuses to make the kind of superfine distinction between white and pinkish white that interests Molinists:

> Let Molinists distinguish, 'Souls washed white
> Were red once, still show pinkish to the eye.

> (IX. 1489–90)

Half-Rome tells how Pompilia's story became darker and darker, 'Till all is black or blood-red in the piece'. And as red can fade into either black or white, so too it can consort with either.

Red and white are peculiarly Caponsacchi's colours, for he is the poem's St George. Red and white are the colours of his family arms, and the arms of his town, Fiesole. They are the proper colours of all Christian soldiers, who should be 'White-cinct, because in white walks sanctity', but who should also wear red to proclaim their 'Unchariness of blood when blood faith begs'. Arrezzo watched while the dragonish Guido was making his leisurely meal of Pompilia. 'Where are the men-at-arms with cross on coat?', asks the Pope, and answers his own question, 'Aloof, bewraying their attire'. Only Caponsacchi, the dancing priest, 'Sprangst forth to fight', and earned the right to wear the red and white uniform of St George. But even his redness is not simple. It is the mark of his courage, but it may also be a worldly stain. It completes, but also compromises, his white livery. When Pompilia begs Caponsacchi to help her escape from her husband, his first response is worldly:

> The plan is rash: the project desperate.
> In such a flight needs must I risk your life,
> Give food for falsehood, folly or mistake,
> Ground for your husband's rancour and revenge.

> (VII. 1448–51)

This is the voice of common sense, and common sense is stained with the world. But it is a transient dye. To Pompilia, Caponsacchi is:

> one star
> Turning now newly red that was so white before –
> One service apprehended newly: just
> A word of mine and there the white was back.

> (VII. 1453–6)

Caponsacchi escapes with Pompilia dressed not as a priest but as a cavalier, sword hanging by his side. His enemies use the fact to slander him. But Caponsacchi, so puzzling is the world, was truly cavalier when he dressed as a priest, and never more priestly than when he dresses as a knight. Then he assumes the red cross of the crusader, and becomes what the Pope calls him, 'my warrior-priest', What the Pope sees clearly, and what many fail to see, is how to distinguish the red stain of worldliness from the red badge of courage.

Caponsacchi is the type in the poem of the active Christian, heroic in deed, just as Pompilia is the type of the devotional Christian. His red and whiteness is inferior to Pompilia's pure whiteness in so far as the active life is inferior to the contemplative life. It is the poem's chief flaw that Browning pretends that this is so without ever believing it. Caponsacchi, rash, indignant, brave, is splendidly realised. Pompilia's brand of sweet all-forgivingness, though it scarcely excuses Guido's behaviour, does enough to make the reader suspect that being married to a saint might not be a condition to be envied.

Red may be the proper complement of white, but it goes just as well with black. Guido makes the point that just because he married for money does not mean that he is willing to forgo all the less substantial delights that a young bride can offer:

> Why quaff life's cup blown free of all the beads,
> The bright red froth wherein our beard should steep
> Before our mouths assay the black o' the wine?

> (XI. 1077–9)

The metaphor is a good example of Browning's worrying ability to enter into sexual perversity. It reaches out beyond its logical point into areas that make the reader flinch. Sex becomes an unholy sacrament.

Caponsacchi and Guido confront each other only once, at the inn where the runaways are found together. It is the dramatic climax of the poem, described both by Caponsacchi and Pompilia, and it is built out of dramatic contrasts between red, white and black. Guido bursts into Pompilia's room and wakes her. She opens her eyes in a room lit by a red sun, and takes for sunset what is really dawn. The incident is important to Browning's plot because it explains the discrepancy between Pompilia's narrative and Caponsacchi's that Hyacinthus makes so much of. Pompilia:

> makes confusion of the reddening white
> Which was the sunset when her strength gave way,
> And the next sunrise and its whitening red
> Which she revived in when her husband came.

> (III. 1184–7)

She had woken in the carriage as the horses were being changed for the last stage to Rome, and told Caponsacchi that she would die if she were not allowed to rest. It was sunset: 'The sky was fierce with colour from the sun / Setting'. Guido arrives at dawn, and Caponsacchi leads him to Pompilia's chamber. She is asleep, 'Wax-white, seraphic', and the sun 'filled the window with a light like blood'. Guido takes his stand against the window:

> By the window all a-flame with morning red,
> He the black figure, the opprobrious blur
> Against all peace and joy and light and life.

> (VI. 1499–1501)

When she wakes and sees her husband there, Pompilia grabs his sword and tries to strike him down. It is her one action of fierce goodness, and it is proper than Caponsacchi records it, for she wears in that moment his white and red livery. He remembers:

> That vision in the blood-red daybreak – that
> Leap to life of the pale electric sword
> Angels go armed with ...

> (VI. 1576–8)

Pompilia, wax-white, and Guido, the black figure, confront each other in a world dyed red by the rising sun. It is the redness that Pompilia remembers, the redness of the dawn and of the previous sunset:

> As in his arms he caught me, and, you say,
> Carried me in, that tragical red eve,
> And laid me where I next returned to life
> In the other red of morning, the two red plates
> That crushed together crushed the time between,
> And are since then a solid fire to me ...

> (VII. 1563–8)

The two red plates crushed time, and they also crushed Pompilia. She, innocently mistaking one red for another, parodies the terrible human inability to distinguish the red of worldly corruption from the red of spiritual courage for which she suffers and dies.

Red in *The Ring and the Book* is the representative colour. It is God's colour and it is the world's, as are all colours. Guido loves colour. His wife, he says, is too Florentine for his taste, too much like a Raphael or a Fra Angelico madonna. He would like a woman more Venetian:

> Give me my gorge of colour, glut of gold
> In a glory round the Virgin made for me!
> Titian's the man, not Monk Angelico …

> (XI. 2112–14)

Such love of colour betrays Guido's worldliness, his low sensuality. It is so different and yet so like Caponsacchi's praise of Pompilia as a saint painted on gold leaf. He demands to tell his story of his flight with Pompilia:

> Which poured forth would present you one pure glass,
> Mirror you plain, – as God's sea, glassed in gold,
> His saints, – the perfect soul Pompilia.

> (VI. 1142–4)

Gold is the colour of Guido's central vice, his avarice, but it is the colour, too, of grace. Pompilia's body knows that she is pregnant before her mind. She feels a sudden happiness, as if 'A broad yellow sunbeam was let fall / From heaven to earth'. Blue is the colour of heaven. Pompilia, dying, finds happiness. The dark skies above her break to allow 'one glimpse of quiet and the cool blue, / To show her for a moment such things were'. In the misery of her marriage Caponsacchi is the one 'blue gap' in a black sky. Blue is heaven's colour, but it is just as certainly a colour of hell. The idea came to Guido that he could solve his problems by killing Pompilia and her parents 'i' the blue of a sudden sulphur-blaze'.

Colours are the light of heaven refracted, and they are also the light of hell. The Pope pronounces Guido 'midmost blotch of black / Discernible in this group of clustered crimes'. But evil, like good, is refracted by cirumstance into colour. Guido's brother, the Abate, arranger of his marriage, is yellow to Guido's red:

> This fox-faced horrible priest, this brother-brute

> The Abate, – why, mere wolfishness looks well,
> Guido stands honest in the red o' the flame,
> Beside this yellow that would pass for white.

(x. 876–9)

In Girolamo, the youngest brother, who tries to seduce Pompilia, he finds a new vice:

> For there's a new distinctive touch, I see,
> Lust – lacking in the two – hell's own blue tint
> That gives the character and marks the man
> More than a match for yellow and red.

(x. 902–5)

Yellow Paolo, blue Girolamo, and red Guido; hypocrisy, lust and violence, complete a spectrum of the black sun of hell. It is perhaps only a happy coincidence that Browning chooses here not the primary colours of light, but the primary pigments. Mixed together them form not white light but a blotch of black.

Colours may be good and may be bad, because they derive from two different sources: from the sun, the fount of God's light, and from 'a mere Druid fire on a far mount'. That is why the Pope awards:

> More praise to him who with his subtle prism
> Shall decompose both lights and name the true.

(x. 1819–20)

The Ring and the Book locates the ambiguity in the phrase, the light of the world: it seeks to distinguish the divine light that shines on us from the putrescent glare that we ourselves emit, to distinguish the whiteness of innocence from the spurious whiteness of worldly honour. The poem decomposes both beams into colour, into red. But the result is still puzzling, for our eyes find it hard to distinguish the redness of courage from the redness of crime. We cannot tell the sun from a druid fire except by examining their spectra, and we cannot know if a colour is true or false unless we know its source. Browning and the Pope look for a way out of this dizzying hermeneutic circle. Despite the sympathy with Molinisn both seem to feel, neither is an admirer of irrational enthusiasm. They argue strenuously, and yet both come to rely in the end on intuition. They find at last only the faith, even the blind faith, that in trusting our intuition we do not maroon ourselves in a world lit only by our own prejudices. They can only trust that what we feel to be true is not a truth merely for us, a 'truth, reverberate, changed, made pass / A spectrum into mind, the narrow eye'. They find no logic to secure this faith, except a logic that proves such faith to be necessary.

The Ring and the Book is a specimen of high Victorian realism, and it is also the life of a saint. Browning appears throughout in a dual role, as realist poet and as hagiographer. The two roles seem discrepant, but it is not so. Whiteness is at once the poem's sign for goodness and for truth. Browning insists that seeing the real is not a passive, or a neutral, or a scientific activity, but a miracle. It is a miracle that he works hard to achieve – Browning has little time for miracles that come easily – but his best efforts cannot secure it. That is why he must begin the poem with a prayer for intercession to his own private saint, his 'lyric love, half-angel and half-bird'. He is looking for the truth, and to do that is to hope for a miracle:

> Red, green, and blue that whirl into a white,
> The variance now, the eventual unity,
> Which makes the miracle.

(I. 1354–6)

12

By White and Red
Describing Human Flesh

Red Cotton Night-Cap Country begins with the kind of daft argument one could only have with a friend. Browning has rented a house in Normandy for the summer, and finds that his old friend, Anne Thackeray, is his near neighbour. Anne Thackeray is planning a little book on this as yet 'un-Murrayed' region. Taken by its sleepy innocence she has christened it 'White Cotton Night-Cap Country'. Browning replies that there is more than one kind of nightcap, and gives a guided tour of an imaginary exhibition of famous nightcaps; Pope's, Hogarth's, Cowper's, the red nightcap forced on the grinning head of Louis XVI for the delight of the mob that howled beneath his window. At last, he gets to the point:

> White Cotton Night-Cap Country: excellent!
> Why not Red Cotton Night-Cap Country too?

> (I. 146–7)

He sets himself the task of proving that the district is as aptly termed red as white. But first he drifts away into some recent local history. The local church, *La Ravissante*, together with 'her sisters Lourdes and La Salette' is one of 'the three safety-guards of France'. It houses a particularly potent image of the Virgin. The statue had been lost when the Norsemen sacked the region. Long afterwards it was found buried and taken in triumph to the church at Londres. But the Virgin, 'liking old abode and loathing new / Was borne – this time by angels – back again'. The Virgin has performed miracles ever since, and is especially adept at easing rheumatic pains. It had long been the wish of the townsfolk that their Virgin should be honoured by the Pope with the gift of two crowns, one for her and one for the child. After much Vatican intrigue they had their way. The Pope agreed that the two crowns, paid for by the local citizenry, should be presented to the church in his name. The crowns were borne to the church at the head of a

144

glorious procession, and the day would have been quite perfect had it not rained.

The poem is by now more than 500 lines long, and seems to have been made up entirely of inconsequential chatter. Browning was fond of presenting himself in his late years as a genial, eccentric, talkative old buffer, and in this poem the act is so convincing that one can hardly blame readers who are taken in. But he has at last sidled towards his subject. The Virgin's crown is dominated by a large sapphire, the gift of a rich jeweller, Miranda, who has retired to the district. The poem goes on to tell Miranda's story.

Miranda is brought up in the faith, and grows from a religious boy to a religious young man. Then he leaves Normandy for Paris and enters the family business. He works hard, is obedient to his parents and punctilious in his devotions. But young men who live so are apt to feel that life is passing them by. Miranda begins at last to sample some of the wider opportunities that Paris offers the young. He begins to drink, to attend variety theatres and to take mistresses. But all is done discreetly. He shirks neither his duty at work nor to his family, and, though he knows that he is living a less than Christian life, he is sure that advancing years will see him safely back in the arms of Mother Church.

The story is so commonplace as not to be worth telling, not that is until one New Year, when Miranda takes his seat at 'The Varieties', notices a young woman seated near him, and falls violently and incurably in love. She is Clara de Millefleurs, of noble birth but impoverished. Her father's early death had left her with the responsibility of supporting both herself and her widowed mother. She had beauty, talent. The stage seemed the best recourse, but she shrank from exposing to the Parisian public her grand old family name, and resolved to make the experiment in London. Things promised well. A dazzling career lay open before her, until a conspiracy of jealous rivals ruined her chances. Alone, in a foreign land, without money, with her elderly mother entirely dependent on her, she was too vulnerable to the blandishments of an 'aged but illustrious Duke'. She became his favourite, palaced in splendour, decked with diamonds, the arbitress of London fashions. The Duke offered his hand in marriage, but 'her better angel interposed'. She fled to Paris where his frantic letters still reach her by every post.

So she tells Miranda, but later has to confess that the story is not strictly true. She was born Lucie Steiner, the illegitimate daughter of a milliner. She came with her mother to Paris, and married a tailor who lodged with them. The young couple failed in Paris, went to London, and failed there too. She returned to Paris alone, and became the mistress of someone rich enough to set up her and her mother in a comfortable apartment.

The confession has its effect on Miranda: it transforms his passionate devotion into steadfast love:

> Monsieur Léonce Miranda took his soul
> In both his hands, as if it were a vase,
> To see what came of the convulsion there,
> And found, amid subsidence, love new born
> So sparklingly resplendent, old was new.

(II. 761–5)

Miranda's brother dies, then his father. He is left in sole possession of the family business, left free to regulate his own life and devote it, if he chooses, to Clara. But then her husband reappears. He has at last found success, has a shop opposite Miranda's, and is reckoned the best cutter of riding clothes in Paris. His only concern is lest his wife claim some share in his new prosperity, and he demands a divorce. It is granted, but Miranda feels that he can no longer stay in Paris after such a scandal. He and Clara retire to Normandy, where they re-build the family seat in a fanciful Parisian style, and live a life of elegant amusement. Miranda dabbles in music, painting and literature, collects, and enjoys the company of a few select Parisian friends. Their life is quietly content, until Miranda, on one of his visits to his mother in Paris, is berated by her for the expense of his building projects and the profligacy of his life. Miranda rushes from her house and throws himself into the Seine. He is fished out, and returns to Normandy where Clara nurses him back to health. Then his mother dies and his cousins put it to him that her death is a direct result of the irregularity of his domestic affairs. He promises to make amends, withdraws into another room, and there he thrusts both his hands into the fire, burning them quite off. He agrees to give up his association with Clara. But his resolve does not last. He sells the business to the cousins and returns with Clara to Normandy, where he continues to paint and write, learning to hold the brush and pen in his mouth, but he occupies himself also in extravagent charities to the poor and to the church. His life seems once again to have achieved an even tenor until one day he mounts the belvedere, the high ecclesiastical tower that he has capriciously built to crown his house, and plunges from it to his death. He leaves his money to the church, but Clara is given management of it during her lifetime. His cousins dispute the will, contending that Miranda was insane, but their suit is rejected.

Browning's story is based on the life and death of Antoine Mellerio.[1] He follows the events of Mellerio's life closely, and retained in his original version the names of the real protagonists, only changing them when he was alerted to the possibility of actions being brought against him for libel. It was a story that excited him almost as much as finding the Yellow Book. He wrote to Isa Blagden: 'I have got *such* a subject for a poem, if I could do justice to it.'

But to compare *Red Cotton Night-Cap Country* with *The Ring and the Book* would be misleading. Browning is obtrusively present throughout *Red Cotton Night-Cap Country*, stage-managing the narrative – 'Now comes my moment, with the thrilling throw / Of curtain from each side a shrouded case' – offering his own extensive, often acid commentary on the action, remaining aloof from each of his characters. *The Ring and the Book* presents a world of saints encompassed by villains: in *Red Cotton Night-Cap Country* a neurotic is hounded to his death by nothing more vile than tawdry respectability. Pompilia's rapt faith is replaced by Miranda's pious hysterics. Miranda needs therapy rather than absolution. It is an utterly modern poem, written only three years after the death of the man who is its hero. It is modern in its grotesquely humdrum story, and modern too in the bizarre shifts of tone that mark its narrative. It is appropriate that the poem is addressed to Anne Thackeray, for if the manner in which Browning tells his story resembles anything in Victorian fiction it is her father's masterpiece, *Vanity Fair*. But not even Thackeray risks the kind of brutal detachment from his characters that Browning often displays. Miranda, whose 'heart was wise according to its lights / And limits', is in the end too stupid to earn Browning's respect. Clara loved Miranda truly, but with a love that was irredeemably selfish, the love of a caterpillar for its leaf. As for Miranda's mother and his cousins, their piety serves only to give them the courage of their moral sadism. Various ecclesiastics appear, but in them religion has become a kind of greed less comprehensible than the avarice of the cousinry, for they are greedy not for themselves but on behalf of the institution that they serve. The poem ends with Browning imagining Clara in the years to come, when 'o'er this life of hers distaste would drop /

Red-cotton-Night-cap-wise'. It would be easy, but wrong, to claim
that the red nightcap had already fallen over Browning's perception
of life.

It would be wrong because Browning's savage comic detachment
is punctuated by odd moments of intense sympathy. It may be
sympathy with the distasteful. Miranda in his moderately profligate
youth lay, as it were, face down on the turf, 'And let strange
creatures make his mouth their home'. Clara, whatever her
shortcomings, is not to be thought of in the same company as some
'Red clout called woman too!.' Browning presses the image, and
fallen woman becomes 'a twist of fetid rag', a 'cupping-cloth' that
should be thrown into a sewer. The whimsical symbol, the red
cotton nightcap, suddenly releases what looks like a spasm of
menstrual disgust. Clara, in contrast, is a piece of 'cambric' only
stained with 'iron mould': the stain on her handkerchief is delicate.
The effect is unnerving. Browning is momentarily implicated in
Miranda's neurotic dilemma, in love both with the Virgin and a real
woman, his love of each besmirching his love of the other. But
Browning does not only sympathise with the noisome. Miranda's
love for Clara is movingly celebrated, and the poem is full of those
extended metaphors through which Browning characteristically
expresses the agitated moral urgency that marks his writing at its
most serious. It is a funny, bitter, pitying, contemptuous, tender
tale. It is difficult to describe the manner of its telling, and it is just as
hard to say what it is told for.

The poem's alternative title is 'Turf and Tower', and these are its
two organising symbols. It could be said that they derive from
Browning's story, from the tower or belvedere that dominates
Miranda's country house, and looks out over the turf of his *'jardin
anglais'*. But the attempt to weave the poem's symbols into the fabric
of its narrative is no more than a gesture. The symbols are
presented, explained and applied to the story by the narrator. In *Red
Cotton Night-Cap Country* Browning is as concerned to show his
workings as he is in *The Ring and the Book* (apart from its first book) to
conceal them. The turf stands for the immediate sensory buzz, the
whirl of sound, smell, taste, touch and sight, that is for each of us
the basis of all our experience, the 'cool slush' in which Caliban lies
while 'small eft-things course / Run in and out each arm and make
him laugh'. The tower is any structure of belief that man builds in an
attempt to reach out from the chaos of his sensory life to some
transcendental truth that he dimly perceives and hankers after.

Miranda's tower is the church, and it is crumbling slowly back on to the turf from which it arose. To climb such a tower is to risk death if one sets foot on a rotten stone and plunges downwards amidst the crushing masonry. Human history is the construction of a sequence of such towers. Each does service for a time, each is hailed as the one true church, but each at last crumbles or crashes to the ground. In the later nineteenth century the tower of Christianity that has been building for centuries is crumbling, rotting, being slowly invaded by the turf from which it climbed. But man must climb, leave the turf and clamber perilously upwards, and, for Miranda, no other tower is available. Miranda climbs on a rotten structure and dies.

The poem's third symbol is the tent. It, too, is echoed in Miranda's house with its 'mansard' roof. The tent is the alternative to the tower, a bivouac within which one may shelter as one lies on the turf. It offers protection not so much from the weather as from bewilderment in the face of the ceaseless flux of sensory experience that is the turf-dweller's only reality. But the tent offers only a precarious illusion of stability. Browning asks us to understand Miranda's story as that of a man who feels he must choose between tower and turf but cannot. He is not content to live with Clara in a tent, nor can he leave her and climb alone into his tower. He jumps from the belvedere in a mad act of faith that the Virgin will support him and bear him to the feet of her statue. Such madness is his only sanity, for the miracle will prove to him that his love for Clara and his love for the Virgin are compatible, and only proof of that could make his life tolerable.

If we understand *Red Cotton Night-Cap Country* through its organising symbols, it becomes a poem about how hard it is to be a Christian, a poem about the wrenching, impossible division between the way of Jesus and the way of the world, between the soul and the body. But it has none of the serious modesty of *Easter-Day*. Browning never suggests that the problem from which Miranda suffers is anything more than a personal freak. Miranda believes in flying Virgins, and Browning contemplates the difficulties of such a man with amused, irritated, pitying detachment. He invites a very English response to Roman flummery. To understand what engages Browning with Miranda's story one must turn to its other pair of symbols, symbols that pervade the poem rather than organise it, for their significance is elusive.

Anne Thackeray names this district of Normandy 'White Cotton Night-Cap Country'. Browning asks 'Why not Red Cotton Night-Cap Country too?' The question seems simple. White is the colour of

innocence, red of guilt. Normandy is White Cotton Night-Cap
Country because it is inhabited by quiet, god-fearing folk. How can
a district be anything but white when its most notorious criminal is a
citizen fined for smuggling half a pound of tobacco? If such a crime is
the utmost 'Impingement of the ruddy on the blank' that Saint-Rambert offers, then the village may properly be called white. Whiteness
is goodness, then, but goodness of that special kind that is at once
admired and laughed at. The white spire of Saint-Rambert's church
is the town's proper emblem, a giant white nightcap publishing the
truth that the town beneath it is sunk in 'one snowy innocence'.
Sunk in because such innocence is sleepy. Anne Thackeray has
looked for, and found a 'Subsiding-into-slumber sort of name', a
name for a district where good folk live, but folk one admires
somewhat condescendingly, for their 'snowy innocence' is scarcely
to be distinguished from the 'righteous flat of insipidity'. When
Browning promises to show a red stain on the white expanse his
project is ambivalent. He plans to show the redness of sin
compromising snowy innocence, and this will at once compromise
the purity of the region, and raise its inhabitants to a level at which
we can regard their doings and feelings uncondescendingly, with
the level gaze with which we ought to look at our fellow human
beings.

Browning invites us to compare his poem with the travel book
that Anne Thackeray is planning. He is politely self-deprecating.
His poem will only 'Play ruddy herald-star to your white blaze'. But
he seems all the same well satisfied with his achievement. As he
paced the sands with Anne Thackeray something struck him 'in a
flash', and his poem is:

> that moment's flashing amplified,
> Impalpability reduced to speech,
> Conception proved by birth ...

(IV. 983–5)

A heady self-confidence gives zest to the lines. His hero, Miranda, is
a dilettante. He knows just enough of art to know that its proper
practice 'demands life whole and sole'. The lot of the artist is to wear
himself out in battle with his age, and Miranda has no taste for any
business so strenuous. Browning celebrates the artist as hero:

To be the very breath that moves the age
Means not to have breath drive you bubble-like
Before it – but yourself to blow: that's strain;
Strain's worry through the lifetime, till there's peace;
We know where peace expects the artist-soul.

(II. 1056–60)

When a poet so profoundly conscious of the artist's task presents one of his major poems as an advertisement for a travel book he must be suspected of an empty gallantry. When he splashes Anne Thackeray's canvas with red, he does so in conscious mastery, like Turner electrifying the cool, grey sea in his 'Helvoetsluys' by adding to it on one of the varnishing days before the Academy exhibition 'a round daub of red-lead somewhat bigger than a shilling', and with that single gesture overpowering the Constable that hung alongside – 'He has been here', said Constable, 'and fired a gun.' Or perhaps more like Corot. Browning compliments Anne Thackeray by reminding her of all the picturesque details of Normandy life that she will certainly not have missed, among them the 'stalwart strider by the wagon-side / Brightening the acre with his purple blouse'. Browning knows with Corot how a landscape may be vivified by a little dab of red paint. He dips his brush in red and shows Anne Thackeray the difference between a writer and an artist by turning her travel book into a poem.

But my analogy is evasive. However Browning proposes to achieve this effect, he cannot do it, like Corot, by the careful positioning of a purple blouse. Two passages help to make the method clearer. Browning's guided tour of famous nightcaps ends, somewhat incongruously, with the red nightcap pushed on Louis XVI's head as he was forced towards an upper window of Versailles to be acclaimed by a jeering mob. Browning remembers the story from Carlyle's 'story-book', and his interest, like Carlyle's, is focused on the response of a single witness, the Corsican lieutenant, Bonaparte:

Had I but one good regiment of my own,
How soon should volleys to the due amount
Lay stiff upon the street-flags this *canaille*!
As for the droll there, he that plays the king
And screws out smile with a Red night-cap on,
He's done for! Somebody must take his place.

(I. 325–30)

Later, Browning imagines Anne Thackeray inspecting Saint-Rambert's collection of nightcaps, and finding them all snow-white, 'virginal, no Rahab-thread / For blushing token of the spy's success'. Red, it seems, is the colour of revolution, worn by the *sans-culottes* to brandish their republicanism, and it is also the colour of the prostitute, the colour appropriate to Rahab. Neither association seems much to Browning's point. No district seems less politically active than Saint-Rambert, where the placards on which the defeated Napoleon III called on his subjects to take up arms against the invading Prussians are so little regarded that the local people do not even bother to remove them:

> No: rain and wind must rub the rags away
> And let the lazy land untroubled snore.

> (I. 137–8)

The search for colleagues of Rahab in the district seems just as futile:

> As to the woman-kind – renounce from those
> The hope of getting a companion-tinge,
> First faint touch promising romantic fault!

> (I. 368–70)

Even Clara, Browning properly insists, is no 'red clout'. The redness that Browning seeks is neither the redness of revolution not the redness of the prostitute, but a quality that inheres both in Rahab's story and in Napoleon's.

Joshua, the Jewish warlord, is preparing to move against the Canaanites. He sends spies ahead of him to reconnoitre Jericho before marching his army across the Jordan. What lies before him is the promised land: his task is to establish the kingdom of Israel. Rahab's role in such a large historical process seems likely to be no more than that of an unremembered casualty. But news of the spies' presence in Jericho reaches the king. Rahab hides them, and helps their escape. Her reward is a promise that when Joshua puts Jericho to the sword, she and her family will be spared. They need only identify their household with a scarlet thread. The chronicler makes no comment on Rahab's motives, whether she acted out of selfish fear or out of pity. But for one brief moment history works itself out through her. In being at once a traitor to her people and an unlikely Jewish heroine she is an embodiment of the ambivalence of all historical change. Napoleon is not much like an enigmatic, and presumably uncomprehending, Canaanite prostitute. He looks at the king and at the mob both with thin-lipped disdain. But in the end he differs from Rahab chiefly in that he is self-conscious, aware that history has reached a decisive turn, and aware too that the direction it takes can be determined, or at least decisively influenced, by him.

Red Cotton Night-Cap Country is one of the many poems in which Browning is preoccupied with the nature of historical change. But he is not interested in political history. The dynastic wars that fascinate him are wars of ideas. *Sordello* is the story of 'the development of a soul: little else is worth study'. As with people, so with history. Browning is not interested in the succession of events, but in the succession of states of mind. The towers that are built tall and proud only to tumble back upon the turf from which they rose are not emperor's castles but imperial ideas. They rise and fall: there is no cessation of time, no end of change. That is why all ages are, to themselves, ages of crisis. What makes a man representative, and hence a fit subject for a poem, is that he suffers more completely than his fellows the crisis peculiar to his age. Sordello lives at the dawn of the renaissance: the hero as warrior is about to give way to a rival ideal, the hero as artist. Sordello is a representative man, a man fit to figure in a major poem because he so completely suffers the crisis of his own page of history. It is for the same reason that Miranda, for all that he is dull-witted, credulous, and often quite absurd, is nevertheless for Browning a true hero. The crucial movement of the nineteenth century plays itself out within his soul, so that, whatever his limitations, he truly represents his age.

Miranda's mother lives a life of respectable piety 'bent o'er her bezique' with 'Monsieur Curé This and Sister That'. Piety for her means a strict obedience to the decalogue and a lofty scorn of sinners. She is the custodian of a Christian tradition that is moribund. The life of the Church in the later nineteenth century is aptly figured in the life of a censorious old widow who whiles away her time at cards. Even the street she lives in, the Quai Rousseau, hints that the values to which she pays devout lip-service have been overtaken by history. The Christian tower is rotten, crumbling. Beside it a clean, new edifice is being constructed. Its spokesman is the physician Beaumont, a kindly man, a doctor for the mind as well as the body, who patches up Miranda after his suicide attempt and again after his self-mutilation. He thinks Miranda insane, and believes such casualties inevitable 'as long as priests may preach / Spiritual terrors'. He is a rationalist and a materialist: 'Body and soul are one thing, with two names / For more or less elaborated stuff'. This heady doctrine comes to us recommended by Beaumont's kindliness and his good sense, but it is at once undercut by Browning's dry comment: 'Such is the new Religio Medici, / Though antiquated faith held otherwise ... '. Beaumont believes that science will succeed faith, and do away with the 'terrors' that torment Miranda. He does not know that scientific materialism will itself become a tower, and inspire in its defenders the same homicidal and suicidal zeal with which Christianity inspired its early adherents. He learns his lesson, briefly, violently, and Browning notes it in the dry, comic style that is recurrent in the poem:

> I note these old unscientific ways.
> Poor Beaumont cannot: for the Commune ruled
> Next year, and ere they shot his priests, shot him.

> (III. 508–10)

It is Miranda, not his mother or his doctor, who is the representative man. He is alive equally to the claims of the spirit and the claims of the material world, and he can surrender neither the one nor the other. *Red Cotton Night-Cap Country* is Miranda Agonistes, and his agon is the agon of the age. Miranda's mother, as she demands that her son abandon his mistress, is 'one white appeal'. In death she becomes simply a 'stretch of rigid white'. Against her Beaumont raises a banner that will soon become the red flag of the communards. But it is Miranda and neither of them who is fully human, plunging his white hands into the red fire, or, more movingly, at his mother's funeral plunging his red face into white snow:

> the poor fellow in his misery,
> Buried hot face and bosom, where heaped snow
> Offered assistance, at the grave's black edge.

> (III. 347–9)

Confronted by his mother's death Miranda can still choose neither white nor red. All he can do is to bury his flushed face in white snow and feel how cold burns as he is later to feel how fire burns. Miranda is not a great sinner – his sins are not really 'as scarlet' – but the Bible tells of another kind of red stain, the stain on the sheep marked for sacrifice. Miranda is marked as one of history's sacrificial victims, and in that marking he confirms his representative humanity, 'By White and Red describing human flesh'.

Miranda spends most of his life hiding from his own internal self-contradictions; hiding in sensuality from piety, and in piety from the throb of the sensual life. His chief activity is in forging weak reconciliations between things incompatible. In Normandy he seeks to reconcile town and country, with the result that his house looks absurdly incongruous, like a Parisian hotel transplanted, the Hôtel de Normandie. He seeks to reconcile the strenuous life of the artist with the ease of the gentleman and becomes a dilletante. He tries to reconcile turf and tower by living with Clara and at the same time giving to the church with mad generosity. He tries to write his life as a pastoral poem, where living is at once rural and citified, where the stressful life of the artist becomes the negligent ease of the piper, and where sensuality is freshly innocent, and he knows that to yearn for the pastoral life is to yearn for Eden. Browning indulges his nostalgia, imagines him descending from his belvedere one springtime:

> Then he descends, unbosoms straight his store
> Of blessings in the bud, and both embrace,
> Husband and wife, since earth is Paradise,
> And man at peace with God.

(I. 691–4)

References to Eden punctuate the description of Miranda's life with Clara in Normandy, and they are, in their way, charming. But Browning is the least pastoral of all great English poets, incapable of imagining even heaven as uncompetitive.

The pastoral dream is sufficient only for Clara. Browning describes how she passed him one day, some time after Miranda's death:

>   she wore a soft and white
> Engaging dress, with velvet stripes and squares
> Severely black, yet scarce discouraging
> Fresh Paris-manufacture!

(I. 829–32)

She walks with her attendants, but tripping behind her come 'Two great goats and two prodigious sheep':

>   one great naked sheep-face stopped to ask
> Who was the stranger, snuffed inquisitive
> My hand that made acquaintance with its nose ...

(I. 891–3)

There is an odd incongruity between the strange, dream-like pageant, and Browning's crisply comic naturalism. The narrative voice exposes the procession as unreal. Clara has taken the moral antonyms of human experience, black and white, sheep and goats, and transformed them into costume. Browning can describe her face only as 'singularly colourless'. She has given up her whole life to the service of Miranda, as content to join him in prayer as to join him in bed, and the consequence of such self-surrender is that she has given up her part in the kind of experience that Browning finds challenging and become a fit inhabitant of a false Eden. Browning is well enough pleased with her characterisation: she is 'a finished little piece'. But this is nothing to be proud of, for 'the incomplete / More than completeness matches the immense'.

Miranda is Browning's hero, not in his kindliness, nor in his moral uprightness, but in his moments of madness: when he throws himself in the Seine, when he plunges his hands into the fire, in his final leap from the belvedere. Not that Browning admires such actions in themselves. He takes the sensible view that they are pathetic and ridiculous. They expose Miranda's weak-mindedness, but they show too his inability to hide from the truth of his experience. Browning's verdict on Miranda's action is chilling:

>   Hold a belief you only half-believe,
>   With all momentous issues either way, –

And I advise you imitate this leap,
Put faith to proof, be cured or killed at once.

(IV. 353–6)

Miranda's leap from the tower does not represent a choice between
Clara and the Virgin. He never half-believes in the Virgin any more
than he half-believes in his love for Clara. He believes utterly in
both. His doubt is whether he can be true to each of his mistresses
without betraying both. He leaps in the faith that the Virgin will
intercede, that he will be carried through the air and brought
gently to rest at the feet of her statue. In interceding the Virgin will
prove her power to a sceptical world, and, in making Miranda the
instrument of her miracle, she will signify that she is as tolerant of
Miranda's love for Clara as Clara is of his love for the Virgin. His
hope is that, his flight over, he will rise and meet Clara, and find
that her past has been magically expunged, and that she may now
become his wife. His leap, and Browning's approval of it, registers
the final conviction of them both that if man cannot serve two
mistresses, he had better have done with it and die.

The Virgin does not come to Miranda's aid. Supernatural powers
in the nineteenth century are sadly shrunken and seem not to
extend much beyond the cure of minor rheumatic aches. Miranda
crashes on to a gravel path and is killed. As a fitting conclusion to
the black comedy of his career, his death achieves what his whole
life could not. Clara and the Virgin, his two incompatible
mistresses, are reconciled, for the terms of his will dictate that until
her death 'Clara represent the Ravissante'. So it is that turf and
tower, grass and stone, are reconciled in the moment of Miranda's
death:

A flash in middle air, and stone-dead lay
Monsieur Léonce Miranda on the turf.

(IV. 340–1)

Browning may praise Miranda 'according to his lights' for his last
mad act of faith, but the pity is that he had such lights. He lived not
far from Browning's friend, Joseph Milsand. Had Miranda applied
to him Milsand would have shown him how to repair his mutilated
body with 'artificial hands of caoutchouc' and shown him too how
to repair the injuries to his soul. He would:

> counsel justice – to yourself, the first,
> To your associate, very like a wife
> Or something better, – to the world at large,
> Friends, strangers, horses, hounds, and cousinry –
> All which amount of justice will include
> Justice to God.
>
> (III. 773–8)

He would have shown Miranda how the rival duties that pull him apart are, in fact, complementary. The passage in which Browning celebrates the wisdom of his old friend ends with what looks like a graceful but extraneous compliment:

> Milsand, who makest warm my wintry world,
> And wise my heaven, if there we consort too.
>
> (III. 781–2)

But it is the key to the whole poem, for Milsand's quiet common sense is the miracle that Miranda died seeking. It proves that we can find comfort in the here and now, accept what warmth we find in a wintry world, without giving up our hope of heaven.

The poem begins with Browning walking from his rented cottage down to the beach. He walks through a field of 'emerald luzern bursting into blue', treading as he passes on wild-mustard flowers, his feet 'Bruising the acrid aromatics out', until he tastes the 'good salt savour of the sea'. The beach is richly tactile: 'first, the sifted sands, then sands in slab / Smooth save for pipy wreath-work of the worm', and then the line of sea-weed 'Burnt cinder-black, with brown uncrumpled swathe / Of berried softness, sea-swoln thrice its size'. It is Browning at his most Caliban-like, swimming before ever he reaches the sea in a liquid bath of sensual stimuli. But his luxurious sensuality does not indicate a confinement within the physical. He likes Saint-Rambert because it is so ordinary. It serves to remind him that:

> One place performs, like any other place,
> The proper service every place on earth
> Was framed to furnish men with: serves alike
> To give him note that, through the place he sees,
> A place is signified he never saw,
> But, if he lacks not soul, may learn to know.
>
> (I. 59–64)

He looks through sensual appearances just as willingly as he surrenders to them, and the two impulses are not self-contradictory but mutually supporting. A unitary, transcendental truth anchors his delight in the welter of his bodily experience, and that welter, in its turn, saves him from the blank abstraction to which the service of the soul might otherwise reduce him. All life, like Miranda's, has the texture of 'shot silk', its blankness inwoven with colour, its white with red. Miranda sees those colours garishly opposed, but Milsand and Browning both indicate another possibility. They show how the red and white may come together in the subtle mottling that is the defining tint of human flesh.

13

The Crimson Quest

In *Numpholeptos* a nymph, like the moon, bathes the man who loves her in a cool, silvery light. From the 'magic hall' where the nymph lives her light 'Rays forth' through the 'fantastic world'. But the hall is 'Like the gem / Centuply angled o'er a diadem', and the light, as it shines through the walls, is refracted into colour. The lover's penance is to follow one after another each shaft of coloured light through all the world, and then to 'retrack' his steps, and find that the coloured beam ends where it began 'in your blank pure soul', 'alike the source / And tomb of the prismatic glow'. The lover imagines that by bathing in the light that shoots out from the nymph he will achieve a soul as 'blank' as her own, and become her fit companion. But the light he steeps himself in is not white but coloured, and he returns after each pilgrimage dyed, grotesque, further from the completion of his quest than he was when he set out. So, he returns from the yellow ray:

> Here I reek suffused
> With crocus, saffron, orange, as I used
> With scarlet, purple, every dye o' the bow
> Born of the storm-cloud. As before you show
> Scarce recognition, no approval, some
> Mistrust, more wonder at a man become
> Monstrous in garb ...

(82–8)

In a fit of pique he protests at the futility of the task he has been set. But by the end of the poem he has once again submitted to his penance, and sets out to follow the red ray in the hope that this, 'the crimson quest', will prove successful.

Browning's characteristic manner of verse argument is densely figurative, but in *Numpholeptos* the figure is allowed to exist independent of the argument. The result is one of Browning's few symbolist poems. Perhaps for this reason Browning is able to gather together in *Numpholeptos* themes that had engaged him in many

earlier poems. In its concern with impossible, ideal love *Numpholeptos* looks back to *Alastor* and *Endymion*, the key influences on
Browning's first major poems, and this signals Browning's return to
the cluster of themes that had engaged him in *Pauline, Paracelsus* and
Sordello. The poem's central image, a moony light refracted into
colour, points back to the lunar rainbow of *Christmas-Eve*. The
lover's weariness, condemned to pursue a quest to which he can see
no end, reminds one of *Childe Roland*, and his querulousness, his
feeble protests at the demands of an unreasonable mistress and his
final resignation take the reader back to *Andrea del Sarto*. *Numpholeptos* sends shafts of light shooting out over a large part of Browning's
poetic output, which makes it depressing that the major portion of
the critical treatment that the poem has received has been devoted
to speculation on what the poem might be thought to suggest about
Browning's feelings for his dead wife.

Browning's own remarks on the poem, in a letter to Furnivall, are
helpful, if cagey. He describes it as

> an allegory ... of an impossible ideal object of love, accepted
> conventionally as such, by a man who, on the whole, cannot quite
> blind himself to the demonstrable fact that the possessor of
> knowledge and purity obtained without the natural consequence
> of obtaining them by achievement – not inheritance – such a being
> is imaginary, not real, a nymph and no woman: and why such an
> one would be ignorant of a lover's endeavour to emulate the
> qualities which the beloved is entitled to consider as pre-existent
> to earthly experience, and independent of its inevitable results.[1]

This is prose a little after the style of Paracelsus's lectures, but it can
be disentangled. The key notion is that the lover's predicament is a
type of the 'inevitable results of human experience'. It is inevitable
and natural that the lover should return after each journey and find
himself grotesquely dyed, reeking of yellow. Forty years before
Browning had written of 'the shifting hues of our common nature
when subjected to the prism of circumstance'.[2] *Numpholeptos*
explores that metaphor. A human being, unlike a nymph, cannot
exist independently of circumstances, for we come to exist as
individuals only when our common human nature shines through
the particular circumstances of our lives. These circumstances act as
a prism: our common human nature, as it shines through them, is
refracted into colour. The lover, being human, can do no other than

follow his coloured lights, 'swim and swathe / In yellow licence'.
When he believes that his bath has left him 'Monstrous in garb', he
is shamed by the badge of his own human nature. He feels
humiliated, as Sordello had before him, that his inner light must be
thwarted, must be broken into rainbow flakes. But the only
alternative is death.

The lover wants to become one with his mistress, to bathe in her
light until it becomes his light. But he can never arrive at whiteness,
only steep himself in colour. This is one of his complaints. The other
is that his mistress's light is cold and pale, like moonlight. Her
silvery smile is 'sad, petrific'. The significance of her gaze is elusive,
showing 'Scarce recognition, some / Mistrust, more wonder', but
it is elusive because it is 'blank'. Like Miranda's Clara she is
'singularly colourless', a blank on to which the lover may project the
erratic play of his own emotions. He yearns not only to share her
whiteness, but for her whiteness to pass the 'pallid limit', and be
transformed to 'sunlight and salvation'. This is the hope with which
the poem ends:

> Who knows but this – the crimson-quest –
> May deepen to a sunrise, not decay
> To that cold sad sweet smile?

> (150–2)

The lover carps because he experiences only refracted light, and
carps too because his beloved shines only with reflected light. His
quest is to transmute his colour into her whiteness, but it is also to
intensify her moonlight into dawn. He wants to transform the
coloured lights of mortal circumstance into white light, and to
transform the reflected light of the moon-nymph into the direct light
of the sun. The poem works at once to sanction both dreams, and to
expose their futility.

His demand that the moonlight be changed into sunlight is a
covert recognition of this. Sunlight, unlike moonlight, warms, and
is the proper type of love. He pines for the sun, but even as he does
so he stumbles on the truth that, were his dream to come true, it
would kill him. He looks in his nymph's eyes for what:

> if born would blind
> Mine with redundant bliss, as flesh may find

The inert nerve, sting awake the palsied limb,
Bid with life's ecstasy sense overbrim,
And suck back death in the resurging joy ...

(29–33)

To dream of the sun is to long for a joy so intense that it would kill. But it is less important to know that the sun might kill than that it would blind. To gaze at the moon is to raise one's face to a chill light, to gaze at the sun is to be blinded.

The lover's life is spent alternately gazing in loving disappointment at the blank moon and trudging wearily along shafts of coloured light. The poem is spoken just after the lover's return from his pilgrimage on the yellow ray, just before he sets out on 'the crimson-quest'. The yellow ray has been a disappointment. He has returned dyed yellow, 'absurd / As frightful', and is oddly peeved that the yellow ray has yielded nothing but yellowness. He suspects it is the quality of the yellow that disappoints him. He has assumed only a 'sulphur-steeped disguise', like the yellow sheet in which heretics were taken for burning, and feels cheated of the 'priestly cloth of gold' that he had hoped would mantle him. But 'sulphur' registers a sense of self-disgust rather than a precise hue. He complains, 'Here I reek / With crocus, saffron, orange', and it must be a remarkable cloth of gold that could please a man who finds such colours offensive. He has known:

                              no stay nor stint
To yellow, since you sanctioned that I bathe,
Burnish me, soul and body, swim and swathe
In yellow licence.

(79–82)

But he has chosen to think of his sojourn in the yellow ray as a penance not as a gift. It is so nearly otherwise. He learns there 'What agency it was first tipped the crests / Of unnamed wildflower', and gave its marking to 'the burrowing snake'. He is offered a Wordsworthian education, 'wonder, linked / With fear', but he is an ungrateful pupil, for he seeks knowledge independent of the process by which it is gained, knowledge such as is bestowed on the priest at the moment of his ordination. The poem charts Browning's belief that no such knowledge is available.

The lover seeks sunshine: he longs for dawn:

> true blood-streaked, sun-warmth, action-time
> By heart pulse ripened to a ruddy glow
> Of gold above my clay.

(12–14)

But all he is granted is 'yellow licence' followed by a 'crimson-quest'. He feels cheated, but looked at another way he has been given what he wants, for yellow and red are the two disguises in which we can look at the intolerable white light of the sun. He can look at the sun at dawn, and see it as 'a ruddy glow / Of gold'. If his gaze remained fixed on the sun as it climbed the sky it would drop its coloured disguise and blind him. The lover's eyes could not bear to gaze directly at the light of the sun. He can look safely at the sun's light only when it is reflected as moonlight or refracted as colour. He feels as a constraint what is really a mercy.

There is no pleasing the man. He complains of reeking, 'With scarlet, purple, every dye o' the bow / Born of the storm-cloud'. And then he complains that the nymph has reneged on her promise to him:

> you promise shall return
> Your pilgrim jewelled as with drops o' the urn
> The rainbow paints from, and no smutch at all
> Of ghastliness at edge of some cloud-pall
> Heaven cowers before, as earth awaits the fall
> O' the bolt and flash of doom.

(119–24)

He complains that he has been rainbow-dyed, and that he has not been rainbow-painted. He wants, it seems, to be decorated by rainbow tints that are not 'Born of the storm-cloud', that are free from the complication of 'wonder' and 'fear', of beauty and storm, free from the painful contrarieties of mortal life. He finds that no such rainbow exists and feels, quite unreasonably, betrayed.

All he has to do, it might seem, is to embrace his mortal experience rather than feel constrained by it, to turn his back on the moon-nymph and her cold, unattainable whiteness, to stop hankering after a sun that if he gazed on it would blind him, and luxuriate instead, one after another, in baths of coloured light. He should give up the alchemist's vain search for some truth that transcends the defining limits of mortal life and find his happiness in the chemist's patient study of earthly fact. The lover seeks within his experience for something outside his experience. It is a futile quest, and he should abandon it, just as Browning found himself as a poet only when he abandoned the succession of Romantic heroes who, in *Pauline*, *Paracelsus* and *Sordello* act out the futility of demanding that the finite world accommodate itself to infinite yearnings. He should settle, as Browning learned to settle, for light refracted: the white light of truth divided into the play of coloured beams that images the only life available to men and women. The lover in *Numpholeptos* is right to regret his 'querulous outbreak', right to address himself once again to his human task, and set out on his journey along the red ray. His mistake is that he submits wearily rather than striding robustly forwards, and that he hopes still that redness, mortal colour, might yield something other than itself.

This seems to me a misreading of both *Numpholeptos* and of Browning's whole achievement, for neither in *Numpholeptos* nor elsewhere does Browning suggest that it is enough to delight in experience for its own sake. Caliban, as he lies in the warm mud and surrenders himself to his physical sensations, is an attractive beast. As his mind lifts itself from the primal ooze, and he imagines a God with the mind of a spiteful child, he becomes deformed. But whereas his sensuality, however engaging, is bestial, in his deformity he is recognisably human. He finds, and we find in reading the poem, that we are human not simply in the quality of our sensations, but in our need to explain them; that we are defined by our need to find or to imagine some still point uninvolved in the whirl of our sensory experience. Caliban becomes fully human when he knows that there is something above his spiteful god, and that whatever it is it must be 'quiet'.

The best commentary on *Numpholeptos* is Shelley's fragmentary *Essay on Love*:

> We dimly see within our intellectual nature a miniature as it were of our entire self, yet deprived of all that we condemn or despise, the ideal prototype of every thing excellent or lovely that we are capable of conceiving as belonging to the nature of man. Not only the portrait of our external being but an assemblage of the

minutest particles of which our nature is composed: a mirror
whose surface reflects only the forms of purity and brightness: a
soul within our soul that describes a circle around its proper
paradise which pain, and sorrow, and evil dare not overleap. To
this we eagerly refer all sensations, thirsting that they should
resemble or correspond with it.[3]

What the lover in *Numpholeptos* yearns for is what we all yearn for,
some image of ourselves that 'reflects only the forms of purity and
brightness'. It is ourselves, but ourselves deprived of all that in us
that we 'condemn and despise'. Browning's lover is in love with
exactly such an ideal creature. As Browning himself told Furnivall:
'such a being is imaginary, not real, a nymph and no woman'. She is
imagined free of all the lover's human limitations. She has no
sympathy with his defects, because she has no knowledge of defect.
She possesses all the lover's knowledge and purity, but possesses
them 'without the natural consequence of obtaining them by
achievement'. So she shines whitely, the possessor of knowledge
gained without undergoing any experiental process. In her
presence the lover looks at himself and is humiliated by his body
rankly dyed with colour. He despises himself, and, inevitably,
transfers the contempt that he feels for himself to her:

                     O that ear
All fact pricks ruddy, that thrice-superfine
Femininity of sense, with right divine
To waive all process, take result stain-free
From out the very muck wherein ...

(143–7)

He resents her because she shines with a light that is devoid of all
that he despises in himself, because she is his ideal, not his real,
prototype. He resents her for the same reason that he loves her. His
is, as he recognises, the 'true slave's querulous outbreak'.

In *Numpholeptos*, as in *Childe Roland*, life is imaged as the pursuit of
an object perfectly pure and therefore unattainable, for the harder
the pilgrim strives the more the grime of experience will stick to him,
and the less fit will he be to win his goal. Life is absurd, futile. The
speaker of *Childe Roland* is driven into neurosis. His vision of the
utterly pure leaves him only with a sickly sense of the world as ugly,

diseased, so that to see a bare patch of grass is to shrink, as at leprosy. There is something of him in the speaker of *Numpholeptos*. But it need not be so. It is possible to believe that life is the pursuit of the unattainable, absurd, and yet to celebrate its absurdity. Shelley describes 'the invisible and unattainable point to which love tends', but his argument is closed only when he recognises the incurable frustration which is our lot as the guarantee of all that is best in our human nature, for it is the struggle to attain the unattainable that 'urges forth the powers of man to arrest the faintest shadow of that without the possession of which there is no rest nor respite to the heart over which it rules'. It is a frustration that secures the openness to experience the only alternative to which is death.

Numpholeptos ends when the speaker recovers from his querulousness, recovers at any rate a wan hope, and sets out once more on his impossible pilgrimage:

> Forth at your behest
> I fare. Who knows but this – the crimson-quest –
> May deepen to a sunrise, not decay
> To that cold sad sweet smile? – which I obey.

(149–52)

Part Three
Gerard Manley Hopkins

14

Pure Blues

A Vision of the Mermaids is an odd poem. For one thing we see little of the mermaids, largely because they are so over-dressed. A crest made of some gossamer stuff stretches from 'crown to tail-fin'. They have fins on their shoulders, their hair is elaborately decorated with coral, sea-weed, shells, sea anemones and so on, and they wear long skirts. Some of them play with the sea-weed, others dive or splash:

> But most in a half-circle watch'd the sun:
> And a sweet sadness dwelt on every one ...
>
> (116–17)

In his illustration to the poem[1] Hopkins leaves out the sportive mermaids. Those he draws are arranged in several groups and stand in the sea, stiff and ill at ease, looking at the sunset. The eye travels easily over these forlorn creatures, the rock around which they gather and the sea, which is drawn with fussy conventionality, and comes to rest on a dramatic sunset sky. The sky is brilliantly lit. Dark storm clouds writhe across it, and there are rents, vaginal in shape but horizontal. In the poem the effect is preserved:

> Plum-purple was the west; but spikes of light
> Spear'd open lustrous gashes, crimson-white ...
>
> (7–8)

Not only is their spearing, but throbbing, panting, gasping and lips:

> Now all things rosy turn'd: the west had grown
> To an orb'd rose, which, by hot pantings blown
> Apart, betwixt ten thousand petall'd lips
> By interchange gasp'd splendour and eclipse.
>
> (19–22)

171

Bridges believed the poem to have been submitted by Hopkins for his school poetry prize, but this seems unlikely. It reads more like the kind of thing that gets passed around under the desks.

In the sketch the eye moves from the mermaids to the sunset, but in the poem the sunset introduces the description of the mermaids, and it arouses expectations that Hopkins scarcely fulfils. He 'gazed unhinder'd' at the sunset, but as soon as the mermaids appear his inhibitions become painfully apparent. He describes their dress, and then, possibly unsure of what to do with them, he turns a Homeric simile:

> Soon – as when Summer of his sister Spring
> Crushes and tears the rare enjewelling,
> And boasting 'I have fairer things than these'
> Plashes amidst the billowy apple-trees
> His lusty hands, in gusts of scented wind
> Swirling out bloom till all the air is blind
> With rosy foam and pelting blossom and mists
> Of driving vermeil-rain; and, as he lists,
> The dainty onyx-coronals deflowers,
> A glorious wanton ...

> (84–93)

Summer has 'lusty hands', he 'deflowers', he is a 'wanton'. The scattering of blossom becomes Summer's rape of Spring, his sister, and the incident is described with vivid relish. It is quite unclear what it is in the mermaids' behaviour that releases such emotions, but it is no wonder that when they reappear they are chastened, sweetly sad.

A Vision of the Mermaids is, of course, an exercise in the manner of Keats. Technically, it is proficient imitation. Hopkins has, for example, read *The Eve of St Agnes* and noted Keats's handling of the alexandrine: 'Down that dark rock o'er which their lush, long tresses weep'. He is a good deal less succesful in his attempts to match Keats's rich sensuality. He does not fail for lack of skill, for he is at least as competent a versifier as Keats was when he wrote *Endymion*. He fails because he does not trust his own sexuality, and he is right not to. Only once in the poem does he achieve the special Keatsian kind of intimacy, and that is when he turns from the mermaids' beauty to their sorrow. He wonders whether they are sad because they 'ring the knells' of drowned sailors:

> or that it is a pain
> To know the dark depths of the ponderous sea,
> The miles profound of solid green, and be
> With loath'd cold fishes ...

(121–4)

That is not, I suppose, very good, but it is very like Keats. Elsewhere the gorgeous diction seems only to mime sensuous apprehension:

> An intense line of throbbing blood-light shook
> A quivering pennon: then, for eye too keen
> Ebb'd back beneath its snowy lids, unseen.

(16–18)

The effects of light and colour are observed with real precision, but the epithets – 'throbbing', 'quivering' – seem mechanically excited.

I mention *A Vision of the Mermaids* to make two points. First, Hopkins is not free to receive any vital influence from Keats's poetry until he has committed himself to rejecting a life of sensual pleasure for a life of spiritual contemplation. Four years later, in 1866, he wrote *The Habit of Perfection*. One by one, the senses are addressed and disciplined:

> Palate, the hutch of tasty lust,
> Desire not to be rinsed with wine ...

The palate is dismissed, but only after it has been offered a phonetic feast. Keats is the best poet in English at finding sounds that seem not to be so much pronounced as tasted, but Hopkins here is very nearly his equal. The sense of touch is similarly celebrated as it is rejected:

> O feel-of-primrose hands, O feet
> That want the yield of plashy sward ...

It is traditional to note in Hopkins a conflict between sensuality and spirituality, but it seems truer to say that he found his sensuality and his vocation together, that he can turn with delight to the 'ruck and reel' of the visible world only in the confidence that such a world is mortal and subordinate.

Second, in *A Vision of the Mermaids* Hopkin's sensuality has a distinctive cast. The western sky is 'Plum-purple' but torn by 'crimson-white' gashes like 'water-lily flakes' in 'beryl lakes'. The zenith is 'crimson' and is reflected by 'rosy-lipp'd waves' and by the cliffs which seem decorated by 'garnet wreaths and blooms of rosy-budded fire'. The mermaids' crests are coloured as if 'sapphire molten-blue' were 'vein'd and streak'd' with 'dusk-deep lazuli', as if 'tender pinks' were stained with 'bloody Tyrian dye'. Their hair, 'pansy-dark or bronzen', is decorated with 'rosy weed' or a 'turquoise-gemm'd / Circlet of astral flowerets'. There are 'fans of amethyst', 'crimson streams', a 'body rosy-pale', 'sapphire hail', 'crimson-golden floods', 'vermeil rein', 'clouds of violet', 'threads of carmine' and a 'blood-vivid clot'. The poem is less a vision of mermaids than of colours. The characters and the objects work only to fix momentarily a kaleidoscope of dazzling, shifting colour. The poem ends not so much when Hopkins rows away and the mermaids disappear as when the colours all disappear into the blank whiteness of the rock around which the mermaids had clustered:

> White loom'd my rock, the water gurgling o'er,
> Whence oft I watch, but see those Mermaids now no more.

> (142–3)

Throughout the poem Hopkins's excitement is expressed through, or disguised as, a play of colour. This is not so surprising, for Hopkins's love of colour is clear in all his verse, and clearer still in his notebooks. He does not only delight in colours, he studies them:

> Note on green wheat. The difference between this green and that of long grass is that the first suggests silver, latter azure. Former more opacity, body, smoothness. It is the exact complement of carnation. Nearest to emerald of any green I know, the real emerald *stone*. It is lucent. Perhaps it has a chrysoprase bloom. Both blue greens.[2]

It is an educated love of colour, and the quotation is enough to indicate that the principal teacher has been Ruskin.[3]

Colour, for Ruskin, is the ground of all visual experience: 'Everything that you see around you presents itself to your eyes only as an arrangement of patches of different colours variously shaded.'[4]

Our knowledge of form derives from experience: our knowledge of colour is direct. Painting, at least its 'technical power', depends upon the painter's ability to release us from the hackneyed adult perception of the world as an assemblage of various objects belonging to some category, such as man, tree, cirrus cloud:

> The whole technical power of painting depends on our recovery of what may be called the *innocence of the eye*; that is to say, of a sort of childish perception of these flat stains of colour, merely as such, without consciousness of what they signify, – as a blind man would see them if suddenly gifted with sight.[5]

We can, if we wish, read Millais's *The Blind Girl* as figuring Ruskin's point. It is the child who looks back at the flat coloured landscape, and the blind girl stares at us as a way of prompting us to see the landscape more innocently than even the child sees it, to see it as the blind girl would if she could, for the first time.

The phrase that Ruskin stresses, the innocence of the eye, is so famous that it is easy to blind ourselves to the fact that Ruskin means just what he says. The painter strips from things the veil of familiarity that obscures the adult's view of them, and he does so by retaining the ability to see like a child. So much Ruskin has in common with Wordsworth, but Wordsworth's sense of the imaginative truth of the child's perception has merged with a Victorian sense of childhood innocence. To see like this, to see 'flat stains of colour, merely as such, without consciousness of what they signify', is to be free from guilt. This seems so odd that it is worth stressing that it is not one of Ruskin's passing eccentricities, but a considered and, for Ruskin, consistently held belief. It is why Ruskin so often celebrates colour as 'the purifying or sanctifying element of material beauty'.[6] To delight in colour is to feel a childish joy, and so to affirm that within the corrupt adult self the innocent child lives on. The great masters of pure colour are the 'Gothic' painters, pre-eminently Fra Angelico, who is Ruskin's type of innocent seeing; pure-minded, innocent, like a child.

Like, it needs to be added, the child Ruskin, for the first experience of beauty that Ruskin remembers is of 'flat stains of colour', the pattern on the carpet in his parents' house.[7] This may be important, but more important still is Ruskin's fear of his own powerful sexuality. The story of Ruskin's marriage has been told too often to need repeating, and is too sad for me to want to tell it over again. It is unfair that Ruskin's brave attempts to come to terms with the body, of which the best mark is his winning through to a passionate admiration of painters such as Titian and Correggio, are less well known. But his efforts, heroic though they were, left him still maimed, destroying the erotic sketches of Turner, the artist he best loved, able to fall in love only with a little girl. It is surely crucial to Ruskin's sense of the innocent eye that it is prepubescent. The stains of colour in which it delights are 'flat', not rounded into the dangerous curves that threaten the purity of the adolescent's visual experience.

When Ruskin celebrates the innocence of the eye he yearns for a kind of seeing that he can no longer quite share, for he is not only recommending a visual habit or a painterly technique, but yearning for his own lost childhood. I doubt whether Hopkins had to learn this from Ruskin: he would have known it for himself. He wrote once to Canon Dixon: 'insight is more sensitive, in fact is more perfect, earlier in life than later and especially towards elementary impressions: I remember that crimson and pure blues seemed to me spiritual and heavenly sights fit to draw tears once.'[8] Hopkins is characteristically more reticent than Ruskin; more, to use a favourite word of his, manly; and he has a firm, adult sense that to find the spiritual and heavenly in blobs of colour is not quite serious. But all the same when he speaks of 'pure blues' he makes Ruskin's connection between a pure colour and a pure mind, the elementary simplicity of the impression and the innocent simplicity of the child.

Moments when he sees colours purely, 'as a blind man would see them if suddenly gifted with sight' are doubly precious for Hopkins, precious because at such moments the experienced eye is shocked out of its callousness, and precious, too, because the adult regains for a moment his ability to respond to the natural world purely, innocently. It is such a moment that Hopkins records in a fragment on a rainbow:

> See on one hand
> He drops his bright roots in the water'd sward,
> And rosing part, on part dispenses green;
> But with his other foot three miles beyond
> He rises from the flock of villages
> That bead the plain; did ever Havering church-tower
> Breathe in such ether? or the Quickly elms
> Mask'd with such violet disallow their green?[9]

The rainbow falls on the church tower and the elms as a mark of special grace signalled by the gentle shock of their change in colour. But the colour changes in kind as well as quality. The tower and the trees are no longer pigmented: they do not have the colour of solid bodies, but shine instead with the disembodied colours of divided light. Such colours, the colours not of matter but of air, for both Ruskin and Hopkins are the types of perfect purity.

The point is made explicit in *The Caged Skylark*. The soul is imprisoned in the mortal body like 'a dare-gale skylark scanted in a dull cage'. The analogy has its dangers. Hopkins risks tempting us to think of the God who imprisons our spirits in a 'bone-house, mean house' in something of the same way that we think of people who put skylarks in cages. But what he wants is the feeling that the caged bird is both 'beyond the remembering his free fells', and yet still aware that the cage is not his proper home. The memory of the wild bird and its life remains for the caged bird only as a bleak consciousness of being out of place, trapped in alien surroundings. Both the imprisoned spirit and the imprisoned bird 'droop deadly sometimes in their cells'. Their weariness is not like that of the wild bird, though the wild bird sometimes also needs to rest:

> Why, hear him, hear him babble and droop down to his nest,
> But his own nest, wild nest, no prison.

Death and the resurrection can now be presented as a homecoming, the soul finding again its own nest, freed at last from the awkward misery of a body that unnaturally, painfully constrains it. In heaven the spirit will not be bodiless: it will find its own body, its proper body, just as the wild skylark finds its own nest:

> Man's spirit will be flesh-bound when found at best
> But uncumbered: meadow-down is not distressed
> For a rainbow footing it nor he for his bones risen.

The resurrected body will rest as lightly on the spirit as a rainbow on a meadow. Freed from its mortal weight the body is unconstricting, rainbow-light. But it is surely more than its lightness that makes the rainbow the proper type of the risen body. When he wishes to imagine flesh purified, Hopkins imagines it transformed into colour. The colour of the rainbow is the perfect choice, for a rainbow is nothing but colour: it is light divided, colour without matter, it can be seen but not touched.

Colour purifies, makes clean. In a letter to Bridges, Hopkins remembers a line from a poem by Dixon, a 'miraculous' line: 'Wind and much wintry blue then swept the earth'.[10] The metaphor is not so much dynamic as housewifely. The blue sky is a nurse's cool uniform as she sweeps her ward clean with the wind. When in his own poetry Hopkins becomes dangerously engaged with the senses, he tends to withdraw into colour. *Hurrahing in Harvest* is the best example. Hopkins greets the barbarous beauty of the summer as a girl greeting her lover. Desire pushes aside fear as she gazes at his 'wilder, wilful-wavier' male energy:

> I walk, I lift up, I lift up heart, eyes,
> Down all that glory in the heavens to glean our Saviour,
> And, eyes, heart, what looks, what lips yet gave you a
> Rapturous love's greeting of realer, of rounder replies?
> And the azurous hung hills are his world-wielding shoulder
> Majestic – as a stallion stalwart – very-violet sweet.

The erotic energy of the season is compacted into the muscled shoulder of the hills, of a stallion, of Christ, but the vision ends, and Hopkins can turn to consider its significance only when the bone and muscle have been softened into the blueness of the hills, only when their violence has been softened into violet.

Hopkins withdraws into 'violet', disengages his more intimate senses the better to contemplate the meaning of his experience. There is no sense, I think, that he flees from the painful joys of eros to the more restful pleasures of the picturesque. But *Hurrahing in Harvest* was written after Hopkins had achieved a measure of emotional security, after he had fallen 'in love' with Christ. *A Vision of the Mermaids* was written before he had found any such self-assurance. It is an adolescent poem, not at all in the sense that Keats is sometimes accused of being adolescent, but because its sensuality is at once frenetic and mechanical. Hopkins purifies his response to the mermaids by dissolving their bodies into a play of colour, but the effect, to use Ruskin's terms, is not at all Gothic, unlikely to remind anyone of Fra Angelico. Unable to confront directly his own eroticism, Hopkins disguises intense feeling as intense colour, but the colours refuse to remain 'flat stains'. Spikes spear open gashes, colours throb, pant and swell into rosy lips. Hopkins's eye is exact and excited, but scarcely innocent. The reds and yellows of the sunset sky are smudged by the young man's troubled yearnings. He cannot see the colours 'merely as such, without consciousness of what they signify': all too clearly they offer themselves to him loaded with covert meaning. He cannot see as a child because he is not a child, and even if, in his later life, when he found in his priesthood a measure of the assurance, the self-acceptance, that as a young man, like most young men, he lacked, and became able once again to see as a child, he could do so only at a cost, the cost of ignoring much in his experience of himself and in his experience of the world around him.

15

Two Flocks, Two Folds – Black, White

'All men, completely organized and justly tempered, enjoy colour,' writes Ruskin: 'it is meant for the perpetual comfort and delight of the human heart: it is richly bestowed on the highest works of creation, and is the eminent sign and seal of perfection in them, being associated with *life* in the human body, with *light* in the sky, and with *purity* and hardness in the earth, – death, night, and pollution of all kinds being colourless.'[1] Beautiful colour is the mark of perfection in nature: love of colour is the badge of health in man. The celebration of colour seems simple and complete. But it is not so. All through his life Ruskin's love of colour vied with other impulses which persuaded him that colour was not at all the most important of material qualities, and love of colour not the best sign of an upright character.

Ruskin insists, for example, that form is more important than colour, and although he will sometimes qualify his judgement so thoroughly that it all but disappears, he never retracts it. Form is in the object, colour in the object and the eye that perceives it together. Form may be seen truly or falsely, whereas if we would speak strictly we cannot speak of colours being truly or falsely represented at all. Colour is a 'secondary and uncertain quality'. We cannot possibly tell whether two men see the same colour, but only whether they 'use the same name for it': 'One man may see yellow whereas another sees blue, but as the effect is constant they agree on the term to be used for it, and both call it blue, or both yellow, having yet totally different ideas attached to the term.'[2] Colours, then, have no place in the public world of shared experience. They give no solid evidence of the world we live in, and they offer no basis for stable aesthetic judgement. It follows that the artist's essential function is to represent the forms of the world around him. The man who sees only the 'flat stains of colour' imprinted on his retina is confined to a kind of seeing in which his private fancies and the facts of the external world are inextricably mixed up. The painter's proper task must be to look through those stains of colour to the form which, because it is 'positive in the object', offers firm knowledge of things as they are.

It was one of Ruskin's misfortunes that he learned to despise German philosophy without having read any. When he thinks philosophically he has nowhere to turn for a model of the mind's relationship with the world except to Locke, and Locke's model is not always appropriate. Ruskin is very ready to ignore the 'secondary and uncertain' status of colour when it suits him. But I do not believe that his subordination of colour to form can be explained just as a genuflection to philosophical orthodoxy. Ruskin has a consistent awareness that the sense of colour is at the mercy of one's mood and one's physical condition, easily disturbed by petulance or indigestion, and so not quite trustworthy and not quite serious.

Ruskin wrestled throughout his career with the rival claims of form and colour. He divided painters into two classes? the chiaroscurists, who subordinated colour to form, and the colourists, who subordinated form to colour.[3] The colourists he thought of as members of the Gothic school, or of the school of crystal, whereas the chiaroscurists were Greek, members of the school of clay. Ruskin's love of the Gothic, of the school of crystal, is countered by a stern sense of duty that pulls him towards Greek art and the school of clay, and at last, though the struggle never ended, it was his sense of duty that won:

> If you want to paint... in the Greek School, the school of Leonardo, Correggio and Turner, you cannot design coloured windows, nor Angelican paradises. If, on the other hand, you choose to live in the peace of paradise, you canot share in the gloomy triumphs of the earth. ... For my own part, with what poor gift and skill is in me, I belong wholly to the chiaroscurist school.[4]

The contrast between the two schools is a contrast between childhood and adulthood, innocence and experience. No chiaroscurist can match the charm of Fra Angelico, nor his innocent purity, but, for all that, the chiaroscurists have 'the highest powers of thought'. To move from the school of crystal to the school of clay is to be conscious, first of all, of loss, of colours dimmed and become turbid, of innocent purity clouded, but to refuse to make the transition is to remain forever a child. Angelico's purism, however delightful, is childishly fanciful in comparison with the naturalism of the great masters. But Ruskin yearns for childhood innocence even as he rejects it. He delights in showing his Oxford students the work of the Gothic colourists:

> As long as I can possibly keep you there there you shall stay – among the almond and apple blossom. But if you go on into the veracities of the school of Clay, you will find there is something at the roots of almond and apple trees, which is – this – and that [here he showed his audience two dragons; one by Turner, one by Michelangelo]. You must look at him in the face – fight him – conquer him with what scathe you may: you need not think to keep out of the way of him.[5]

Dragons, for Ruskin, live inside and outside the head. The dragon binds together Ruskin's hatred of nineteenth-century materialism, its loss of faith in the spirit, and nineteenth-century ugliness, its factories spitting out fire and smoke. To ignore 'the veracities of the school of Clay' is to remain a child, to turn away from the dark side of the human mind, and to evade the pressing realities of modern life, its industrial squalor and economic cruelty. The heroic man confronts this compound monster: he does not shrink from it into a world of 'almond and apple blossom'. But the dragon is not Ruskin's most powerful symbol for this complex of ideas. In 1884 he announced that the middle of the nineteenth century had witnessed the birth of a new kind of weather, the storm-cloud of the nineteenth century, a dark, louring cloud driven by an east wind, a plague wind, that blotted out the sunlight for weeks together over all the western world.[6] It is not like any storm-cloud that the world has known before. Those clouds gave birth to the rainbow, and if they hid the sun they hid it 'through gold and vermilion'. The new cloud simply obscures. It steeps the sun in its own murk. The effect is exactly what we would gain were we to 'throw a bad half-crown into a basin of soap and water'. Ruskin insists that his lecture is matter of fact, his concern only to describe a new weather condition. But it is not a lecture at all: it is the vision of an unhinged prophet. Ruskin is growing old: the east wind is not good for his rheumatism. His eyes, once so sensitive, are not what they were. He looks at the Turners he loves and their colours seem sadly faded. He looks at the sun as it sets over Coniston, and its reds and golds seem bastard sons of the colours he saw in his youth. He looks inside himself and finds depression darkening his mental landscape. In a grandiose gesture he takes the dark cloud that sits in his own head and spreads it over all Europe. But it is not just this, for Ruskin was never quite mad. In the storm-cloud Ruskin's private perturbation reaches out to join with the pall of sooty smog that rests over every industrial city of the West, until a personal cry of pain becomes a prophetic rage. In *The Storm-Cloud of the Nineteenth Century* Ruskin finally joins the chiaroscurist school. He paints a picture in some black, much grey, and a little white like 'a bad half-crown'. The storm-cloud marks the school of crystal, the school of Gothic colour, as dead, irrelevant. Only chiaroscuro can model the truths that Ruskin now finds it urgent to announce.

The young Hopkins found in Catholicism the best defence against what he calls 'the sordidness of things': 'this is (objectively) intensified and (subjectively) destroyed by Catholicism'.[7] That is to say, man and his works seem even more sordid to the convert, but he learns not to mind about it. Working men may still spit in the gutter, but such things pass, and there will be no bronchitis in the kingdom of heaven. We do not know how Hopkins's Jesuit superiors responded to this painful refinement, but it may be no coincidence that they sent him, early in his priesthood, to Liverpool and to Glasgow. God is one refuge from 'the sordidness of things': nature is another. This is the octave of Hopkins's *Spring*

> Nothing is so beautiful as Spring –
> When weeds, in wheels, shoot long and lovely and lush;
> Thrush's eggs look little low heavens, and thrush
> Through the echoing timber does so rinse and wring
> The ear, it strikes like lightnings to hear his sing;
> The glassy peartree leaves and blooms, they brush
> The descending blue; that blue is all in a rush
> With richness, the racing lambs too have fair their fling.

One is grateful, of course, for such bounding joy. It is a touch unfair to place next to it one of Ruskin's moral landscapes:

> It is a little valley of soft turf, enclosed in its narrow oval by jutting rocks and broad flakes of nodding fern. From one side of it to the other winds, serpentine, a clear brown stream, drooping into quicker ripple as it reaches the end of the oval field, and then, first islanding a purple and white rock with an amber pool, it dashes

away into a narrow fall of foam under a thicket of mountain-ash and alder. The autumn sun, low but clear, shines on the scarlet ash-berries and on the golden birch-leaves, which, fallen here and there, when the breeze has not caught them, rest quiet in the crannies of the purple rock. Beside the rock, in the hollow under the thicket, the carcass of a ewe, drowned in the last flood, lies nearly bare to the bone, its white ribs protruding through the skin, raven-torn; and the rags of its wool still flickering from the branches that first stayed it as the stream swept it down. A little lower, the current plunges, roaring, into a circular chasm like a well, surrounded on three sides by a chimney-like hollowness of polished rock, down which the foam slips in detached snow-flakes. Round the edges of the pool beneath, the water circles slowly, like black oil; a little butterfly lies on its back, its wings glued to one of the eddies, its limbs feebly quivering; a fish rises, and it is gone. Lower down the stream, I can just see, over a knoll, the green and damp turf roofs of four or five hovels, built at the edge of a morass, which is trodden by the cattle into a black Slough of Despond at their doors, and traversed by a few ill-set stepping-stones, with here and there a flat slab on the tops, where they have sunk out of sight; and at the turn of the brook I see a man fishing, with a boy and a dog – a picturesque and pretty group enough certainly, if they had not been there all day starving.[8]

If the comparison suggests that Hopkins would have done better when looking at the spring landscape to think of the poor, then it is grossly unfair. The poor may always be with us but we cannot always be thinking of them. It is rather that Ruskin sees the Scottish valley in autumn more comprehensively than Hopkins sees the landscape that he describes. Ruskin sees the rowan, as Hopkins sees it elsewhere, 'bead-bonny', and he is fascinated, as Hopkins always is, by the complex beauty of moving water. But he sees too the carcass of a drowned sheep, and a butterfly struggling feebly in the water until it is gulped down by a fish. No such incidents compromise the pure beauty of Hopkins's *Spring*, and they could not do so, for the beauty that he describes is incompatible with such things. He is an exponent, here, of what Ruskin calls the purist ideal; that is, he finds the beauty that he seeks by purifying the natural world of everything but the beautiful. Such idealism, writes Ruskin, 'results from the unwillingness of men whose dispositions are more than ordinarily tender and holy to contemplate the various forms of definite evil which necessarily occur in the daily aspect of the world around them'.[9] The work of such men is 'always childish, but beautiful in its childishness',[10] and it is *'always* an indication of some degree of weakness in the mind', an incapacity to confront the chequered truth of our experience.[11] Ruskin's remarks may seem moralistic to modern readers, but he is tactful and generous in his severity. He insists that purism is a lesser form of art than naturalism, but he insists too that scorn of the purist ideal is the sign of a greater weakness than any the purist is guilty of. He would have us see that these men are not the greatest of artists, but he would have us love them first.

May is Mary's month, and Mary born 'without spot' secures the connection Hopkins finds between springtime, childhood innocence and an unfallen world. In springtime he hears:

> A strain of the earth's sweet being in the beginning
> In Eden garden.

He knows that spring is a passing season. He celebrates an innocence that he accepts can only be glimpsed before it is corrupted. Childhood innocence, 'Innocent mind and Mayday in girl and boy' can last no more than spring, and natural innocence is everywhere threatened by the depradations of fallen man. It is just that he presents such things as threatening natural beauty and his poetic vision together.

In *The Sea and the Skylark* he stands with one ear turned to the beat of the waves, one to the song of the bird, but his eyes rest on a Welsh town. The sounds are 'two noises too old to end', and they have also 'the cheer and charm of earth's past prime'. Together they 'ring right out our sordid, turbid time, / Being pure'. The sea and the skylark give him a sense of the town's sordidness that is '(objectively) intensified and (subjectively) destroyed'. The study of towns becomes a branch of scatology, the type of urban architecture a sewage system:

> Our make and making break, are breaking, down
> To man's last dust, drain fast towards man's first slime.

But at the same time the town becomes insubstantial, 'shallow and frail'. It will be survived, as it was preceded, by the sound of the sea and the song of the skylark. The sea and the bird intensify Hopkins's sense of the town's vileness, but as they do so they expose the town as little more than an illusion, a passing nightmare.

Ruskin notes that the distinguishing characteristic of modern colour is its cloudiness.[12] A painter such as Turner cannot match the flat purity of Angelico's colours, and it would be wrong were he to try. Angelico is childish in his refusal to admit the cloudiness of daily life, but his is a genuine childishness. Ruskin had nothing but contempt for the German Nazarenes, who, it seemed to him, mimicked Angelico's methods without sharing his vision. Hopkins, just as clearly as Ruskin, knows that man is fallen, that the pure colours of Eden are clouded:

> And all is seared with trade; bleared, smeared with toil;
> And wears man's smudge and shares man's smell ...

His is a 'sordid, turbid time'. But still he celebrates what he can only glimpse momentarily:

> Have, get, before it cloy,
> Before it cloud, Christ, lord, and sour with sinning ...

He speaks to Christ. He might as well be talking to himself.

I say might as well, but I mean might better. Hopkins is rather too ready to credit Christ with his own fastidiousness. There is something weak and disturbing in Hopkins's dismissal of the bugler boy:

> Let me though see no more of him, and not disappointment
> Those sweet hopes quell whose least me quickenings lift ...

He ought not, one feels, to be more concerned with his own feelings than with his priestly duties. In a letter to Bridges the weakness spills over into viciousness:

> I enclose a poem, the Bugler. I am half inclined to hope the Hero of it may be killed in Afghanistan.[13]

It would be wrong to suggest that Hopkins's inclination to hope that the bugler is quickly killed is an expression of the same prayer that ends *Spring*:

Have, get, before it cloy,
Before it cloud, Christ, lord, and sour with sinning,
Innocent mind and Mayday in girl and boy,
Most, O maid's child, thy choice and worthy the winning.

But it would be just as wrong, surely, to claim that the two are quite
unconnected. Both are expressions of Ruskin's purism, not the
purism that he describes – for Ruskin cannot share Angelico's vision
of a world perfectly and always beautiful any more than Hopkins
can – so much as the purism that he feels in himself, a fastidious
flinching from ugliness, a readiness to see it only as the enemy of
natural beauty and of the beautiful in art. The souring of spring
freshness and the sordid Welsh town can exist within *Spring* and *Sea
and Skylark* only as threats to the beauty that the poems celebrate,
and hence as threats to the poems themselves. They make the
beauty more intense by making it precarious, but they also limit it. It
is a beauty defined by its exclusion of much that is most pressing in
what Ruskin calls 'the daily aspect of the world', and it is akin to the
beauty that Hopkins sees in the bugler boy. Aware only of boyish
innocence Hopkins can see contact between him and the rough
soldiery only as a desecration. He prays that the boy will live safe
within his innocence as within a magic circle, an 'our day's God's
own Galahad', but he has no confidence in his prayer. Hopkins's
inclination to hope that the boy is killed is consistent with the poem,
for only by death can the boy be protected not only from his fellow
soldiers but from all that in the boy that finds no place in Hopkins's
exclusive vision. The vision must be preserved even if the boy has to
die to preserve it.

'Let me though see no more of him', Hopkins prays, and
confesses in the prayer that his concern is less for the bugler than for
himself. He betrays, as Ruskin has it, his Angelican disposition, the
'unwillingness of men, whose dispositions are more than ordinarily
tender and holy, to contemplate the various forms of definite evil
which necessarily occur in the daily aspect of the world around
them'. But is it really only the impurity of the rough soldiers, the
sordidness of the outside world that moves Hopkins to dismiss the
bugler boy so callously? Hopkins is tremblingly alive to the boy's
lissomness, his 'limber liquid youth'. When touched, he 'Yields
tender as a pushed peach'. His charming moral impressionableness
tiptoes on the edge of becoming a dangerous physical succulence.
His wish to see the boy no more betrays, surely, not just Hopkins's

fears for the boy's soul, but for his own. A reading of *The Bugler's First Communion* does not compromise Hopkins's success in poems such as *Spring* and *Sea and Skylark*, but it shows that they are successful within strict limits. Hopkins has only to turn his gaze from a countryside seen as 'pure', perfectly innocent and perfectly beautiful, to a human being for the gasp of naïve awe to tumble into a vicious sentimentality.

When Ruskin struggles away from the colourists, the school of crystal, towards the chiaroscurists, the school of clay, he is not simply announcing – though that is part of it – that Tintoretto is a greater painter than Fra Angelico. It is a struggle against all that in himself that would rather sit under almond and apple blossom than take up the sword against the dragon. His struggle is Hopkins's struggle, too. In *Andromeda* Perseus meets the dragon. In *Tom's Garland* Hopkins turns, as Ruskin had before him, to consider the unemployed, the waste matter ejected by a society that now operates like one of the industrial processes that enrich it. The contrast is clearest if one turns from *Spring* to the sonnets of 1885. In *Spring* Hopkins is a colourist:

> The glassy peartree leaves and blooms, they brush
> The descending blue; that blue is all in a rush
> With richness; the racing lambs too have fair their fling.

But the late sonnets are written in chiaroscuro:

> I wake and feel the fell of dark, not day.
> What hours, O what black hours we have spent
> This night! what sights you, heart, saw; ways you went!
> And more must, in yet longer light's delay.

The harmony of colour, the leaves and blossom of the pear tree against a blue sky, has given way to a stark opposition between darkness and light. Hopkins struggles with a 'dark' heaven, a Christ with 'darksome devouring eyes'. He can no more find comfort that 'blind / Eyes in their dark can day'. He has lived through a night, a year, 'Of now done darkness'. And the darkness is interrupted only by brief flashes of light, as when Hopkins understands that the pain he feels is a kind of threshing: 'Why? that my chaff might fly: my grain lie, sheer and clear'. Or when his inner darkness is suddenly lit by God's smile, 'as skies / Betweenpie mountains – lights a lovely mile'.

At the threshold, between the world of colour and chiaroscuro, is the sibyl who minds the gate to the underworld. *Spelt from Sibyl's Leaves*, written, it seems, early in 1885, introduces the terrible sonnets written later in that year by announcing Hopkins's allegiance to the Greek school, the school of chiaroscuro:

> Only the beakleaved boughs dragonish damask the tool smooth
> bleak light, black,
> Ever so black on it, Our tale, O our oracle! Let life, waned, ah let
> life wind
> Off her once skeined stained veined variety upon, all on two
> spools; part, pen, pack
> Now her all in two flocks, two folds – black, white; right, wrong;
> reckon but, reck but, mind
> But these two; ware of a world where but these two tell, each off
> the other; of a rack
> Where, selfwrung, selfstrung, sheathe- and shelterless, thoughts
> against thoughts in groans grind.

All colours, all 'veined variety', disappear in the darkness leaving only 'boughs dragonish' silhouetted against the sky, leaving only 'black, white'. All the glancing coloured lights and coloured shades of the daytime earth, earth's dapple, is at an end, and seems now only a distraction from the stark opposition, the stark choice, 'black, white; right, wrong'. And as Ruskin warned his students of the perils of such a world even as he showed it to them, so Hopkins warns, 'ware of a world where but these two tell'. But to beware is to be aware, and once aware there is no return to a world where the eye delights in subtle gradations of colour. All colours are gathered on to two spools, and the black and white jar against each other. They make 'a rack / Where, selfwrung, selfstrung, sheathe- and shelterless, thoughts against thoughts in groans grind'.

16

Dappled Things

In *Spring* Hopkins looks at the fresh beauty of a daytime world, but the only spiritual truth that such a world can figure is the truth of childhood innocence, 'Innocent mind and Mayday in girl and boy'. When Hopkins wishes to figure the truths of adult experience, he looks at a night landscape, a landscape in which nature's 'stained veined variety' is obscured, and the eye, undistracted, can turn inwards to contemplate the grating of 'thoughts against thoughts'. To look at nature is to be distracted, too, from death. Nature is everywhere vital: 'weeds, in wheels, shoot long and lovely and lush'. The blue daytime sky, 'all in a rush', distracts us from our mortality. Night-time reminds us that man is a spark in the darkness that flashes momentarily, and is then 'in an enormous dark / Drowned':

> Manshape, that shone
> Shear off, disseveral, a star, death blots black out; nor mark
> Is any of him at all so stark
> But vastness blurs and time beats level.

It is a fragile star set amidst blurring, levelling darkness that best figures the precariousness of man's life, and concentrates his mind on its proper business: death and the resurrection. In these late poems, *Spelt from Sibyl's Leaves* and *That Nature is a Heraclitean Fire and of the comfort of the Resurrection*, the daytime world is rejected in favour of night-time, and the concentration that night-time encourages on death and the reality of inner experience, thoughts.

To compare *Spring* with *Spelt from Sibyl's Leaves* is to find a contrast between colour and chiaroscuro, childhood innocence and adult experience, the fact of sensual experience and the terrible spiritual truths from which joyous sensuality can only distract us. Hopkins wrote also a group of poems that mediate between these poles, and these poems are surely his richest achievement. Colour may be reconciled with light and shade rather than opposed to them: it may be dappled.

Again the proper comparison is with Ruskin, for Ruskin is at his most critically sure not when he is opposing colour and chiaroscuro, but when he is celebrating their reconciliation. Titian, born a colourist, becomes a perfect painter when he assimilates all the truths of the chiaroscurist. Turner, born a chiaroscurist, becomes almost perfect when he assimilates all the truths of the school of colour. In his praise of Turner and Titian Ruskin reconciles, if only briefly, his love of beauty with his respect for truth, his love of nature with his love of man. He looks at the great works of Turner and Titian, neither Gothic nor Greek, neither of the school of crystal nor of clay, and finds in them the type of his own hard-won and short-lived inner harmony. Titian and Turner are exponents of the naturalist ideal, men who look hard at the world and see it as it is, loving the beautiful but not flinching from the ugly, and creating at the last a beauty that is stronger than the purist's, for it comprehends all that the purist has had to exclude because it does not fit his weaker, more childish vision. Ruskin's central concern in the final three volumes of *Modern Painters* and in the second and third volumes of *The Stones of Venice* is to define a single aesthetic ideal, naturalism, and these books represent his greatest critical achievement.

In comparison with Titian or with Turner, Hopkins is a minor artist, but all the same dappling is best thought of as Hopkins's version of Ruskin's naturalist ideal. *Pied Beauty* is a naturalist's manifesto:

> Glory be to God for dappled things –
> For skies of couple-colour as a brinded cow;
> For rose-moles all in stipple upon trout that swim;
> Fresh-firecoal chestnut falls; finches' wings;
> Landscape plotted and pieced – fold, fallow, and plough;
> And all trades, their gear and tackle and trim.
> All things counter, original, spare, strange;
> Whatever is fickle, freckled (who knows how?)
> With swift, slow; sweet, sour; adazzle, dim;
> He fathers-forth whose beauty is past change:
> > Praise him.

The painterly point is that dappling includes contrast and gradation of light and shade as well as contrast and gradation of colour. It is the technique that Ruskin thought of as Titianesque, Turnerian. But the power of Ruskin's criticism depends on his rare ability to wield a rhetoric that insists on the interdependence of the breadth of a painter's technique and the breadth of his moral vision, and the same is surely true of Hopkins. In *Spring*, Mayday innocence is threatened by clouding and by souring, but in *Pied Beauty* the sour and the dim just as much as the sweet and the adazzle have their place within a more comprehensive ideal of beauty. The result is that adult experience and adult industry, seen in *Spring* and *Sea and Skylark* only as sinning and sewage, threats to the beauty that the poems celebrate and so threats to the poems themselves, can be included within a naturalistic vision. There is place here for 'all trades, their gear and tackle and trim'.

God's Grandeur might seem in contrast to be a purist poem, for it prizes a 'freshness' that has now retreated 'deep down things', away from man. God's grandeur flames out only intermittently, or it oozes through a surface of experience that men have utterly besmirched:

> all is seared with trade; bleared, smeared with toil;
> And wears man's smudge and shares man's smell.

As in *Spring* and as in *Sea and Skylark* blearing, smearing and smudging seem only threats to the pure and the fresh. But it is not really so. For one thing God's grandeur is 'like the ooze of oil / Crushed', and it would be a startlingly incompetent poet who presented oily ooze as the fresh antithesis of blearing and smearing. And in any case the simple contrast between the pure and the dirty is nullified in the poem's magical conclusion:

> And though the last lights off the black West went
> Oh, morning, at the brown brink eastward, springs –
> Because the Holy Ghost over the bent
> World broods with warm breast and with ah! bright wings.

The world is 'bent', crooked, fallen, but it is 'bent' too in acceptance of the authority and the love of the Holy Ghost. The poem ends when it finds the connection between the fact of man's depravity and the miracle of God's mercy. For God to 'brood' over the world, to meditate sadly on man and his plight, is the same as for him to cherish it with a 'warm breast', as a mother bird her egg. In the final line there is a 'black West', a brown eastern horizon, and the 'bright wings' of dawn. The poem ends, we might say, when Hopkins realises that you need not use oil just to make yourself and everything around you dirty. You can use it to paint with.

Hopkins did not, of course, make a neat progress from purism to naturalism. *God's Grandeur, Spring* and *Pied Beauty* were written in that order within a few months of each other in 1877. I do not mean the terms to denote stages of development but alternative reflexes in response to mixed experience. In one mood Hopkins embraces the pure, and registers the sour and the dim only as threats to his vision. In another he accepts both, and tries to win from the clash between them a vision in which they are reconciled.

The Wreck of the Deutschland begins with Hopkins in 'dread' of God, pinioned between the 'frown of his face' and 'the hurtle of hell'. But his fear of God is at once the fear of 'lightning and lashed rod' and the ecstatic nervousness of a bride at her wedding to a lusty groom:

> The swoon of a heart that the sweep and the hurl of thee trod
> > Hard down with a horror of height:
> And the midriff astrain with leaning of, laced with fire of
> > > > > stress.
>
> > > > > > > (15–16)

He becomes 'soft sift / In an hourglass'. He is reduced to a recognition of his own mortality, but at the same time his being disintegrates into a crumbling swoon within a body now swollen into stiff womanly curves. The verse throughout this opening passage is palpably erotic:

> Thou hast bound bones and veins in me, fastened me flesh,
> And after it almost unmade, what with dread,
> Thy doing: and dost thou touch me afresh?
> Over again I feel thy finger and find thee.
>
> > > > > > > (5–8)

It gains its momentum from Hopkins at once shuddering at the 'lashed rod' and shivering at the subtle pressure of a lover's finger, and knowing that both responses are alike recognitions of the deep love that God feels for him. In the poem's first four stanzas Hopkins tells the story of an inner drama which is resolved when sensuality and spirituality, and love and dread are accommodated one to another, when Hopkins can name the same thing as a 'pressure' and a 'principle', when he can feel his own mortality as 'Christ's gift'. Hopkins finds peace, and in that peace he can open his eyes and look at the world around him. He sees a night sky at once stormy and starry and with sunset still discolouring the western horizon. He kisses his hands to the stars 'lovely-asunder' and to the 'dappled-with-damson west'. This is Hopkins's first use in verse of the word 'dapple'. It marks a moment when the chill beauty of the chiaroscurist, an arrangement in light and dark, is varied by damson stains, and the two together make a sky on which Hopkins can gaze and find the proper type of his spiritual repose.

The mental buffeting that Hopkins endures in the opening stanzas of the poem prefigures the 'buck and flood' of the waves that sweep over the *Deutschland* when the ship founders on a sandbank off the Kentish coast. Hopkins, who finds the love of God in his spiritual terror, prefigures the glory of the tall nun who finds Christ's love in her drowning. Even the nuns' exile from Germany has its counterpart in Hopkins's distance from family and friends 'On a pastoral forehead of Wales'. Hopkins finds the nun's plight in himself, but the effect is not at all egotistical. He makes no claim to share in her heroism:

> I was under a roof here, I was at rest,
> And they the prey of the gales ...

> (191–2)

It is just that in order to pay her proper tribute he must understand how it was for her, and he can only do so by searching his own, more humdrum life for what in his own experience is the shadow of her glory.

His discovery that God's 'terror', 'the frown of his face', is only an aspect of God's love helps him to understand how the tall nun can see in all that is before her – the waves breaking over the deck, icy fingers losing hold, people rolling 'With the sea-romp over the deck' – a clear indication of Christ's love for mankind. She sees the majesty of the terrible: it becomes the pomp and ceremony of the wedding procession bringing her bridegroom to her, and she cries, 'O Christ, Christ, come quickly'. She 'christens her wild-worst best',

as Hopkins too had done, only less grandly, and like him she is
rewarded by calm joy:

> For how to the heart's cheering
> The down-dugged ground-hugged grey
> Hovers off, the jay-blue heavens appearing
> Of pied and peeled May!
> Blue-beating and hoary-glow height; or night, still higher,
> With belled fire and the moth-soft Milky Way …
>
> $$(201-6)^1$$

Hopkins saw a night sky patched with storm cloud, but with stars
still visible, 'lovely-asunder', and a 'dappled-with-damson west'. A
natural sky is appropriate to his victory, but in token of hers he
offers a miracle; all at once a blanket of low winter cloud, snow
cloud, the blue skies of spring, and the 'moth-soft' Milky Way. For
him the dark sky is mottled in the west by the dark purple of
damsons. These purplish remnants of sunset are purified into the
'jay-blue' skies of spring, and just as Hopkins speaks of the
'dappled-with-damson west' he introduces here his other word for
dappling: the blue sky is the sky of 'pied' and peeled May.

For Ruskin and for Hopkins naturalism reconciles beauty and
truth, and it also reconciles physical fact with spiritual meaning, the
scientist's world of things with the human and divine world of
values. To pursue beauty at the expense of truth is to be guilty of one
kind of childishness; to pursue spiritual truth at the expense of
physical fact is to be guilty of another. Hopkins looks kindly on it.
He admires, for example, Dixon's poem *Fallen Rain*:

> It is the most delicate and touching piece of imagination in the
> world. While on the one hand delighting in this play of
> imagination a perverse over-perspectiveness of mind nudges me
> that the rain could never be wooed by the rainbow which only
> comes into being by its falling nor could witness the wooing when
> made any more than the quicksilver can look from the outside
> back into the glass. However it is the imagination of the
> 'prescientific' child that you here put on.[2]

Hopkins is, I suspect, only polite in calling his objection perverse (in
his own poems on rainbows he is careful to avoid such blunders).

He likes Dixon's poem, but he is aware too that however charmingly Dixon may express the imagination of the prescientific child such an imagination can now only be 'put on'.

Hopkins does not believe that one honours the spiritual by disregarding the material. One of the last of the long line of literary projects that Hopkins never carried through was to be 'a sort of popular account of Light and the Ether'. The book was to correct not the materialism of contemporary science, but its abstraction:

> The study of physical science has, unless corrected in some way, an effect the very opposite of what one would suppose. One would think it might materialize people (no doubt it does make them or, rather I shd. say, they become materialists; but that is not the same thing: they do not believe in Matter more but in God less); but in fact they seem to end in conceiving only of a world of formulas, with its being properly speaking in thought, towards which the outer world acts as a sort of feeder, supplying examples for literary purposes.[3]

Contemporary science retreats from God, but it retreats too from the material world. Its purpose is to abandon God and the material world together in favour of a mental vacuum peopled by abstract presences, mathematical formulas. I take Hopkins's account from a letter to Dixon, and it may be that he took a not quite kind pleasure in convicting the scientists of exactly that failing that he had gently indicated in Dixon's *Fallen Rain*, using the world only as 'a sort of feeder, supplying examples for literary purposes'. In any case, the ambition of his own poetry is clear enough: he wishes to praise God and the material world together, so that the more accurately the material world is described the more accurately it will reveal the presence of its maker.

Hopkins's religious vision includes near its centre a faith in God's presence within the material world. The key moments in history are those when God affirms that presence; in the Creation, in the covenant God made with Noah after the flood, the covenant signed by a rainbow, and, most wonderfully, in the life of Christ. Hopkins was devoted to Mary because the incarnation took place within her. She gave 'God's infinity':

> Welcome in womb and breast,
> Birth, milk, and all the rest ...

(20–1)

Through her the rich sensuality of human experience was divinely sanctioned. In all his poems on Mary, Hopkins celebrates the wedding of spirit and flesh, of God with the material universe. The most considerable of these is *The Blessed Virgin compared to the Air we Breathe*.

The poem is in two parts. The first begins from the fact that we must breathe in order to live:

> This air, which, by life's law,
> My lung must draw and draw ...

(13–14)

As we need air, and as air is all around us, so we need Mary, who is also all around us. What we need is Christ in Mary, Christ in the act of accommodating himself to a human body, and we need that because the fact that Christ could live within Mary's body is the guarantee that he may live within ours.

> Of her flesh he took flesh:
> He does take fresh and fresh,
> Though much the mystery how,
> Not flesh but spirit now
> And makes, O marvellous!
> New Nazareths in us ...

(55–60)

This section of the poem works to reveal the full significance of the word *spirit*, which means both breath or air and the immaterial. What Hopkins would have us see is that with every breath we take, as the life-giving oxygen mingles with our blood, we figure the incarnation. By breathing a man allays 'The death-dance in his blood'; he calms the buzzing pressure that we feel whenever we hold our breath, and this is the natural sign that Christ's promise of eternal life is here, now, if we will only accept it:

> Men here may draw like breath
> More Christ and baffle death.

(66–7)

In the act of breathing, drawing air or spirit into the body, life is sustained. For Hopkins the choice of whether to live in the exercise of religious faith or whether to live as an atheistic materialist was a choice between living and choosing not to live at all. Materialists can offer no account of even the simplest human experiences. Their account of hearing stops at the ear, of seeing at the eye. But it is obvious that, though an ear might register sounds, it could never listen to them. It could register, for example, a noise, but it could not understand a word. The eye might allow flat stains of colour to be imprinted on its retina, but it could never see a tree. Living, as opposed to the mere existence of inert matter, requires that at each moment the material be impregnated with spirit, and for Hopkins this crucial truth is figured in the fact that our bodies are kept alive only by drawing into themselves every few seconds 'air's fine flood'. It is important to Hopkins that the word *spirit* is a pun. But if he were to leave it there he would be guilty of a Dixonism; for air, even if it can penetrate the 'fleeciest, frailest-flixed snowflake' is, after all, still matter. That is why he does not compare the air we breathe to Christ, but to Mary, who was 'Merely a woman'. The one meaning of the word *spirit*, air, contains the other meaning not by a loose and untrue natural analogy but by a miracle, as Mary's body contained God.

The poem's second part begins from the fact that the sky is Mary's colour, blue:

> Again look overhead
> How air is azured …

> (73–4)

Rays of sunlight hit the earth's atmospheric cocoon at an angle and are fractured. The most refrangible are bent back to form the blue of the sky. For Shelley that fact figures the limitations of mortal experience – life lived in motley under 'a dome of many-coloured glass' cut off from the white radiance of eternity. But Shelley thought that because, though not a materialist, he was what Hopkins robustly termed a 'pagan'. He cannot be right. He is disproved by the fact of the incarnation. What Hopkins stresses is that:

> this blue heaven
> The seven or seven times seven
> Hued sunbeam will transmit
> Perfect, not alter it.
>
> (86–9)

Hopkins accepts that when they hit the earth's atmosphere some
light rays must be fragmented or the sky would not be blue, but he
insists that this cannot be true of all rays, for, if that were so, the sky
would be the only blue thing we ever saw: no blue rays could
penetrate the atmosphere and be reflected back to us in, for
example, the blue of the bluebells that Hopkins loved. Hopkins
presents the blueness of the sky as the proof that we are bathed in
the white light of eternity, not that we are cut off from it:

> The glass-blue days are those
> When every colour glows,
> Each shape and shadow shows ...
>
> (83–5)

Hopkins's version is truer – it has a stronger factual basis than
Shelley's – but it is not quite true enough for Hopkins. He is not
content with the paradox that the sky is at once 'glass' and 'blue':
perfectly transparent and coloured. He knows that air, atmosphere,
does alter the colour of objects, and alters it the more perceptibly the
more air intervenes between the object and the eye. Distant hills, for
example, are blue because the air is, ever so slightly, blue. Hopkins
claims only that the light dust of blue that the air sprinkles on distant
things makes them prettier:

> Or if there does some soft,
> On things aloof, aloft,
> Bloom breathe, that one breath more
> Earth is the fairer for ...
>
> (90–3)

This is a major concession. Hopkins is forced to give up the claim
that in the atmosphere of mortal life beauty and truth may be

perfectly reconciled. He is forced into the purist or childish preference for the pretty rather than the true, but he is forced into that position not because he has too little respect for facts, but because he has too much respect for them. He is too wary of Dixonism to pretend that the air is not slightly coloured.

If it were not for the sky, 'This bath of blue':

> the sun would shake
> A blear and blinding ball
> With blackness bound, and all
> The thick stars round him roll
> Flashing like flecks of coal,
> Quartz-fret, or spark of salt,
> In grimy vast vault.
> So God was god of old ...
>
> (96–103)

The sky, the atmosphere, diffuses sunlight. Without it the sun would be a 'blinding ball' set in black space, and we could see only a contrast between the horror of black darkness and the appalling majesty of God. The universe would be displayed to us 'all in two flocks, two folds – black, white; right, wrong', and Hopkins would have us be 'ware of a world where but these two tell'. It is the world of the Old Testament, as God was 'of old'. We are separated from it by the fact of the incarnation, which at once changes nothing, and utterly transforms everything. It cannot change the nature of God, for his nature is immutable, but it changes our perception of his nature, and Mary is praised as the instrument of that change of perception:

> Through her we may see him
> Made sweeter, not made dim,
> And her hand leaves his light
> Sifted to suit our sight ...
>
> (110–13)

In the Old Testament God demands that he be recognised and obeyed, and he still insists on that no less clearly, but the duty has become sweet, because through the incarnation God has made himself lovable. The 'glass-blue days' are those:

When every colour glows,
Each shape and shadow shows ...

(84–5)

They are dappled days, days when the truth of the colourist is
reconciled with the truth of the chiaroscurist. To look at God's
majesty, his 'glory bare', is to be reminded that each one of us is
justly damned and condemned to live forever in darkness, in the
'grimy vasty vault'. We ought to know that, but to know too that
through Christ we may be saved, not by God's simple sense of
justice, but by the higher justice of his love. The blue sky interceding
between blind blackness and blinding light becomes for Hopkins a
badge of the trust in Christ's love that is the only thing that can
sustain us. Dappling, colour reconciled with light and shade,
becomes a sign of God's justice reconciled with God's love. Hopkins
loves colour because colour figures for him his hope of salvation.

17

Gold-Vermilion

The Blessed Virgin compared to the Air we Breathe is an important poem, but for all its charm it is in the end more important as a clear statement of ideas important to Hopkins than for itself. It is diffuse, and Hopkins seems uncomfortable with the short line and the rhyme scheme, a mixture of couplets and triplets. He knew as much: 'It is partly a compromise with popular taste, and it is too true that the highest subjects are not those on which it is easy to reach one's highest.'[1] *The Windhover*, though, he described as 'the best thing I ever wrote':[2]

> I caught this morning morning's minion, kingdom of daylight's
> dauphin, dapple-dawn-drawn Falcon, in his riding
> Of the rolling level underneath him steady air, and striding
> High there, how he rung upon the rein of a wimpling wing
> In his ecstasy! then off, off forth on swing,
> As a skate's heel sweeps smooth on a bow-bend: the hurl and
> gliding
> Rebuffed the big wind. My heart in hiding
> Stirred for a bird – the achieve of, the mastery of the thing!

What Hopkins catches, seizes in a moment of understanding, is the relationship between the bird and the wind. The bird rides the wind as a cavalier his horse, at once accommodating himself to the horse's movement and subduing the horse's will to his own. In flight the falcon proclaims its self, selves. The pressure of air that sustains the bird does not limit but defines the falcon's selfhood. The falcon 'Rebuffed the big wind'. In his comments on Loyola's *Spiritual Exercises* Hopkins notes: 'when I compare myself, my being-myself, with anything else whatever, all things alike, all in the same degree, rebuff me with blank unlikeness'.[3] What the falcon feels as it tenses its muscled wing against the heavy air is the wind rebuffed, and the bird gloriously confirmed in sole and perfect possession of its own selfhood. Its inner being and its outer being are fused, and fused to one end, the bird's proclamation that it is itself. Such a state Hopkins calls ecstasy.

The metaphors present the falcon as a royal bird, the darling prince of the kingdom of day, as a horseman and as a skater. Each metaphor points to a mastery that is won by recognising and rejoicing in dependence. The freedom that the skater feels as he sweeps a smooth curve is a freedom won in an act of submission to the physics of speed, steel blade and ice. The case of the horseman is similar, and the prince is supported in his state by the people over whom he rules. They bear him up in his majesty as the air the falcon. If this dependence were resented or refused the horseman would fall, the skater stumble, the prince would be deposed. The octave of the sonnet explains a paradox, that ecstasy is the triumphant display of mastery, and that one wins mastery in an act of submission.

As he watches the falcon Hopkins is stirred:

> My heart in hiding
> Stirred for a bird – the achieve of, the mastery of the thing!

What the sentence insists on is a sad contrast between what Hopkins sees in the falcon's flight – flamboyance, an absoluteness of self-display – and his own locked up emotions. At its simplest what he sees is the bird finding in flight the means to let its self play through its body, and he feels weigh heavy on him his formal clerical dress and the conventions that inhibit the physical behaviour of a gentleman and a priest. It is not much different from what he feels in *Epithalamion* when he comes across boys swimming:

> how the boys
> With dare and with downdolphinry and bellbright bodies
> huddling out,
> Are earthworld, airworld, waterworld thorough hurled, all by turn
> and turn about.

He is stirred – 'The garland of their gambol flashes in his breast' – and he hurries to a neighbouring pool, takes his clothes off and delights in the touch of the earth on his bare feet and the 'flinty kindcold' water on his body. Swimming was a great pleasure to Hopkins, largely, perhaps, because it was one of the few activities in which a priest might permit himself the luxury of physical self-expression.

But what Hopkins feels as he looks at the falcon is more than that, and not only because he can swim but cannot fly. When he describes his heart 'in hiding' he is not thinking just of conventional inhibitions. To live in obscurity, in hiding, is the lot of most of us, and it is the life that, in becoming a Jesuit, Hopkins expressly chose. St Ignatius had lived in Rome 'so hidden a life' that after his death, when moves were afoot to canonise him, a cardinal said 'that he had never remarked anything in him more than in any edifying priest'.[4] It is the Jesuit's duty to imitate in this the founder of his order, and to find consolation for surrendering all thought of earthly fame in the example of St Ignatius, and the example, too, of Christ. Hopkins writes that 'the hidden life at Nazareth is the great help to faith for us who must live more or less an obscure, constrained, and unsuccessful life'.[5] In contrast the falcon is dazzling, the prince of sunlight, its flight a miracle of unconstrained achievement. What stirs Hopkins as he gazes at the bird is, in part, a painful sense of all that he has given up to become a priest. In a letter to Dixon, Hopkins quotes the remark of the Blessed John Berchmans, 'and the text is famous among us, "Common life is the greatest of my mortifications" '.[6] Seeing the royal, unconstrained bird mortifies Hopkins by sharpening his sense of the common life that he has chosen.

The falcon is knightly, a soldier horseman. Hopkins is stirred by it as he always is by martial display. He took pleasure in military parades, especially of mounted soldiers. He is as dazzled by a red coat as a flighty girl in a Jane Austen novel, and what stirs him surely is the contrast between the soldiers' showy scarlet uniforms and his own subdued clerical black, their lives dedicated to glorious exploit and his own dedicated to obscurity. What he feels is not envy, a sin of which Hopkins seems incapable, but the wistful pleasure that good men feel when they see others enjoying a pleasure from which they are debarred. He tells Bridges that news of friends marrying makes him feel 'spoony', and that is, I think, the exact word for what he feels when he looks at soldiers. He feels it even though he knows that they are, most of them, 'but foul clay':

> the heart,
> Since, proud, it calls the calling manly, gives a guess
> That, hopes that, makesbelieve, the men must be no less;
> It fancies, feigns, deems, dears the artist after his art;
> And fain will find as sterling all as all is smart,
> And scarlet wear the spirit of war there express.

Hopkins's heart leaps at the sight of a scarlet coat, for the coat is, or one can pretend that it is, an outward display of the soldier's inner self, 'the spirit of war'. It is this, not that both are killers, that ties together the falcon and the soldier. Both stir Hopkins by showing him the possibility of a life devoted to the display of the self, a life quite different from the life he has chosen.

As he gazes at the falcon, Hopkins is reminded by contrast of his own 'common life', and is stirred by a sharp recognition that this common life is the greatest of his mortifications. That is, I think, true, but it is only partly true. The falcon embodies a life given over to glorious self-display, and for Hopkins that is the life not only of princes and soldiers, but of poets. He would surely have understood Auden's characterisation of poets, 'Encased in talent like a uniform', who 'can dash forward like hussars'. Verse-making is to the poet what Hopkins imagines the falcon's flight is to the bird. Both are activities through which the poet and the bird delight in the self that they display, and this is why during the first years of his priesthood Hopkins felt the practise of poetry to be inconsistent with his vocation. Even in 1881, in a letter to Dixon, he notes that literature can be valued by Jesuits 'only as a means to an end'. Very few Jesuits have written poetry, and this is because poetry 'has seldom been found to be to that end a very serviceable means'.[7] This is soberly put, but he adds that if the lives of those few Jesuits who have written poetry are examined, there will be found something 'counterbalancing in their career'. He instances Southwell and the historian, Thomas Campion, and he goes on to make the staggering assertion that what is 'counterbalancing' in their careers is their martyrdom. His letter is written on the 300th anniversary of Campion's death. He had planned to write an ode to mark the occasion, but nothing remains of it. This is unsurprising when one reads what he writes of Southwell: 'he wrote amidst a terrible persecution and died a martyr, with circumstances of horrible barbarity: this is the counterpoise in his career'.[8]

It is the common currency of Hopkins criticism to note that Hopkins found it difficult to reconcile his priestly vocation with his other calling, poetry. But what he is grappling with in his letter to Dixon is something other than a tricky problem. His admiration for Campion's 'eloquence like Shakespeare's' is winningly enthusiastic, like a schoolboy's for his home team's centre forward, and it comes up sharp against the clear implication that Campion could safely give vent to that eloquence even in the very narrow compass to which he confined himself only because he was to be washed clean in his own blood.

The defining mark of the poet is that he would have us delight in 'the achieve of, the mastery of the thing'. The poet's proper goal, like the soldier's, is fame, and 'individual fame', Hopkins reminds Dixon, 'St Ignatius looked on as the most dangerous and dazzling of all attractions'. The proper model for the Jesuit writer is Francisco Suarez, 'our most famous theologian: he is a man of vast volume of mind, but without originality or brilliancy: he treats everything satisfactorily, but you never remember a phrase of his, the manner is nothing'.[9] Suarez is praised for his dullness. He was dull out of duty, piously refraining from any exhibition of eloquence that might call attention to the author, and he is praised for it by Hopkins, the most original and brilliant of nineteenth-century poets, the arch phrase-maker, the poet in whom manner is everything.

When Hopkins is stirred by the falcon, he is stirred by the vision of a life from which he is excluded, and this is mortifying. But he is stirred, too, because he sees something in the bird that he feels in himself, and this is both exhilarating and dangerous. The bird is a type of the artist, like Henry Purcell, the 'great stormfowl' who:

> whenever he has walked his while
> The thunder-purple seabeach plumed purple-of-thunder,
> If a wuthering of his palmy snow-pinions scatter a colossal
> smile
> Off him, but meaning motion fans fresh our wits with
> wonder.

Carelessly, easily, the bird shakes its wings, and displays 'the sakes of him'. Purcell's music is 'none of your damned subjective rot'.[10] It expresses Purcell's 'abrupt self' as accidentally as the falcon, intent only on flight, expresses its being. To display oneself perfectly and at the same time negligently is the highest reach of art, but it is not at all clear that such self-display should be any concern of the Christian let alone of the priest. Perhaps it was not just Purcell's protestantism that persuaded Hopkins to begin this sonnet hoping that Purcell will be spared damnation. Hopkins is pledged to a life 'in hiding'. When he is stirred by the bird's arrogant mastery of flight, its effortless, careless self-display, he is stirred by a temptation. In the octave of the sonnet he yields to it. He contrives a verbal display that so wonderfully describes the falcon's because it is a match for it. The octave ends with a colossal smile as Hopkins exclaims at 'the achieve of, the mastery of the thing!', at once the bird's mastery and his own.

I do not mean, of course, that in writing *The Windhover* Hopkins committed a sin, but I mean something scarcely less odd, that for Hopkins each and every poem begins in sin and has to struggle towards salvation. A large part of Hopkins's correspondence is taken up with his responses to criticism of his poems by Bridges, Dixon and Patmore on account of their oddity, their extravagant mannerism. He is by turns ruefully apologetic and obstinately defensive. But when replying to his poet friends Hopkins stands only at the bar of Victorian taste. He recognises, as he tells Dixon, a higher judge: 'the only just literary critic is Christ'.[11] We can understand *The Windhover* as the defence of his own sense of beauty before the only just literary critic: it is entitled 'The Windhover: To Christ our Lord'. Hopkins takes the stirring in his heart as he gazes at the barbarous beauty of the falcon's flight and converts it to a different kind of stirring, a stirring that signals not a delight in mortal beauty but the love of Christ. One recalls his sweet, sad words to Bridges: 'the only person that I am in love with seldom, especially now, stirs my heart sensibly'.[12] Prayer is for Hopkins a kind of stirring: 'this sigh or aspiration or stirring of the spirit towards God'.[13] He must transform one kind of stirring into the other, he must turn from the falcon to Christ. But it is not enough for him simply to turn from one to the other, rather the falcon must yield Christ as a poem yields its meaning:

> Brute beauty and valour and act, oh, air, pride, plume, here
> Buckle! AND the fire that breaks from thee then, a billion
> Times told lovelier, more dangerous, O my chevalier!

The 'here', the mastery of the falcon in flight, must yield the 'then' of Calvary, the 'brute beauty' of the falcon, the beauty of concentrated power, must yield the tender beauty of Christ in his passion. To this end Hopkins's description of Christ is compacted out of his vocabulary of mortal beauty. Christ is a 'chevalier', a knightly horseman, like the falcon. He is 'dangerous' like mortal beauty. Fire breaks from him as it breaks from the kingfisher. The diction insists that the beauty of Christ can be buckled to, held together with, the beauty of the falcon. The falcon is, after all, supported by the 'steady air' over which it rules. The bird's is a paradoxical mastery, inseparable from submission, and can be fitted together without too much strain to the mastery of Christ on the cross who conquers by giving his body to be killed. But to buckle means also to arm for combat, and in this sense of the word the falcon is not fitted together with Christ but vanquished by him. The octave echoes the Dauphin's praise of his horse in *Henry V*,[14] and the poem records the falcon's Agincourt. Christ proves 'a billion / Times told lovelier, more dangerous'. The phrasing suggests a tournament rather than a war. The falcon and Christ joust, rival lords of Hopkins's heart, the falcon is worsted and Christ rules supreme. The brute beauty of the falcon meets the divine beauty of Christ, and buckles, crumples.

These lines are notoriously difficult to paraphrase, and I do not expect the details of my reading to be generally accepted. But what I would insist on is that the lines fuse the two movements of *To What Serves Mortal Beauty*. In the first movement of the poem mortal beauty is accepted, in the second it is repudiated. In these lines the falcon is at once redeemed, seen as a type of Christ and discarded as the embodiment of a brute beauty that is eclipsed by the beauty of Jesus. The falcon at once yields, and yields to Christ. That done the falcon is finished with. Hopkins has met it, owned it. Now he can 'leave, let that alone'.

And as he does so he finds that he has gained a new acceptance of his life in hiding, his more or less obscure, constrained and unsuccessful life. The sequence of feeling is clear enough. The falcon in flight stirs his heart by offering him a vision of a life of ecstasy, a life quite different from his own. But he recognises that the bird is beautiful only in so far as its beauty figures the beauty of Christ, and at last he can look anew at his own life of 'sheer plod' and find in it a beauty that may more aptly figure the beauty of Christ than the flight of a falcon however majestic. The poem ends by finding beauty in the humdrum.

It is a movement of thought that Hopkins repeated in his sonnet *In Honour of St Alphonsus Rodriguez*. There the progression is from warrior glory, the glory that is 'flashed off exploit', to the glory of Christ in his crucifixion and the martyrs in their deaths, and at last to the glory proper to St Alphonsus, the glory of the humdrum. For forty years Alphonsus acted as hall porter to the College of Palma in Majorca, and Hopkins ends his sonnet, disastrously, meditating on the even passage of those years:

> while there went
> Those years and years by of world without event
> That in Majorca Alfonso watched the door.

It is pleasant to see examples of humble diligence such as this rewarded in the New Years Honours list, but when the prize is a place in the calendar of saints the effect is bathetic. The problem is not just that Hopkins seems to have no clear notion why Alfonso was canonised. Hopkins chastens his style, attunes it to the humdrum life that he is celebrating. He tries for a ringing flatness of the kind that Wordsworth might have achieved, but the effect is just flat. When Hopkins turns away from barbarous beauty to the beauty of common life, life in hiding, he does not have a style to turn to.

The danger that threatens at the end of *The Windhover*, when Hopkins turns to celebrate the beauty of a life of 'sheer plod' is that he will be able to record his spiritual victory only by assuming a style like Suarez's, dull. The danger is wonderfully circumvented:

> No wonder of it: sheer plod makes plough down sillion
> Shine, and blue-bleak embers, ah my dear,
> Fall, gall themselves, and gash gold-vermilion.

Chivalric metaphors are replaced by a ploughman and a coal fire. Virgil had seen the light flash from the ploughshare as it broke through the crumbling earth, but I suppose that Hopkins had seen it for himself. It becomes his image for the hidden beauty that he finds in Harry Ploughman, so sturdily buckling down to his life's labour: 'cragiron under and cold furls / With-a-fountain's shining-shot furls'. He ends with a fire, its drab covering of ashes slipping and crumbling, and exposing the gold-red of live coals. Hopkins told Dixon: 'we cultivate the commonplace outwardly and wish the beauty of the king's daughter, the soul, to be from within'.[15] As the ashes slip, the inner beauty is revealed as the proper type of the fire that breaks from Christ. To accept a common life was the greatest of the mortifications that Hopkins knew, which is why he can properly find in it a beauty that is the shadow of the beauty of the crucifixion. *The Windhover* ends with a domestic hearth, but two other images play around it. Hopkins was moved by just fallen chestnuts, their pale green husks split so that he could glimpse the shiny conker inside. He notes in his journal: 'Chestnuts bright as coals or spots of vermilion'.[16] In *Pied Beauty* he praises God for 'Fresh firecoal chestnut falls'. Second, in *Felix Randal* he ends, as he had ended *Harry Ploughman*, glorying in the flash that signals the beauty hidden at the heart of the farrier's life of humble labour:

> When thou at the random grim forge, powerful amidst peers,

Didst fettle for the great grey drayhorse his bright and battering
sandal!

He celebrates the moment when the blue-grey metal emerges from
the forge transfigured, bright as gold. The fire, the chestnut and the
forge all move Hopkins as moments when the humdrum displays,
for a moment, its inner beauty, its beauty like that of 'the king's
daughter, the soul', and the suddenness of that beauty and its glory
is figured on each occasion by a muted colour, blue-bleak embers, a
pale green husk, grey iron, flashing out reddish gold.

Hopkins celebrates such moments within his poems, but in
another sense it would be true to say that those moments are his
poems. He believed, and it would be impertinent to disagree with
him, that to devote his life to poetry would be a sin. If he
nevertheless found a way of justifying to himself spending some
small part of his life in writing poems, then it was surely that he
could think of his poems as gashes, rents in the 'blue-bleak' surface
of a priest's life that allowed the heart in hiding to flare out
momentarily and bear witness to the beauty hidden within. At that
moment, and only for a moment, the hidden life is revealed, and
flashes out in a burst of glorious colour, 'gold-vermilion'.

Conclusion

Beginning this last chapter, I am uneasy, like the hero of *Numpholeptos* confronting again the moon-white nymph, feeling himself further from completing his quest than ever. I started with an idea, and I tried to show through a discussion of particular poems that the idea was well-founded. It seemed a sensible procedure. But individual poems never simply confirm a general truth. They stain us with their own particularity, until we look down and find ourselves reeking with crocus, saffron, orange, as far as ever from the white light of the thesis. That repetitive, endless shunting between the general and the particular, between an experience of literature and an understanding of it, seems to me to characterise almost all literary criticism. If I am not struck dumb, it is because I think it true not just of literary criticism, but of most of our dealings with the world.

When I look at a rainbow I cannot see it for what I know it is, a continuous gradation of colour. What I see is red, yellow, green and violet indistinctly banded, and I cannot see otherwise, because my words for colours are a part of my experience. My language reaches out to what I see and orders it, only for what I see to dissolve the order that language imposes. Sensation is not independent of understanding, but neither is it identical with it. Human experience is always and necessarily fluid, not so much an endless shunting to and fro as a dance in which the understanding reaches out to what we feel, only to find the sensation slip between its fingers.

To experience so purely that the understanding is obliterated is a powerful human dream. Keats entertains it when he longs for a life of sensations rather than of thoughts. It is what makes Browning's Caliban, as he splashes in his warm mud pool – before he starts to think – so engaging. But it is a dream, unrealisable. Ruskin may claim that 'the whole technical power of painting' depends on the recovery of the power to see innocently, to see the world as 'flat stains of colour', but when he considers the matter further, he is willing to admit that the innocence that 'sees' only what is imprinted on the retina can never be regained, that seeing is always and necessarily sophisticated by the understanding. To see the world as flat stains of colour can only be a sophisticated accomplishment. When Browning sees flowers as 'reds and whites and yellows' we are just as likely to think of Monet as of the innocent eyes of a child.

The opposite dream is just as powerful; experience wholly accommodated to the understanding, life become a perfect allegory. It is how God sees the world, and it is the vision that a religious poet like Hopkins tries to share. But although, because he is a Christian, he must try to see like God, because he is a man, he must fail. He is committed by his faith both to the attempt and to its failure. He must find the truth that the windhover figures, but he must show too that for him the fact of the bird cannot entirely be subdued to an apprehension of its value.

In all the poems that I have discussed there is a flickering between two poles; experience and understanding, or fact and value. It is an opposition figured in the contrast between white light and colour with which I have been repeatedly concerned; between moonlight and, in *The Ancient Mariner*, the iridescent water snakes, in *Endymion* the green earth, in *Christmas-Eve* the rainbow, and in *Numpholeptos* the shafts of coloured light. But even when, as in these cases, the oppositions seem similar, the similarity dissolves as soon as it is grasped. In *The Ancient Mariner*, we think perhaps of a contrast between innocence and experience, in *Endymion* between dream and reality, in *Christmas-Eve* between God's truth and man's understanding, in *Numpholeptos* between an idea and the process of experience that the idea at once informs and is derived from. Even at this heady level of generality the poems pull apart. This is unsurprising. Any figure that attempts to extricate one from another fact and value is bound to fail because, independently of the other, neither can exist. What is offered at most is a contrast between value stained by sensation and sensation bleached by value. The figures cannot help but share in the dance of experience that they seek to define.

Neither white light, nor colour, nor the contrast between them arrives in the poems that I have discussed at any stable value. That they fail to do so does not in itself tell us anything about the differences between poets. The instability is evident within a group of poems written by a single poet, even within a single poem. What it illustrates is the ground on which nineteenth-century writers, all of them and regardless of their philosophical, religious and political differences, work out their representation of what it feels like to live. They begin by establishing a discrepancy between fact and value or experience and understanding, and their effort is to resolve the discrepancy. This can be done, but only by demonstrating that fact and value, experience and understanding, cannot be distinguished.

Looked at in one way this is a solution: looked at otherwise it creates a new problem, for if our facts are not separable from values, then values cannot be authenticated by an appeal to facts, and facts cannot be shown to be facts by demonstrating their independence of values. This circling, unending and unendable argument is central to nineteenth-century literature, as evident in the novels as it is in the poems.

Browning is the writer with whom I have been centrally concerned only because, of all nineteenth-century writers, he seems to me to have the sharpest understanding of this situation. In his work words for colours are rarely content simply to mark colour experiences. Words for physical sensation are presented to us freighted with moral meanings, and would become symbols if only the meanings they carried remained stable. But redness in *The Ring and the Book* can figure anything; gaucheness, innocence, worldly pride or murderous violence. In *Red Cotton Night-Cap Country* it is scarcely any less elusive. Browning repeatedly looks back to the pure life of the sensations, to Caliban in his warm mud pool, as if he were confident of finding in these primal facts a touchstone for reality. Just as often he looks forward to a 'pure white light', an absolute truth next to which all the relative truths of our mortal life can be tested. But he looks back and looks forward from a middle ground where facts and truths move together and part bewilderingly, in a way appropriately figured by the dizzyingly various significances that Browning attaches to the word *red*.

In Browning, much more often and more clearly than in Keats and Hopkins, the contrast between white light and colour is a central structural device. But the contrast is as variously significant as are the words for colours themselves. In *The Ring and the Book*, for example, Browning confidently announces that it needs only for a poet to run through the full spectrum of human experience for the various colours to 'whirl into white'. In *Numpholeptos* the speaker – and nothing in the poem contradicts him – seems to have resigned himself to the discovery that such a journey is tiring and futile: at its end he will be dyed more grotesquely than he was when he set out. White light may figure the solid truth that partial minds refract into colour, or it may figure a dream, an imaginary ideal that serves only to make us disgruntled with the coloured realities of our mortal experience. Throughout the nineteenth century colours may figure the truth that this world, and our life in this world, is illusion, and may equally well figure the truth that our living experience is our only reality. Browning is representative in entertaining both these views only to shy away from either of them, to some middle ground where the pressing truth is no longer what the discrepancy between the actual and the real, or, looked at the other way, between fact and fancy, might signify, but that the discrepancy exists. What white and what red mean is very hard to say. What the contrast between them betokens is just as difficult. And yet Browning is prepared to insist that it is 'white and red', and the difference between them, that best describes human flesh.

The Ring and the Book rests on two premises. First, that the truth may be 'evolved' from a complete knowledge of the facts, and so may command an objective rather than a subjective assent. Second, that facts in themselves are valueless, and that to seek to evolve a value, truth, from facts is absurd. Both positions are robustly argued, which does not save them from being contradictory. Browning appeals to the facts to authenticate the values that he finds in his story, and he also admits that the facts are inert, unworkable, like pure gold, until they are fused with a living soul. Browning is not stymied by this contradiction, he is energised by it. It drives him through the whole of a huge, unwieldy poem. His failure to resolve it does not irk him as a badge of his philosophical naïvety, it is a failure that he brandishes as a badge of his representative humanity. What he implies is that in this matter the alternative to being self-contradictory is being callow.

For Browning a religious faith was a stratagem designed to meet the particular emergency with which he was confronted. It was something to be made and re-made almost every day. Hopkins would have judged him a pagan. His was not a natural religion. In so far as the demands of his faith were at one with the rquirements of his human nature, this was only a happy coincidence. In so far as they failed to coincide, so much the worse for his nature. Browning's attempt to ground his faith on the facts of his sensory experience would have seemed to Hopkins not only futile but misguided. He was freed by his Catholicism from the need; that troubles Browning because it seemed at once so pressing and so impossible, to deduce his values from the facts of his experience. But all the same, in poem after poem, Hopkins attests to his need to record what he sees before celebrating the faith that releases him from bondage to the senses. His concern may be to subdue the facts of his experience to the value of his faith, but he remains characteristically Victorian in finding in the forging of some bond between them the plot of almost all his completed poems.

It is not enough for him to find the religious truth that the falcon signifies. The bird must be realised before it is read, or, to use Ruskin's terms, he must savour the bird's vital beauty before he can go on to consider its beauty as theoretic or typical. Browning confronts the discrepancy between his experience of life and his understanding of it, a discrepancy that reappears despite all his attempts to resolve it, and he is exhilarated. 'Incompleteness more than completeness matches the immense', and so his incomplete vision heartens him with the promise of an eternity of strenuous effort. For Hopkins the discrepancy is no less real, though for him it is a more chastening reminder of the limitations of his mortal vision. The windhover is a bird and it is a lesson, and the fact of the bird rebuffs Hopkins's best efforts to understand what the fact teaches: the octave of the sonnet is followed, without being quite super-seded, by the sestet.

The asymmetry of the sonnet, eight lines matched with six, is one of the ways Hopkins registers that his experience and his faith, despite all that he can do, remain discrepant, or can be resolved only in the inexplicable mystery of form. The opposition of white light and colour is another; between the sun as a 'blear and blinding ball' and sunlight as it is diffused and refracted in the 'glass-blue' days of spring, between life's 'skeined stained veined variety' and the 'black, white' of salvation and damnation. No more than in Browning does the contrast achieve a stable value. In *The Blessed Virgin compared to the Air we Breathe* the contrast signals the difference between the Old and the New Testaments, the black and white of simple justice against the blue of justice tempered by love, but in *Spelt from Sibyl's Leaves* the coloured lights of life, its stained variety, are a distraction from terrible realities, at once a mercy and dangerously seductive. Colours may figure the 'ruck and reel' of the visible world, the welter of appearance, or, as when the ashes slip and gash gold-vermilion, may just as well figure the beauty of the soul that subsists beneath humdrum appearances. Hopkins may oppose cloud and colour, the 'all in a rush' blue sky of childhood innocence threatened by the 'cloud' of sinning, or he may reconcile them as in the 'pied and peeled May' of the nun's vision, or in the dappled things for which he praises God.

Hopkins's faith, unlike Browning's, is stable, and yet, almost as if he had no control over the matter, he searches his faith for the paradoxes that will enable him to share in the central plot of his time. His poems are suspended between two principles: that God is immanent in the world, so that to worship the beauty of the creation is to worship the beauty of God; and that the world is fallen, and its beauty only a dangerous distraction from the issues on which the fate of our souls depends. One principle holds up the promise of a perfect reconciliation between our sensual experience and our religious duty: the more keenly we delight in the 'rose-stipple' of the trout the more aptly we worship its creator. The other principle insists that whatever the claims of mortal beauty we must in the end 'leave, let that alone', and focus our mind on a reality that can never be revealed to us through our senses, 'God's better beauty, grace'.

Browning and Hopkins would both of them have seemed 'irritable' to Keats, both 'reachers after fact and reason'. They search for some solution that will accommodate their reason to their understanding, only for the solution to dissolve, to become a dissolution, leaving them free to reach again. The movement of their verse shares in this restlessness: neither tries to match Keats in his ease, his 'wayward indolence'. It may have been apparent that of the three poets it is Keats that I love best, and what I love best in him is his 'indolence', his ability to be at ease with himself and with his world. Browning's rugged optimism in the face of pain and sorrow, and Hopkins's firm faith both seem to be fine things, but not so fine as Keats's talent for being happy. When Madeline wakes and finds Porphyro by her bed, they are both of them for a moment frozen. Then 'into her dream he melted'. Into her dream, and into her arms. It is the poem's 'Solution sweet'. The bitter conundrum entangling dream and reality, what is and what only seems, is at once solved and dissolved. Apollonius solves the riddle of Lamia, and the sign that he does so is that she dissolves. His solution is her dissolution. The world of *Lamia* is ugly and competitive, not like *The Eve of St Agnes* where Madeline and Porphyro solve and dissolve together.

Keats knows that reality is the weaving together of dream and fact, of the world inside and the world outside our heads. It is precarious, elusive, apprehended in a moment only the next moment to fade. That is why its proper figure is colour, the colour of the woven rainbow. But in the poems of his that I like best – in his happiest poems – *The Eve of St Agnes* and *To Autumn*, the knowledge does not leave him, as it leaves Browning and

Hopkins, restless or insecure, but rather, in Keats's special sense of the word, indolent.

In comparison with Keats, both Browning and Hopkins are inhibited, constrained. Henry James admired this reticence in Browning, his insistence on maintaining an impeccably common-place social demeanour and nourishing his creative fires in secret, and in Hopkins it might be said to be an inhibition forced on him by his vocation. But Browning's reticence seems to me to run deeper than can be accounted for simply by a proper contempt for artistic showmanship, and Hopkins seems to find in the Jesuit order a confirmation of what he had known before, that his most intense life must somehow remain 'hidden'. At the centre of the lives of both men was a relationship – Browning's with his wife, and Hopkins's with Jesus – that they jealously guarded: friends and readers are allowed only to glimpse it. That is one reason why both are so different from Keats, whose muse is the 'unchariest', who is so 'unmisgiving'.

In so far as these are differences of temperament, all that one can do is to note them. But this might not be quite all there is to it. In my first chapter I summarised – brutally, for lack of space – the argument that Bernard Harrison pursues throughout his *Form and Content*. Harrison concludes that there is good reason to suppose that people who have a similar ability to discriminate between colours have a similar experience of colours. The importance of this is fairly plain. The experience of colour is just one of the systems of knots that tie us to the world, but it can stand for them all. If I am forced to the position that I can compare my ability to discriminate between colours with my neighbour's ability, but can have no confidence that our experience of colours is at all similar, then I am left alone, trapped in a reality that I can at best assume to be something like the reality that my friends experience. It was so for Ruskin:

> One man may see yellow whereas another sees blue, but as the effect is constant they agree on the term to be used for it, and both will call it blue, or both yellow, having yet totally different ideas attached to the term.[1]

We cannot possibly tell whether two men see the same colour, but only whether they 'use the same name for it'. Browning is saved from the same conclusion only by a confusion:

> Why here's my neighbour colour-blind,
> Eyes like mine to all appearance: 'green as grass', do I
>   affirm?
> 'Red as grass', he contradicts me; which employs the
>   proper term?
> Were we two the earth's sole tenants, with no third for
>   referee,
> How should I distinguish?

('La Saisiaz', 274–8)

Browning saves himself from Ruskin's conclusion only by writing as if particular colour terms were naturally rather than conventionally attached to particular colour experiences. Hopkins arrives by a different route at a similar position. He knows that colour is experienced 'only in the thought / Of him that looks', and so the type of human experience becomes a group of people standing round a waterfall who 'see one bow each, yet not the same to all'. The knot that joins each to the world is the same knot that divides each from the other.

It is given to few of us to be so unmisgiving as Keats, to lay ourselves so open to our friends and our readers. I do not claim – it would be absurd to do so – that this talent came to Keats as a reward for having found a benign solution to a knotty problem of philosophy. Neither do I claim that Browning and Hopkins, had they read and been convinced by Harrison's argument, would have at once been freed from the painful constraints of believing themselves to be trapped within an experience of the world that isolated them from their fellows. My claim is more modest – that happiness, as opposed to short-lived solitary bursts of joy when the blue-bleak surface of the world momentarily cracks, is by nature social, communal. We do not need to believe that we all feel the same before we can be happy any more than we need to feel, before we delight in a rainbow, that other people see exactly the same colours that we do. What we need is only the confidence that their experience is not secret, hidden, but available to us, and that ours is available to them. We need to accept at least this; that Keats's brave openness, his unchariness, is not a futile refusal to accept the truth that we are each of us cut off from other people, marooned in a solitary world from which there is no escape. Harrison offers us this hope. He allows us to believe that Clare, looking at a lark's egg and noticing the 'purply tinges' at the larger end, that Kipling watching the dull red stain spreading on the suicide's shirt, and Hopkins seeing a conker just split from its shell, are recording an experience that we can share, and to believe this is at any rate a first step in the hard task of living without misgivings.

Notes

Notes to Chapter 1: Dull Red

1. Rudyard Kipling, *Something of Myself* (London, 1937) pp. 86–7.
2. Barthes has a good discussion of the importance of framing in nineteenth-century fiction, and of the use of windows to create a frame, in paragraph xxv of *SZ*, 'Le portrait' (see Roland Barthes, *SZ* (Paris, 1970) pp. 67–8).
3. The two best-known examples are *A Christmas Carol* and *Bleak House*.
4. The most lucid deployment of the term of which I am aware is Michael Riffaterre's in his *Semiotics of Poetry* (London, 1980), but even here its sense seems at best loosely metaphorical.
5. See Paul D. Sherman, *Colour Vision in the Nineteenth Century* (Bristol, 1981) p. 72.
6. Brent Berlin and Paul Kay, *Basic Color Terms* (Berkeley and Los Angeles, Calif., 1969) p. 94.
7. Quoted by Bernard Harrison, *Form and Content* (Oxford, 1973) p. 103.

Notes to Chapter 2: Awful Newton

1. Turner's quotation is given in *The Paintings of J. M. W. Turner*, ed. Martin Butlin and Evelyn Joll (London, 1977) vol. 2, p. 5.
2. On Turner's response to Newton, see R. D. Gray, 'J. M. W. Turner and Goethe's Colour-Theory', *German Studies Presented to W.H. Bruford* (London, 1962) pp. 112–16.
3. Butlin and Joll (*Paintings of J. M. W. Turner*, vol. 2, pp. 227–9) believe 'The Fountain of Fallacy' to be identical with the surviving painting 'The Fountain of Indolence'.
4. See ibid., pp. 207–8; John Gage, *Colour in Turner* (London, 1969) p. 252; and Jack Lindsay, *The Sunset Ship: The Poems of J. M. W. Turner* (London, 1966) pp. 56–7.
5. The anecdote is quoted by Gage, *Colour in Turner*, p. 169.
6. Marjorie Hope Nicolson, *Newton Demands the Muse* (Princeton, N.J., 1946).
7. *The Letters of Samuel Taylor Coleridge*, ed. E. L. Griggs (Oxford, 1959) vol. 4, p. 750.
8. Ibid., p. 751.
9. Sir Isaac Newton, *Opticks*, Book One, Part ii, Proposition ii, Theorem ii.
10. *The Letters of Samuel Taylor Coleridge*, vol. 2, p. 709.

Notes to Chapter 3: A Rainbow in the Sky

1. Stephen Prickett, *The Poetry of Growth* (Cambridge, 1970).
2. Compare Paul de Man's description of the Shape all light as 'the figure for the figurality of all signification' in his essay 'Shelley Disfigured' (p. 62) in *Deconstruction and Criticism*, ed. Geoffrey Hartman (London, 1980) pp. 39–73.

3.   *The Complete Works of John Ruskin*, ed. Wedderburn and Cook (London, 1903–12) vol. x, p. 174.
4.   *The Sermons and Devotional Writings of Gerald Manley Hopkins*, ed. Christopher Devlin (London, 1959) p. 35.
5.   The point is made by George P. Landow in 'The Rainbow: a Problematic Image', in *Nature and the Victorian Imagination'* ed. U. C. Knoepflmacher and G. B. Tennyson (Berkeley, Calif., 1977) pp. 341–69.
6.   *Turner's Picturesque Views in England and Wales, 1825–1838*, ed. Eric Shanes (London, 1979) pp. 33 and 41.
7.   C. R. Leslie, *Memoirs of the Life of John Constable, R. A.* (London, 1937) p. 396.
8.   Ibid., p. 118.

Notes to Chapter 4: Blue, Glossy Green, and Velvet Black

1.   *Memoirs of the Life of John Constable, R. A.*, p. 150.
2.   Jack Lindsay has entitled his collection of Turner's verse fragments *The Sunset Ship* (London, 1966).
3.   What Robert Penn Warren identifies as 'the primary meaning' in 'A Poem of Pure Imagination: an Experiment in Reading', in his *Selected Essays* (New York, 1951) pp. 198–305.
4.   See John Livingstone Lowes, *The Road to Xanadu* (Boston, Mass., 1926) pp. 203–8.
5.   *Goethe's Theory of Colours*, trs. C. L. Eastlake (London, 1840) p. 150.
6.   See *The Road to Xanadu*, pp. 35–8.

Notes to Chapter 5: Woven Colours

1.   *Complete Works of William Hazlitt*, ed. P. P. Howe (1930) vol. 5, pp. 1–18.
2.   'The more I understand of Sir Isaac Newton's work, the more boldly I dare utter to my own mind, and therefore to *you*, that I believe the soul of 500 Sir Isaac Newton's would go to the making up of a Shakespeare or a Milton' (Samuel Taylor Coleridge, *Letters* (Oxford, 1956) vol. 2, p. 709).
3.   Quoted by Christopher Ricks, *Keats and Embarrassment* (London, 1974) p. 150. Ricks, too, is inclined to disagree with Trilling.
4.   See *Keats and Embarrassment*, pp. 23 and 50.

Notes to Chapter 6: Purple Riot

1.   In Lasinio's engraving (see Robert Gittings, *John Keats* (London, 1968) pp. 279–81).

2. The revised text and the relevant letters to Woodhouse and Taylor are quoted in *Keats: The Complete Poems*, ed. Miriam Allott (London, 1970) pp. 474–5.

Notes to Chapter 7: Blind Hope

1. See Ford Madox Hueffer, *Ford Madox Brown: A Record of his Life and Work* (London, 1896) pp. 120–1, and *The Complete Works of John Ruskin*, vol. xxiv, pp. 148–51.
2. *The Letters of Robert Browning and Elizabeth Barrett Browning, 1845–1846* (London, 1898) vol. 1, p. 45.
3. Ibid., vol. 1, p. 6.
4. ' "The Jewelled Bow": a Study in Browning's Imagery of Humanism', *PMLA*, vol. lxx (1955) pp. 115–31. See also Park Honan, *Browning's Characters: A Study in Poetic Technique* (New Haven, Conn., 1961) pp. 189–98; and Bernard Brugière, *L'Univers imaginaire de Robert Browning* (Paris, 1979) pp. 469–79.
5. *Letters of Robert Browning and Elizabeth Barrett Browning*, vol. 1, pp. 34–5.

Notes to Chapter 8: Rainbow Flakes

1. *Shelley's Prose*, ed. D. L. Clark (Albuquerque, N.M., 1954) p. 173.

Notes to Chapter 9: Seven Proper Colours Chorded

1. Most modern commentators agree that John has in mind seven single candlesticks rather than the seven-branched candlestick, which, because of its use in Jewish ritual, he was formerly thought to be referring to. But it does not matter to my point which interpretation found favour with Browning.
2. Samuel Taylor Coleridge, *The Ancient Mariner*, ll. 424–5.

Notes to Chapter 10: The Subtle Prism

1. On this see W. C. de Vane, 'The Virgin and the Dragon', *Yale Review*, vol. xxxvii (1947) pp. 33–46.
2. Although, typically of the poem, even cloud is accepted, just once, as benign, even preferable to sunshine:

> Sun-suffused,
> A cloud may soothe the eye made blind by blaze, –
> Better the very clarity of heaven:
> The soft streaks are the beautiful and dear.

(x. 1639–42)

Note to Chapter 11: The Red Thing

1. Park Honan's interesting discussion of Browning's use of colour in *The Ring and the Book* strikes me as unconvincing in its insistence that colours achieve within the poem a stable significance. See Park Honan, *Browning's Characters* (New Haven, Conn., 1961) pp. 189–98.

Note to Chapter 12: By White and Red Describing Human Flesh

1. The relation of Browning's poem to Mellerio's story is summarised by John Pettigrew in *Robert Browning: The Poems* (Harmondsworth, Middx, 1984) vol. 2, pp. 986–8.

Notes to Chapter 13: The Crimson Quest

1. The letter is quoted by W. C. de Vane in *A Browning Handbook* (London, 1940) p. 360.
2. *Robert Browning's Prose Life of Strafford*, ed. H. Firth and F. J. Furnivall (London, 1892) pp. 60–1.
3. *Shelley's Prose*, p. 170.

Notes to Chapter 14: Pure Blues

1. The drawing is reproduced by Gardner and MacKenzie in *The Poems of Gerard Manley Hopkins* (London, 1967) facing p. 8.
2. *The Notebooks and Papers of Gerard Manley Hopkins*, ed. Humphrey House (London, 1937) p. 8.
3. Ruskin's influence on Hopkins is interestingly discussed by Patricia Ball in *The Science of Aspects* (London, 1971).
4. *The Complete Works of John Ruskin*, vol. xv, p. 27.
5. Ibid.
6. See, for example, ibid., vol. v, pp. 321–6; vol. vi, pp. 68–9; vol. vii, p. 415; and vol. x, p. 172.
7. Ibid., vol. xxxv, p. 21.
8. *The Correspondence of Gerard Manley Hopkins and Richard Weston Dixon*, ed. C. C. Abbott (London, 1935) p. 38.
9. Hopkins made three attempts at the final line, of which I quote the version I prefer. See Gardner and MacKenzie, *Poems of Gerard Manley Hopkins*, p. 142.
10. *The Letters of Gerard Manley Hopkins to Robert Bridges*, ed. C. C. Abbott, p. 92.

Notes to Chapter 15: Two Flocks, Two Folds – Black, White

1. *The Complete Works of John Ruskin*, vol. vi, p. 71.

2. Ibid., vol. III, p. 160.
3. John Hayman has a good discussion of Ruskin's handling of this distinction. See 'Towards the Labyrinth: Ruskin's Lectures as Slade Professor of Art', in *New Approaches to Ruskin*, ed. Robert Hewison (London, 1981) pp. 111–24.
4. *The Complete Works of John Ruskin*, vol. XX. pp. 174–5.
5. Ibid., vol. XXII, pp. 61–2.
6. 'The Storm-Cloud of the Nineteenth Century', ibid., vol. XXXIV, pp. 7–80.
7. *Further Letters of Gerard Manley Hopkins*, ed. C. C. Abbott (London, 1956) pp. 226–7.
8. *The Complete Works of John Ruskin*, vol. VII, pp. 268–9.
9. Ibid., vol. V, pp. 103–4.
10. Ibid., p. 105.
11. Ibid., p. 108.
12. Ibid., p. 317.
13. *The Letters of Gerard Manley Hopkins to Robert Bridges*, p. 92.

Notes to Chapter 16: Dappled Things

1. After making this assertion Hopkins retracts it: 'No, but it was not these … '. But in poetry, gifts, once offered, can never be withdrawn.
2. *The Correspondence of Gerard Manley Hopkins and Richard Weston Dixon*, p. 20.
3. Ibid., p. 139.

Notes to Chapter 17: Gold-Vermilion

1. *The Letters of Gerard Manley Hopkins to Robert Bridges*, p. 179.
2. Ibid., p. 85.
3. *The Sermons and Devotional Writings of Gerard Manley Hopkins*, ed. Christopher Devlin (London, 1959) p. 123.
4. *The Correspondence of Gerard Manley Hopkins and Richard Weston Dixon*, pp. 95–6.
5. Ibid., p. 96.
6. Ibid., p. 93.
7. Ibid., p. 94.
8. Ibid., pp. 93–4.
9. Ibid., p. 95.
10. *The Letters of Gerard Manley Hopkins to Robert Bridges*, p. 84.
11. *The Correspondence of Gerard Manley Hopkins and Richard Weston Dixon*, p. 8.
12. *The Letters of Gerard Manley Hopkins to Robert Bridges*, p. 66.
13. *The Sermons and Devotional Writings of Gerard Manley Hopkins*, p. 333.
14. This is pointed out by Gardner and MacKenzie, *Poems of Gerard Manley Hopkins*, p. 267.
15. *The Correspondence of Gerard Manley Hopkins and Richad Weston Dixon*, p. 96.
16. *The Notebooks and Papers of Gerard Manley Hopkins*, p. 120.

Note to Conclusion

1. *The Complete Works of John Ruskin*, vol. III, p. 160.

Index

Addison, Joseph, 22–3
Aeschylus, 94
Allott, Miriam, 50
Angelico, Fra, 175, 181, 186
Armstrong, Isobel, 104
Arnold, Matthew, 36
Auden, W. H., 8, 205

Ball, Patricia, 223n
Barthes, Roland, 9
Bayley, John, 46, 75
Bentham, Jeremy, 54
Berchmans, John, 204
Berlin, Brent, 11–12
Blake, William, 25
Boehme, Jacob, 26
Bridges, Robert, 172, 178, 186, 204, 207
Brown, Ford Madox, 83–4
Browning, Elizabeth Barrett, 84–6, 94–5, 119
Browning, Robert, 81–167
  Andrea del Sarto, 161
  Childe Roland, 161, 166–7
  Christmas-Eve, 104–15, 212
  Deaf and Dumb, 86
  Easter-Day, 104–5
  Fifine at the Fair, 85, 91–4
  Gerard de Lairese, With, 87–91
  Numpholeptos, 160–8, 211, 212, 213
  Paracelsus, 96–7, 161, 165
  Pauline, 85, 96–7, 161, 165
  Red Cotton Night-Cap Country, 85, 144–59, 213
  Ring and the Book, The, 85, 116–43, 147, 162, 213–14
  Saisiaz, La, 127, 217–18
  Sordello, 85, 96–103, 110, 153, 161, 165
Brugiere, Bernard, 222n
Bunsen, R. W., 116
Butlin, Martin, 220n
Byron, Lord George Gordon, 50–1

Campbell, Thomas, 32–3

Campion, Thomas, 205
Caravaggio, 119
Carlyle, Thomas, 151
Chevreul, M. E., 10
Clare, John, 1–4
Coleridge, S. T., 25–8, 29, 36–45, 48, 55, 105
  The Ancient Mariner, 36–45, 114–15, 212
Constable, John, 34–6, 44, 151
Corot, 151
Correggio, 176
Cowper, William, 2

Dante, 46–7
de Man, Paul, 220n
de Vane, W. C., 222n, 223n
Dickens, Charles, 220n
Dixon, R. W., 176, 178, 195–6, 204, 205, 206, 207
Donne, John, 32, 76

Eliot, George, 3, 102

Fisher, John, 34
Flaxman, John, 24
Furnivall, F. J., 161

Gage, John, 220n
Gittings, Robert, 70
Goethe, J. W. von, 20, 25–8, 39
Gray, R. D., 220n

Harrison, Bernard, 217, 220n
Hartley, Davis, 54
Hay, D. R., 10
Hayman, John, 224n
Hazlitt, William, 51–6
Helmholtz, H. L. F. von, 117
Honan, Park, 222n, 223n
Hopkins, Gerard Manley, 31–3, 171–220
  Andromeda, 188
  Blessed Virgin compared to the Air we Breathe, The, 196–201, 213
  Bugler's First Communion, The, 186–8

Caged Skylark, The, 177
Epithalamion, 203
Felix Randal, 209–10
God's Grandeur, 186, 192–3
Habit of Perfection, The, 173
Harry Ploughman, 209
Henry Purcell, 206
Hurrahing in Harvest, 178
In honour of St Alphonsus Rodriguez, 208–9
'It was a hard thing to undo this knot', 31–3
'I wake and feel the fell of dark, not day', 188
Pied Beauty, 191–2, 209
Rainbow, The, 176–7
Sea and the Skylark, The, 185–6
Soldier, The, 204–5
Spelt from Sibyl's Leaves, 189–90, 215
Spring, 183–8
That Nature is a Heraclitean Fire and of the Comfort of the Resurrection, 190
Tom's Garland, 188
To what serves Mortal Beauty, 208
Windhover, The, 202–10
Wreck of the Deutschland, The, 193–5
Hueffer, Ford Madox, 222n
Hunt, Leigh, 66

James, Henry, 119, 217
Joll, Evelyn, 220n

Kay, Paul, 11–12
Keats, John, 25, 46–80, 173
Belle Dame sans merci, La, 78
Calidore, 64
Endymion, 49–50, 65–9, 161, 212
Eve of St Agnes, The, 69–80, 172, 216
Fall of Hyperion, The, 46–7
George Felton Matthew, To, 64
Imitation of Spenser, 65
'I stood tiptoe upon a little hill', 65
Lamia, 47–63, 216
Kipling, Rudyard, 7–9, 13–15
Kirchoff, Gustav, 116

Landow, George. P., 221n

Leslie, C. R., 34–5
Lindsay, Jack, 21, 36
Locke, John, 9, 181
Lowes, John Livingstone, 221n
Loyola, Ignatius, 202, 204, 206

Mallet, David, 24
Malthus, Thomas, 54
Maxwell, James Clerk, 116–17, 12?
Michelangelo, 182
Millais, J. E., 83–4, 175
Milton, John, 24

Newton, Issac, 9, 10, 19–28, 54, 10?
Nicolson, Marjorie Hope, 24

Orcagna, 70

Patmore, Coventry, 207
Pettigrew, John, 223n
Plotinus, 26
Poussin, Nicolas, 35
Prickett, Stephen, 29, 31–2
Priestley, Joseph, 41

Raymond, W. O., 86
Ricks, Christopher, 59–60, 221n
Riffaterre, Michael, 220
Rossetti, D. G., 4–5
Rubens, 34
Runge, Otto von, 11
Ruskin, John, 68, 83, 174–7, 180–8 191–2, 217

Savage, Richard, 26–7
Shakespeare, William, 66, 208
Shanes, Eric, 33
Shelley, P. B.
Adonais, 23, 26–7, 68, 74, 86, 198–9
Alastor, 14–15, 78, 102, 161
Essay on Love, 165–6
Evening: Ponte Al Mare, Pisa, 4
Prometheus Unbound, 47, 63, 94
Triumph of Life, The, 29–31
Shelvocke, George, 37–8
Sherman, Paul, D., 220n
Southwell, Robert, 205
Sterne, Laurence, 1
Stewart, Dugald, 12
Suarez, Francisco, 206, 209

Tennyson, Alfred, 74
Thackeray, Anne, 144, 149–50
Thackeray, W. M., 7, 147
Thomson, James, 2, 19–20, 24–5
Titian, 176
Trilling, Lionel, 58
Turner, J. M. W., 19–24, 33–4, 36,
    44, 151, 182

Warren, Robert Penn, 221n
Wisdom, John, 13
Wordsworth, William, 29, 31–2, 37
    106

Young, Thomas, 117